Guerrilla Marketing Online

2nd Edition

Books by Jay Conrad Levinson

The Most Important $1.00 Book Ever Written

Secrets of Successful Free-Lancing

San Francisco: An Unusual Guide to Unusual Shopping
(with Pat Levinson and John Bear)

Earning Money Without a Job

555 Ways to Earn Extra Money

150 Secrets of Successful Weight Loss
(with Michael Levin and Michael Rokeach, M.D.)

Quit Your Job!

An Earthling's Guide to Satellite TV

Guerrilla Marketing

Guerrilla Marketing Attack

Guerrilla Marketing Weapons

The 90-Minute Hour

Guerrilla Financing
(with Bruce Jan Blechman)

Guerrilla Selling
(with Bill Gallagher and Orvel Ray Wilson)

Guerrilla Marketing Excellence

Guerrilla Advertising

The Way of the Guerrilla

Guerrilla Marketing Online
(with Charles Rubin)

Guerrilla Marketing Online Weapons
(with Charles Rubin)

Books by Charles Rubin

Thinking Small: The Buyer's Guide to Portable Computers

The Endless Apple

AppleWorks: Boosting Your Business with Integrated Software

Command Performance: AppleWorks

Microsoft Works on the Apple Macintosh

Macintosh Hard Disk Management

Running Microsoft Works

The Macintosh Bible "What Do I Do Now?" Book

The Macintosh Bible Guide to System 7

The Macintosh Bible Guide to FileMaker Pro

The Macintosh Bible Guide to System 7.1

The Macintosh Bible Guide to ClarisWorks 3.0

The Little Book of Computer Wisdom: How to Make Friends
  with Your PC or Mac

Guerrilla Marketing Online
  (with Jay Conrad Levinson)

Guerrilla Marketing Online Weapons
  (with Jay Conrad Levinson)

Managing Your Business with Quickbooks
  (with Diane Parssinen)

GUERRILLA MARKETING ONLINE

2ND EDITION

*The Entrepreneur's Guide to
Earning Profits on the Internet*

Jay Conrad Levinson
and **Charles Rubin**

HOUGHTON MIFFLIN COMPANY
Boston • New York   1997

For information about permission to reproduce selections from
this book, write to Permissions, Houghton Mifflin Company,
215 Park Avenue South, New York, New York 10003.

Library of Congress Cataloging-in-Publication Data
Levinson, Jay Conrad.
    Guerrilla marketing online : the entrepreneur's guide to earning
profits on the Internet / Jay Conrad Levinson and Charles Rubin.
        p.   cm.
    Includes index.
    ISBN 0-395-86061-X
    1. Internet marketing. 2. Marketing — Data processing.
3. Internet advertising.   I. Rubin, Charles, 1953– . II. Title.
HF5415.125.L48   1997
658.8'00285'4678 — dc21   97-25296   CIP

Printed in the United States of America

QUM 10 9 8 7 6 5 4 3 2 1

Contents

Acknowledgments

I wish to thank Michael Larsen and Elizabeth Pomada for ushering me into cyberspace and finally joining me there; Robert Pope for clearing the path and removing all the obstacles; John Wathen for filling in the potholes on the online road; Marnie Patterson for seeing and illuminating the path; Bill Gallagher, Jr., for furnishing me with a road map; Candace Jones for proving that it is both the information and the communications superhighway; and my coauthor, Charlie Rubin, for navigating it for me with speed and aplomb. These people continue to prove to me that the Internet is more about people than it is about things.

JAY CONRAD LEVINSON

I would like to thank Arnie Wolen of Sedona On-Line for his unflagging encouragement and support; Diane Parssinen and Michael Sohaski for sharing their online discoveries with me; and Bill Gallagher, Jr., for setting a great example of what it means to be an online guerrilla.

CHARLES RUBIN

Introduction

The online marketplace has changed a lot since we wrote the first edition of this book in 1994, and this new edition brings our readers up to date. Although the basic guerrilla marketing strategies we introduced for the online marketplace in the previous edition are still valid today (even more so in most cases), the locations where you'll carry out those strategies and the specific means you'll use to carry them out have changed considerably.

ACCESS EXPANDS

Internet service providers have multiplied perhaps a hundredfold since 1994, and now there are local service providers in many small towns. Almost anyone in America can now get Internet access via a local phone call for $20 a month or less.

Methods of Internet access have also improved. *Modem* speeds are now up to 56 kilobits per second. Cable TV and satellite operators are now offering access to the *Net* at speeds dozens or even hundreds of times faster than via a dial-up modem. Internet access software has become standard equipment in most new PCs sold at retail. And for those who can't afford a new PC, new devices like WebTV allow Internet access to anyone with a television and a phone line.

What this all means is that there are now more people doing more things on the Internet than ever before.

THE WEB DOMINATES

In 1994, the *World Wide Web* was just becoming a part of our lives. Today, it dominates the Internet and will also dominate the thinking of anyone marketing on the Net.

Graphical Web browsers were only starting to come into use at the end of 1994. Today Microsoft includes its Internet Explorer browser in every copy of Windows. Not to be outdone, Netscape has delivered more than 70 million copies of its Navigator and Communicator browsers.

Older Internet services that were popular before the Web's rise to prominence have faded into the background these days. While our previous edition talked a lot about services such as *Gopher, FTP,* and bulletin board systems, this edition will focus more on the Web. We'll still cover the older services because we believe guerrillas should use as many means of marketing as their resources allow, but we've added new Web-specific material throughout the book. Some new topics covered include:

- how to choose a Web designer
- setting goals for a Web storefront
- planning an information publishing strategy
- receiving orders online
- advertising on the Web
- gaining visibility for a Web site

ABOUT THIS BOOK

This book is a guerrilla's guide to that marketplace and how to successfully attack it. There are many fine books available about personal computer communications, networking, using the Internet or using specific online services, conducting research online, creating Web sites, and programming with *HTML* or Java. This book is not one of them. Our focus is on applying proven guerrilla marketing strategies to the online marketplace.

If you haven't been online or have explored only a small part of the online world, you'll need to get your bearings as to the scope and layout of the overall marketplace. We'll give you enough information to get oriented, but you'll also benefit from reading a more detailed and technical guide to using the online world.

HOW TO USE THIS BOOK

In this book, we'll cover the realities of online marketing. We'll explore detailed weapons and strategies for fighting and winning in the online markets so that you can produce maximum profits with minimum expense. Here are your basic marching orders.

Understand the online marketplace.   The online market is a vast, diverse, and potentially confusing place. There are millions of people exploring tens of thousands of electronic locations on the Internet, *online services*, and bulletin boards. Chapters 1 and 2 will introduce you to this market: how it's organized, what you can do there, who can participate, and how to get started as quickly as possible.

Learn to navigate, communicate, and respond.   Once you have a general idea of how the online terrain is laid out, your next mission is to understand the various online tools and services you can use to market online. Chapter 3 is your guide.

Learn strategies for attacking specific battlegrounds.   Chapters 4 through 9 offer detailed strategies for winning online battles. In these chapters, you'll find out how to maneuver in specific battlegrounds and how to use them to your best advantage.

Choose your weapons.   Chapter 10 lists 100 proven marketing weapons you can use to press your attack, and Chapter 11 offers a dozen strategies you can use to make the most of them.

Develop a strategy.   Chapter 12 offers step-by-step instructions for planning a successful online guerrilla marketing attack. You'll learn how to choose the right battlegrounds, how to build your own custom arsenal of online marketing weapons, and how to create an attack calendar.

Implement that strategy consistently.   Chapters 13 and 14 show how to launch and maintain your marketing attack.

Leverage your online presence.   Chapters 15 and 16 show how to use your online presence to boost other marketing efforts and how to use online resources to gain vital intelligence about your business, your customers, and your competition.

Armed with the resources in this book, you can create an online market presence that will become a significant part of your overall business strategy. You can expand your markets by reaching customers you could never reach before, increase sales by handling many more transactions than you could before, and boost your bottom line by slashing sales and marketing costs to the bone.

All it takes is a commitment to winning, a modest investment in basic computer equipment and services, and the willingness to take action.

PART I

The Online Marketplace

1

Attacking the Online Marketplace

Success in business means selling, and that usually means putting your message, your company identity, and your product or service before as many prospective customers as possible. Since the 1970s, technologies like cable television, fax-on-demand, and 800- or 900-number service have given guerrilla marketers more ways than ever to get their messages out to a wide audience quickly and at lower costs. But nothing we've seen so far comes close to the potential of the online marketplace. Imagine:

- putting your message before a million prospects, or being able to target promotions at very specific groups of prospects in seconds, and for pennies
- opening virtual storefronts in dozens of locations around the world, having instantaneous control over the look and content of your store displays, and being able to take orders day and night
- competing on equal terms with companies ten times the size of yours
- being able to win head-on battles through superior customer service and attitude

The online marketplace makes all this possible. In the online world, you leverage your savvy, guts, and marketing budget far more effectively than you ever have before.

But success in the online marketplace isn't a sure thing, any more than opening a storefront with a good idea is a guarantee of early retirement. The online world has great potential, but in many ways it's a more perilous place than traditional marketing battlegrounds. Already, dozens of would-be millionaires have tested the online waters and have been severely challenged.

In this book, we'll show you how to fight and win in the online marketplace. You'll learn how the marketplace is organized, how different areas of it demand different strategies, how to pick your battlegrounds for maximum success, and how to press your attack for continuing victories and profits.

ABOUT THE ONLINE MARKETPLACE

Anyone who hasn't lived on Mars during the past couple of years has heard a lot about the information highway. Technologies as diverse as computer networks, interactive television, and two-way video telephones have been lumped together under the information-highway banner. Vice President Al Gore has promoted the National Information Infrastructure as a means of streamlining the flow of information among businesses and consumers and of making American companies more competitive.

In the broadest sense, the information highway includes any form of interactive communications technology. That includes everything from the 800 number you dial today to order from a catalog to the interactive TV setup of tomorrow where you point to pizza toppings on the screen to order a hot one from Domino's.

Eventually, interactive computer and television communications may change the way people shop. Already, there are interactive TV trials where you can browse on-screen menus of restaurants or entertainment events and make reservations or order tickets with your TV remote control. Futurists envision a time when you will instruct software *agents* to do your shopping for you. For example, you could have an agent search all online sources for a specific size of refrigerator with certain features and give you a list of options. The agent might suggest the model with the most bang for the buck, or you might even tell it to go ahead and order the appliance for you.

Yes, the future of shopping looks incredible, but if you're planning to leverage online technologies for your business, you'll have to separate what's possible today from what you might be able to do tomorrow. For our purposes, today's information highway is the online marketplace: people using computers and computer networks to connect with one another. This marketplace includes:

- the Internet (or simply the Net), the international matrix of computer networks that links millions of people at university, government, and corporate networks. The Internet includes services such as the World Wide Web, electronic mail, and *discussion groups*.
- online computer services such as America Online, CompuServe, and Prodigy, whose combined subscriber base is more than 10 mil-

lion people. These services require paid subscriptions and offer their own collections of information and their own electronic discussions and clubs. Online services also offer access to the Internet.

- *bulletin board systems* that host some 20 million callers in the United States alone. Many of these offer access to the Internet — and can be accessed via the Internet — as well.

The online marketplace is changing very rapidly. Nevertheless, we've focused on marketing avenues and strategies that should stand the test of time, and we'll show you how to stay in touch with new developments on the information highway.

A MARKET TOO BIG TO IGNORE

Willie Sutton said he robbed banks because that was where the money was. Guerrilla marketers go online because that's where the customers are. Using marketing techniques detailed in other Guerrilla Marketing books, you can reach hundreds, thousands, or even tens of thousands of potential customers by spending a few hundred dollars a month or less.

But with a personal computer and a modem, you can go online and reach millions of people for pennies. Your message will probably appeal to only a tiny fraction of the online population, but with millions of people out there, a tiny fraction is plenty. And, as we'll see, the online marketplace is neatly segmented into special-interest groups, so it's easy to find the groups that will most likely buy your products.

The number of people online is staggering. It's impossible to get a totally accurate count, but estimates range from about 10 million users to more than 40 million users in the United States alone. And the Internet will grow rapidly now, because you no longer need a personal computer to become a *netizen*. For less than $300, you can buy a box that hooks to your TV and phone line and will put you on the Net.

OPPORTUNITIES FOR A GUERRILLA MARKETER

The size of the online market is impressive, but size alone is only the beginning of what makes it attractive for guerrilla marketers. After all, opening a storefront in Los Angeles doesn't guarantee you'll reach even a fraction of your potential customers in southern California. The In-

INTERNET DEMOGRAPHICS

Internet World's annual "State of the Net" issue (December 1996) included statistics for Internet growth and demographics from various research organizations, and the overall picture for online marketers is growing brighter all the time. Among the findings:

- the average Internet user is young (33 years old); educated (53 percent have at least one college degree); and well-off (average salary is $59,000).
- 73.4 percent of users are from the United States, 10.8 percent are from Europe, and 8.4 percent are from Canada and Mexico.
- the number of Internet host computers doubled (from 6.6 million to 12.8 million computers) between July 1995 and July 1996.
- more than 2.5 million people have purchased goods or services on the Net.
- Internet advertising revenues are expected to jump from roughly $200 million in 1996 to $2 billion by the year 2000.

ternet beckons because it gives you incredible leverage over your time and money, lets you zero in on prospects easily, and levels the playing field between you and your competitors, no matter how large or well financed they are.

How do you know if your product or service can make it online? Here's just a sampling of the types of goods and services available on the Internet today:

accounting, banking, brokerage, and legal services

arts and crafts

automobiles and automotive products

board games

books

CD-ROM publishing services

cemetery monuments

clothing

compact disks, laser disks, and videotapes

computer consulting and programming services

computer hardware and software

concert tickets

cosmetics

custom-stained glass

desktop publishing and graphic design services

discount telephone service

employment agencies

eyeglasses

flowers

food

ghostwriting and copywriting

insurance services

international trade consultants

jewelry

legal services

magazines and newsletters

muffins

museum reproductions

musical instruments

original artwork, posters, and prints

personal-care products

promotional products and advertising specialties

real estate

removable tattoos

research services

stamps and coins

training and educational services

travel services

vitamins

X-rated videos, photos, and adult toys

More goods and services appear every day.

NET BUSINESS OPPORTUNITIES

While it's a high-powered market for existing goods and services, the Net has also spawned dozens of new businesses for guerrillas. Here are four Net-based businesses you can profit from.

Internet training service — Train people in your community to use the Net. Offer general courses that show how to get connected and use standard tools like Microsoft Internet Explorer, Netscape Navigator and Communicator, or e-mail programs, and then offer individual training for specific user needs.

Internet-based research service — Charge companies, authors, and others to conduct online research.

Web site design service — It's not that hard to learn a Web authoring package like Microsoft FrontPage, Adobe PageMill, or Claris HomePage. If you've put together a pretty good World Wide Web site yourself, maybe you can get paid to create them for others.

Internet visibility service — You can make local businesses visible on the Net by creating advertisements, listing them in Web directories, or conducting online publicity programs for them.

An advertiser's dream

As with television, radio, or newspaper advertising, on the Internet you can broadcast your message to thousands or millions of people at once. But instead of paying big money to produce an ad, you can create your own online information package and post it yourself.

You can start small, with a few electronic classified ads if you like, or purchase banners or billboards on the World Wide Web or on an online service. You can post different messages in different locations to reach different audiences. You can quickly tell which messages are working best, which are losers, and how many people respond to each one.

For $100 or less, you can create a Web site of your own to advertise your products or services, and anyone with access to the Internet can find you there. You can offer much more information on a Web site than you can in a printed brochure, including pictures, sounds, or even video. And you can easily change your Web site whenever you like.

Even with a $20-per-month Internet account, you can post as many marketing messages and send as much *e-mail* as you like for nothing. Most Internet accounts also include free space for a small Web site. The prices of print ad pages and TV time place severe limits on just how much you can say about your product or service in these media, but you can deliver details, competitive comparisons, testimonials, and even provide catalogs and order forms for customers online for almost nothing. Online florists show color samples of their arrangements, and auto companies like Ford and GM offer interactive demos of cars that you can retrieve and run on your home PC. You can also accept credit cards online.

Finally, the targets of your online advertising are paying attention. People watching TV or skimming through a magazine might devote only a fraction of their attention to any particular ad, but in many cases, online prospects have chosen to read your ad.

Location, location, location

You can be in several places at once in the online marketplace. No matter how adept you are at selling in person, you're limited by your ability to talk with customers one at a time. On the Internet, your message can reach thousands of people at any time of the day or night anywhere around the world.

And with a minimum of expense, your product presentation can be as polished as one from a company ten times the size of yours. The online marketplace puts the smallest company on equal terms with the largest ones.

Customer service

With a Web site, you can display merchandise, offer complete information about it, and accept orders twenty-four hours a day, seven days a week. You can also offer a wider selection of products than you can in a printed catalog because it's less expensive to display information on the Web than to print it.

Niche marketing

While magazine advertising and direct mail can help you focus on particular markets, the Internet lets you attack markets with laserlike precision, and for free. You might pay hundreds or thousands of dollars for a focused mailing list, spend more on producing a direct-mail package, and then spend more on postage. But online buyers have already sorted themselves into topic-specific interest groups. You can place your

message in only the groups that promise high interest in your products.
As members of these groups respond to your messages, you can quickly
build a mailing list of prequalified prospects for future announcements.

Competitive intelligence

By joining the right online discussion groups, you can find out what
people are saying about your competitors' products or respond to questions or complaints about your own. Major companies like Microsoft
and Apple Computer host their own discussion groups to help customers with questions or to conduct focus groups on new products, and you
can do the same. Not sure if a particular marketing message is appropriate? Post it to a discussion group and ask for feedback first. Or, as
companies like Dell Computer do, you can pay one or more employees
to surf the Internet constantly, looking for scuttlebutt about your company or your competition and responding when appropriate.

You can also dig through thousands of computer databases containing millions of reports on business and market activity, corporate financial performance, labor statistics, and other facts that can help you
understand and respond to changing markets.

THE PITFALLS OF ONLINE MARKETING

As with the great California gold rush of 1849, there's a lot of profit to be
had in online markets, but it doesn't come without risk. True guerrilla
marketers survey the terrain and understand the risks in advance so that
they can anticipate and avoid the many traps that lie ahead.

Net savvy

To win in the online market, you must understand the online world:
how to connect, how to explore and exploit various market battlegrounds, where your competition is, and which battlegrounds to choose
for maximum return on your investment. If you're not computer-literate
already, you'll have to invest in some computer and communications
equipment and choose a method of going online, or else pay someone
else to do it for you. Once you are computer-literate, you must become
Net-literate and understand the online marketplace, how to navigate it,
and how to express yourself effectively in it.

When in Rome

Marketing techniques that might seem perfectly natural in the outside world can ruin your reputation online. In a well-publicized case a few years back, the Phoenix law firm of Canter & Siegel *spammed* the Internet, indiscriminately posting advertisements for their immigration law services on thousands of Internet discussion groups. Most of these groups had rules prohibiting such advertising, and most of these groups were about topics that had nothing to do with immigrating to the United States. The spam attack generated a tidal wave of *flames,* or hate mail, back to Canter & Siegel's electronic mailbox. Their Internet access was revoked by their service provider, and although the firm claimed it generated $50,000 worth of business through the effort, Canter & Siegel's online reputation was severely damaged.

Bad news travels quickly

Just as the online market allows you to deliver your marketing messages quickly and easily, it also allows your detractors to spread false or damaging information about you just as quickly and easily. One dissatisfied customer, or one prospect who's offended because you posted a marketing message on a particular discussion group, can pass a summary judgment of you and spread that judgment among thousands of people in seconds with the click of a mouse button. Canter & Siegel and other firms have found this out the hard way. As you pursue your marketing attack, it might be difficult to avoid being flamed entirely, but you can choose your battlegrounds and tailor your strategies to minimize the risk.

The world's largest anarchy

The Internet has been described this way because unlike a television network or a newspaper, the Internet has nobody in charge. When you place an ad in a newspaper, for example, the paper's staff will help you choose a location for maximum impact. On the Internet, you're on your own. Mistakes can be costly to your reputation and future efforts, so it's important to do your homework.

The online market isn't a mass market; it's not one giant fishbowl where you can cast your net for customers. Rather it's hundreds of smaller sub-markets. Many of the market's citizens may never frequent

AVOID SNAKE OIL

At times, the Internet is like the Wild West, and there are a lot of traveling snake oil salesmen out there. From the moment you get an online e-mail account — especially if you sign up on an online service like America Online — you'll be targeted with ads for lists of e-mail addresses, Internet advertising programs, income-generating opportunities, and other come-ons. Don't buy any of these products or services until you've spent enough time online to firmly understand what these products and services offer and how else you might accomplish the same things they promise. In most cases, the offers are either for services or products you don't need or that you can obtain by yourself with a little effort and imagination.

the areas where you post your information. You have to learn how to identify the markets with the greatest interest in your product or service, and how to reach them most effectively.

A thousand words are worth more than one picture

Your marketing efforts must be adapted to the physical realities of the electronic world. You might use photos or pictures liberally in print ads or on television, but these can be costly and time-consuming for prospects to read online. While your customers may well be able to view graphics or even video online, it takes a long time to deliver complex graphical information, and many customers will become impatient waiting for it. Your message must be delivered in such a way that the most likely target groups can see it easily.

Being invisible

In the physical world, you can bombard customers and prospects with passive marketing messages even when they're not particularly looking for them. People see and unconsciously remember print ads, TV ads, billboards, and bus ads as part of their daily lives. You can pay for billboardlike ads on the World Wide Web or online services, but in most cases, messages you post are invisible unless the prospect takes the time to look for and read them. Again, the answer is to be careful about placing those messages in the right locations and to use messages so enticing that people will choose to view them.

Once people are reading your messages, remember that you can't smile and shake hands with customers online. You'll have to learn to engage people with well-written copy, a helpful attitude, and reliable service.

The electronic till

If you actually take orders online, you'll have to decide which payment method to use. Some online marketers only provide product information online and then direct customers to place actual orders over the phone. Others accept credit card numbers online, and still others use secure payment methods that protect financial information from potential interception by computer hackers. Online transaction systems have improved dramatically in the past year and will continue to do so.

Paying attention

The online market is open twenty-four hours a day. As you manage your employees or deal with customers in person, it can be easy to forget that customers may also be waiting on the other side of your computer screen. You'll have to discipline yourself or your staff to monitor your online presence regularly. How often you check your e-mail or other online communication channels depends on the specific marketing strategies and battlegrounds you choose, but all your online customers and prospects expect speedy results, and you must be prepared to oblige them. Follow-up and consistency are even more important than they are when you're selling in person.

High volume can mean high demand

In most cases, your online marketing attack will be only part of your overall business marketing plan. But the Internet market is vast, and your online attacks may generate a staggering volume of e-mail or other electronic traffic. Your marketing plan must be designed to anticipate and deal with the load.

So while going online can boost your visibility and profits, it's also a brave new world that can reward the informed traveler and severely punish the ignoramus. It's no place for second-best, but it promises great rewards for A students.

2

Understanding the
Online Marketplace

The online market exists because millions of people use their computers to communicate. If your computer is connected to a network (either directly or via a dial-up connection with a modem), you can exchange messages with other computer users or gather information from other computers. And where there is communication, there's commerce.

THE BIRTH OF ONLINE SHOPPING

In personal computing's misty past — around 1975 — most communications were private. Companies had their own networks designed for employees only. Universities and government agencies had their own networks that were linked by a government-sponsored data pathway, or *backbone,* so that they could exchange research information. There were online information services, but these were basically collections of statistical data, legal citations, or business-related articles.

As personal computers began to catch on in households and small businesses, some of the companies that had built online business information services opened them up to individual users. CompuServe and others began offering services and information for consumers, such as games, weather, news, encyclopedias, e-mail, and discussion groups on various subjects, all via a phone call from a personal computer. To make connecting as easy and inexpensive as possible, the online services established local telephone numbers in every major city so that subscribers could dial in without having to make a long-distance call.

And when John and Jane Public subscribed to these services and went online, there were marketers ready to greet them. Right there with the games, news, reference libraries, and discussion groups were electronic shopping malls through which shoppers could get product information and order goods. Most online services have electronic shopping malls where you can browse and order everything from compact disks or tapes to flowers, from financial consulting or legal services to computer dating. All you need is a subscriber account to the service, a personal computer and modem, and a telephone line.

Today's online services have millions of subscribers and offer a wide range of services in an effort to appeal to the masses. Subscription fees run around $10 to $20 a month, in general, but you may pay extra for accessing special information or discussion areas on these services or for connecting for more than a few hours per month.

BULLETIN BOARDS

As the big online services were getting off the ground, early electronic entrepreneurs saw a separate market for more specialized online information. Using personal computers and bulletin board software, these guerrillas set up their own online services. Instead of trying to cover every subject and appeal to everyone with a personal computer, a bulletin board service or system (BBS) offers a more focused collection of information to a smaller group of subscribers.

Besides limiting themselves to specific topics, most BBS systems serve only a particular city or portion of a state. And instead of having local dial-in numbers all over the country, most BBSs are reached by only one phone number, so the call is a toll call for anyone outside the immediate area.

Today there are more than 20,000 BBSs in the United States alone, serving around 20 million regular callers. Some bulletin boards don't charge users for access at all — the operators make money selling advertising space or they simply offer the information as a hobby — but most charge from $20 to $100 a year for membership. A typical bulletin board has 1,000 or so subscribers, and BBS topics run the gamut from aviation and astrology through Zen and zoology. But nearly half of the BBSs in the United States specialize in relationships and sex.

ADVENT OF THE INTERNET

In the 1970s and 1980s the online marketplace was a series of islands, large and small, isolated from one another. The online continents were CompuServe, Prodigy, GEnie, America Online, Delphi, Dow Jones

News/Retrieval, and other major information services. The islets were
bulletin boards. But along with these islands was a worldwide computer
information pathway now called the Internet.

The Internet is a data transmission system, or backbone. Originally
called ARPAnet, it was designed as a destruction-proof communications system for researchers at universities, research labs, defense con-
tractors, military installations, and government agencies. The idea was
to distribute computing resources across the country so that an attack in
any one city wouldn't cripple defense research and computer communications.

In the 1980s the National Science Foundation (NSF) expanded the
ARPAnet backbone by setting up regional networks. These networks
were tied together into an entity called NSFnet, which made it easier
for universities to connect with each other. However, commercial activity was still prohibited on this government-funded, research-oriented
system.

In the 1990s this network of networks (now called the Internet) has
been opened up to commercial services and individuals. Along with
the NSFnet, which still links most universities and government agencies, today's Net includes a group of regional network service providers.
These service providers maintain portions of the commercial Internet
backbone or major networks linked to it and also offer connections to
corporations, organizations, and individuals.

Once commercial traffic became possible over the global Internet,
online services and bulletin boards began hooking up to it so that their
subscribers could communicate with people on other online services
and bulletin boards. In addition, companies large and small began tying
their networks to the Internet so that their employees could exchange
information with customers on other company networks or peruse the
vast stores of information available on university and government computer systems.

Today the Net has become the bridge that connects all the islands
and continents of the online marketplace into one colossal whole. It can
link you to hundreds of thousands of Web sites. It carries e-mail for
millions of people, allows billions of file transfers per year, and links host
computers at tens of thousands of colleges and universities, corporations, and government agencies around the world. As of mid-1996, there
were over 12.8 million distinct host computers connected via the Internet.

CLIENTS AND SERVERS

There are two types of Internet participants: *servers* (or *host computers*) and *clients.*

Servers are computers that store information and make it available to individual users or other servers. Servers are also called host computers, because they provide space for (or host) files, e-mail, Web pages, and other types of information.

Any computer can store files, but servers run special software that allows them to make those files available to others who request them. Each Internet s_____ type of server software (although one computer can r_____ ple, an e-mail server _____ news server software,

_____ rporate, government,
_____ that participate in the
_____ ssion group messages,

_____ information stored on
_____ and client programs to
_____ he activities you want to
_____ client program to send
_____ to view Web pages.

_____ networks? Let's look
_____ ss for individual In-

_____ net for years. Nearly
_____ the Internet, and in
_____ igh school networks
_____ rch papers and statis-
_____ ailable on university
_____ hnology researcher in
_____ atest genetic engineer-
_____ in the United States,

_____ he of the earliest members of the Net The United States Census Bureau, Department of Labor Statistics, Library of Congress, Federal Register, Securities and Exchange Commission, Commerce Department, National Weather Service, Smithsonian Institution, and the White House are just a few of the government entities that make information available over the Internet. You can see daily transcripts of White House press briefings, view electronic images from the Library of Congress collection of documents and artwork, look at color satellite weather maps that are updated constantly, or send an e-mail message to President Clinton or to your congressional representative.

Company networks have been joining the Internet in droves since commercial access became available in the early 1990s. Today thousands of companies large and small have their networks connected to the Internet and also have their own Web sites. By connecting their networks to the Net and setting up corporate Web sites, companies can present their products or services to the Internet community, communicate with customers and suppliers, and conduct online research. You can send e-mail to Bill Gates at Microsoft, request a quotation on a new computer from Dell Computer Corporation, or browse the stacks of an online bookstore at www.amazon.com.

Regional backbone providers such as Performance Systems International, UUNet Technologies, BARRnet, and CERFnet maintain regional portions of the commercial Internet backbone and also offer provider (ISP) services to companies and individuals.

Internet service providers *(ISPs)* like Evergreen, Netcom, Panix, and PrimeNet don't maintain parts of the Internet backbone, but they have high-speed connections to the Internet and provide access to the Net via dial-up or leased-line connections with individual computer users or corporate networks. Employees of these companies also sponsor Net-based discussions to help others learn about the Net.

Online computer services such as America Online (AOL), Prodigy, CompuServe, GEnie, and Delphi all offer their subscribers connections to the Internet. With an AOL account, for example, you can access AOL's own services, but you can also send e-mail to anyone else on the Net, participate in Internet-based discussion groups, or view World Wide Web sites.

Bulletin boards are smaller and usually localized and subject-specific versions of online services. Many now provide Internet mail access to their subscribers, and the larger boards act more like online computer services, offering full Internet access.

Individual servers don't provide Net access for subscribers or groups of users but instead offer collections of data or programs for others on the Net to use. For example, Microsoft, Silicon Graphics, Digital Equipment Corporation, Adobe Systems, Apple Computer, and other companies maintain servers that offer software, product information, and technical support for customers or prospects. There are millions of such servers on the Internet.

Individual users are people who are connected to the Net, either via a corporate or educational network or an ISP.

INTERNET SERVICES

The Net links lots of different computers that perform lots of different services.

Electronic mail (e-mail) is carried over the Net between individuals linked via corporate, government, and university networks, online services, bulletin boards, and Internet service providers (ISPs). When you sign up for an Internet account, you get an e-mail address to which others can send mail.

Discussion groups (or *newsgroups*) are like community bulletin boards where anyone can post and read messages. There are thousands of newsgroups on the Net, each focused on a specific topic such as music, politics, or various types of computers or software. Each works like a community bulletin board: you *post* a message with a specific topic, and others can read and respond to that message. You can use a newsgroup reader (or *newsreader*) program to see messages in newsgroups, or you can view them using a World Wide Web browser. You can also view newsgroups from inside most online services, or you can use the most popular Web browsers to view them as well. However, the specific selection of newsgroups you can view depends on which newsgroups your ISP provides access to. Most ISPs offer access to at least 10,000 different newsgroups, but some (online services in particular) don't give you access to newsgroups that discuss sex-oriented topics.

FTP (File Transfer Protocol) servers store text and graphics files. Most FTP servers are at universities. Before the Web came along, you

needed a special program like Fetch, Archie, or Anarchie to search for or
retrieve files via FTP. You can still use these programs (and you need to
use them) to retrieve (or *download*) files from an FTP-only server, but
you can also *upload*, or store files on a Web server and allow users to
retrieve them with a Web browser.

Gopher servers typically store text-only information. Rather than
having to retrieve a file via FTP, you can directly view the text in
documents on Gopher servers. Before the Web came along, you needed
a special program like WinGopher or TurboGopher to access Gopher
servers, but now you can use a Web browser to access them. Once you
access a Gopher server, you can use a search program like *Veronica* to
locate specific documents or other Gopher servers by name.

WAIS (Wide Area Information Servers) store text information, but
you can search for documents by the contents of those documents,
rather than just by title. Typically, you use a Gopher server to access a
program that lets you search for WAIS documents.

The World Wide Web has been around as a Net service since 1990,
but its popularity began taking off with the appearance of easy-to-use
browser programs in 1993. Programs like Netscape Navigator and Microsoft Internet Explorer are used by tens of millions of people as their
main method of accessing the Net. Today, when marketers consider
displaying information on the Net, they're talking about setting up a
location, or *site*, on the Web.

Another reason for the Web's popularity is that it's easy to navigate.
Web servers use a system called the Hypertext Transfer Protocol (*HTTP*)
that automatically links a document on one server with a document on
another. For example, you may be viewing a Web page that lists auto
information, but when you click on the *hypertext* option for Chevrolet,
you're transferred to the main menu of Chevrolet's own Web server. The
connection happens automatically, so it makes navigating to servers
around the world easy.

Although there are still many FTP, Gopher, and WAIS servers on the
Net, the Web has eclipsed these older information presentation methods because it lets you present richer information (graphics, sounds, and
video as well as text), it allows you to search for and view information
more easily, and it requires only one program instead of a handful of
them. Today's Internet user often uses the same browser program to
search for or view information on the Web, send and process e-mail,

view and participate in Internet-based discussion groups, view Gopher documents, and access files via FTP.

Internet Relay Chat *(IRC)* is the Net equivalent of CB radio. *Chat sessions* are real-time discussions in which several people are connected and exchanging text messages at the same time. The Net has hundreds of individual chat sessions, or *channels,* in use around the world via Internet Relay Chat (IRC). Unlike newsgroups, IRC channels are live: several people go online at once to read and respond to others' messages as they're typed. Some chat sessions support hundreds of simultaneous participants. Your screen looks like a script from a play as user names and comments follow one another. We won't spend much time on chat sessions as a marketing tool, however, because they're mostly free-for-all discussions on relatively inane subjects. You might make a sale or two by participating in a chat session, but the time you spent to do it wouldn't be worth it.

However, chat technology is also used in online *conferences,* special events on online services where an authority on a particular topic meets in a chat session with those interested. These are indeed good marketing vehicles, and we'll learn more about them in Chapters 3 and 9.

CONNECTING TO THE INTERNET

There are two ways to establish an Internet connection (see illustration on page 22):

1. Use a computer that's directly wired to a corporate, government, or university network that is connected by a leased telephone line to the Internet.
2. Use a modem on your PC to dial into a corporate or university network, an online service, an ISP's network, or a bulletin board that is connected by a leased telephone line to the Internet.

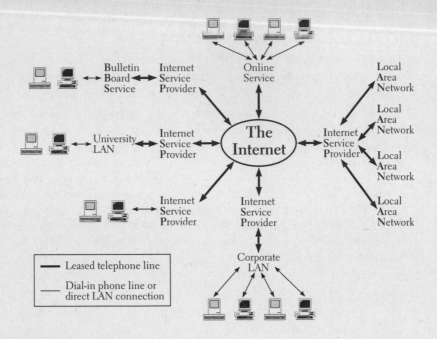

As the diagram shows, for example, an ISP may provide a *direct connection* to a *LAN* (Local Area Network) via a leased telephone line. If a company or university LAN is connected to the Internet, then any computer on it can have access to the Internet, although it's up to the LAN administrator to actually set up access to the Net for individual network users. LAN connections at large companies and universities are *continuous connections.* If your computer is set up for Internet access from the LAN and you have the right navigational programs on your computer, you can cruise the Internet anytime.

ISPs also provide *dial-up connections.* In this case, PC users dial into the ISP's host computer whenever they want to get on the Internet. When you sign up for Internet service with an ISP, the ISP will provide you with the software you need to connect with its network and to surf the Net.

If you use a corporate or university Internet connection, you may pay nothing for it. But if you sign up for an individual account with an online service, bulletin board system, or ISP, you'll pay about $10–$20 per month. This account should allow you unlimited access so that you can connect to the Net any time, any day, for as long as you like.

TYPES OF DIAL-UP CONNECTIONS

Most individual users connect to the Net via a dial-up connection, but not all dial-up connections are the same.

Shell accounts. If your account is with an online service like America Online or Prodigy, you have a *shell account,* in which you don't directly connect to the Net; you ask the online service's computer to do it for you. For example, when you cruise the Web via an AOL account, you click a button to ask AOL's computer to display a browser window, and each time you navigate to a new Web page, you're asking AOL's computer to find the page and display it for you. Shell accounts are easier to set up, because you only have to install one program on your PC — the program you use to dial the online service's host computer. But shell accounts are slower for Net surfing, because your requests must be processed by the service's host computer before they're sent out onto the Internet. Since an online service's host computer is probably dealing with requests from hundreds or thousands of people at once, the response times will vary widely.

IP accounts. If your account is with an ISP, you have an *IP account* (Internet Protocol account), in which you run the Internet communication protocols directly from your PC. These accounts are also known as *PPP* (Point-to-Point Protocol) or *SLIP* (Serial Line Internet Protocol) accounts. In this case, you use various programs on your own PC to do things like check for e-mail, display Web pages, or transfer files. It's a little more complicated to set up an IP account because you'll have to install a handful of programs on your PC, but your Net-surfing will be faster, because your requests for information will go directly from your PC to the Net, rather than having to pass through another host computer as they would on an online service.

CHOOSING AN INTERNET SERVICE PROVIDER

Any ISP can provide you with a connection to the Net, but as a guerrilla marketer, you'll want to make sure you're also getting the services you'll need to be successful online. There are two purposes for Internet accounts.

Access. You'll need an account through which you can access the Net, send and receive e-mail, participate in discussions, view Web sites, and transfer files.

Presence. You'll eventually need an ISP to host your storefront, help you obtain a unique Internet address (or *domain* name), and set up other marketing-related services.

You don't have to use the same ISP for both of those functions. You may want to sign up with an ISP now and surf the Net just to do a little reconnaissance and find out what it's all about, and then choose a different ISP later to host your Web site, for example. Nevertheless, there are several criteria you'll want to keep in mind when looking for an ISP.

Services

Decide which Internet services you want and make sure the connection method offers them. Every ISP and online service offers e-mail, newsgroups, Web browsing, and other basic services. But if you're planning to set up a storefront of your own, find out if the provider can help you with your Internet presence and marketing. Some of the marketing services to look for are:

- *domain name service*, where you get a network address for your company *(For more information about network addresses see "About Internet addresses" on page 26.)*
- *mailbot* (or mail responder) services, where a program automatically sends out a brochure in response to e-mail inquiries
- Web server hosting and design services

When shopping for an ISP, don't just look for a laundry list of services. Get some customer references or ask for a trial account and find out what it's like to use the services. One ISP's e-mail system may be much more cumbersome to use than another's, for example. Check out some of the ISP's other customers, and find out if they're happy with its services. Consider any new online account a trial — you can always change your mind and go with another ISP or online service if you don't like the first one.

Acceptable use policies

Another consideration in choosing an ISP is whether or not the ISP will permit you to conduct the kind of marketing program you want. Every ISP has *acceptable use policies* that spell out such things as how many addresses you can send an e-mail message to at once (which might limit bulk e-mailings), how many different newsgroups you can post the same message to, how much disk storage you can use, and so on. Get a copy of your ISP's policies, and read them to make sure your marketing plans won't be limited.

Reliability and performance

Conducting an online marketing program requires you to have frequent online sessions. Just as you wouldn't use a long-distance provider whose lines went down regularly, you shouldn't go with a cut-rate ISP if that means dealing with a system whose access number is frequently busy, whose Internet connection fails now and then, or whose equipment is so overloaded that your customers can't reach you easily. Ask the ISP for customer references, and check them out to see what sort of experience they've had.

User support

Larger ISPs have full-time technical support staffs who can help you with access or Internet navigation problems. Some offer training sessions, and some even distribute regular newsletters offering tips about surfing the Net. Your own level of technical savvy should determine the amount of service you demand from an ISP. If you think you'll need a lot of help, make sure the ISP offers it.

Cost

Unless you're connecting through a university or a corporation where you're not directly paying the bills, an Internet account will cost you something. You'll pay a monthly service charge, and there may be a monthly rate if you're renting space for a Web server or using a mailbot or other services. Find out what types of account the ISP offers, how each account's services differ, and what they cost.

If you're thinking about a dial-in account, find out whether or not the ISP has a local phone number in your area. Having to dial a long-distance number to access your ISP's computer will add significantly to your monthly Internet connection costs. Some ISPs have 800 numbers you can call to connect for a flat hourly fee, but most use commercial data networks like Tymnet or SprintNet, which have local numbers in most major cities.

If you're planning to use a continuous leased-line connection, find out from the ISP and your local telephone company about the cost to set up and maintain such a connection. Depending on the speed of the line, the connection can cost from $200 to over $1,000 a month.

(For more information about choosing an ISP, see "Choosing an elec-

tronic storefront" on page 91 or pick up one of the Internet user guides listed in the Appendix.)

ABOUT INTERNET ADDRESSES

With millions of users, thousands of servers, and thousands of networks, nobody would be able to find anything on the Net without addresses. (As it is, finding things is hard enough, which is why the Internet has been called an endless line of information dumpsters you can pick through.) Every network, server, or individual PC connected to the Net has a specific address. The address can tell you a lot about how or whether someone is connected, where they're physically located, and which Internet service you use to reach them.

If your online connection is through an online service, you have a user name, or screen name, that identifies you on that service, and to which others on that service send e-mail. For example, Guerrilla Marketing International is a subscriber on America Online (AOL), and its screen name there is GM INTL. However, because AOL is connected to the Internet, every AOL subscriber also has an Internet mailing address. An Internet address includes:

- the user's name
- the name of the network (or *domain*) through which the user is connected
- the type of network it is

For example, the Internet address for Guerrilla Marketing's mailbox on AOL is gmintl@aol.com. Notice that the address is in all lowercase letters. Most Internet-connected systems aren't case-sensitive, but it has become a widely followed convention to use lowercase letters for addresses.

In Guerrilla Marketing's Internet address, the space between *gm* and *intl* has been eliminated. While AOL allows spaces in screen names, the Internet doesn't, nor do most of the systems connected to it. So in this case, the two parts of the screen name are combined. The "at" sign (@) separates Guerrilla Marketing's user name from the network (or domain) name, aol.com. A netizen (an Internet user) would pronounce Guerrilla Marketing's Net address as "GM INTL at AOL dot com."

Domains

Many Internet networks (especially those in the United States) are grouped into different domain types.

.com   =   commercial
.edu   =   educational institutions
.gov   =   government agencies
.mil   =   military agencies
.net   =   network support centers
.org   =   other organizations (for example, nonprofits)

By recognizing these domain types, you'll know if someone sending you e-mail is from a commercial, government, educational, or some other network. There are also *geographic domains*, which usually show up in addresses from countries outside the United States. For example, a user in Canada might have the address abc1234567@freenet.carleton.ca, where the .ca at the end indicates that the network is in Canada.

You can make your one-person company look as large as General Motors by applying for your own domain name. Most ISPs offer a domain name service, which provides your own unique network name even though you're actually connecting via someone else's network. For example, if you sell clothing, you might apply for the domain name gladrags.com and then have a series of mailboxes in that domain, such as info@gladrags.com or sales@gladrags.com, even though you're actually connecting through an ISP like Netcom or PSI. With a custom domain name, your Net address contributes to your marketing effort.

Server addresses and URLs

Network or server addresses follow the same syntax as mailbox addresses but without the @ and user name. For example, a server called Sudsly at the Old Reliable Brewing Company might be called sudsly.olrel.com.

Along with the address of a server, you need to know which of the Internet utilities or searching programs you use to access it. For example, if a server is available via the Gopher search utility, the address might say, "gopher to sudsly.olrel.com" or "gopher: sudsly.olrel.com."

A Universal Resource Locator *(URL)*, which is the most common way to specify server addresses, has a standard format that indicates the type of program you need to reach it, followed by the server's address, and (if necessary) the specific location of a file on that server. For example, the address http://www.marketplace.com tells you that you need an http-compatible browser like Netscape Navigator to reach the World Wide Web (www) server on the network marketplace.com. URL addresses always follow this format. Here are two other examples:

gopher://nstn.ns.ca

ftp://wonders.com/excerpts/android

In the second example, the URL tells us to use the FTP service to reach the *wonders.com* server and then look inside the directory *excerpts* for the file *android*.

FROM NEWBIE TO INTERNAUT IN FIVE STEPS

It's easy to ruffle people's feathers by barging onto mailing lists or into newsgroups and asking all sorts of questions that immediately identify you as a novice, or *newbie*, in cyberslang. If you're careful about your approach to the Internet, on the other hand, you can learn what you need to launch an effective marketing attack without even tipping off the competition that you're coming.

Here's a five-step approach to experiencing the Net and preparing for your marketing attack.

1. Do your homework.   Before you go online, finish this book, get your hands on a good Internet user's guide, and start reading at least one magazine devoted to Net happenings. *(See Appendix for suggestions.)* No single book can tell you everything about the Net, and the pace of new developments is such that you'll need a magazine at first, and ultimately the Net itself, to keep track of what's going on. Magazines will give you an overall perspective about Net trends, and they'll also show you how to reach Net-based resources you can use to stay on top of new developments.

2. Get an Internet account.   Once you have a beginning idea of what's on the Net and which areas you'd like to explore, sign up for an account with a large ISP. *(See Appendix for more information.)* You'll get speedy access to all the major Internet services at a low price, and you'll also get good support if you run into problems. If you want the easiest possible route to the Net, join an online service, but be prepared for slower Internet access.

3. Send some e-mail. Try out the e-mail system and get used to sending, receiving, reading, forwarding, and deleting mail. Start exchanging e-mail with friends, or at least send a few messages to yourself so you get the hang of it. Don't send marketing messages yet, however, or add your e-mail address to your stationery or print advertising. Your explorations may lead you to settle on a different ISP eventually, and you should be sure you want to use a particular ISP before you begin marketing or publicizing your Net address. E-mail will be a fundamental feature of your marketing arsenal, so you should learn to use it as naturally as you use the phone.

4. Explore mailing lists and newsgroups. Use the ISP's search facilities to locate *mailing lists* and newsgroups on subjects related to your business or marketing plans. *(See Chapter 15.)* For the time being, be a *lurker* and just read the newsgroup or mailing list postings. Get a sense of what sorts of things people post, how they express themselves, and what they talk about. Learn from other people's mistakes by observing. Don't make your own contributions yet — save those for the days and weeks down the road when you're more experienced and you know exactly what your marketing plan will be.

5. Prowl the Web. Get on the Web and start poking around. You'll quickly find yourself going from one site to another as you click on various links. To check out sites of other companies that are in your business, use the search feature of your Web browser to locate them by name or industry category. *(See Chapter 15.)* Check out some sites mentioned in magazines, newsgroups, or mailing lists with which you're involved. If you don't like the experience you have with one online service or ISP, try another. Most Net access providers these days have free trial periods; even if they don't, you can always cancel one account and open another. Once you've become familiar with the various Net services and you're happy with the service, you'll be ready to move ahead with your marketing plans.

3

The Electronic Battlegrounds

Marketing is war. It is war against a host of competitors in the same business as yours who are competing with you for the same customers and the same sales dollars. As in the offline world, the online market isn't just one big battlefield; it's dozens of smaller battlefields, each of which has a unique terrain. And as in any war, the success of your online marketing attack will depend largely on your ability to choose battles you can win using tactics you can apply skillfully.

The first key to success in the online marketplace is understanding the characteristics of every battlefield so that you can choose the ones where your unique product, service, and marketing skills can compete most effectively. In this chapter, we'll look at the online battlefields and see how they're being used to market products and services.

As mentioned in Chapter 2, the online world sorts itself into three main areas: the Internet, online services, and bulletin boards. Although the Internet is now providing a link between these three areas, it's useful to look at them separately in terms of their marketing possibilities.

THE INTERNET

The Internet is a relative newcomer to marketing, having been around only since 1991. As a marketing venue, it offers the advantage of reaching millions of people around the world. The key disadvantage is that most of those people aren't likely to be interested in or aware of your product. Unlike online services, the Net is an open community. Nobody is in charge, so there's nobody to help you push your messages out to the people most likely to respond to them. Nevertheless, the Net's potential for commerce is growing by leaps and bounds. The World Wide Web now boasts more than 30 million users, and some studies show that the Net's overall population is growing at the rate of a million users a month.

Internet marketing, especially through the vehicles of mass e-mailings and the World Wide Web, has changed rapidly during the past two years. Most Net users have received dozens, if not hundreds or thousands, of e-mail letters selling something or other, and Web sites have evolved into flashy, interactive selling systems complete with billboards and animation. Further change is a certainty, but we can still look at a few key Net marketing vehicles whose value is unlikely to diminish over time.

E-mail

E-mail allows you to communicate directly with one person or thousands of people, and to do it for the cost of a monthly Internet account and the time it takes to compose a letter.

Individual e-mail is your personal response to an inquiry about your business from someone who has seen a listing in an online directory, read a message you've posted to a discussion group, attended an online conference or chat you've held, or read an electronic document you've published.

Bulk e-mail is promotional mail you send to a list of e-mail recipients. There are hundreds of companies on the Net that will gladly sell you lists of e-mail addresses to which you can send promotional letters, and some of them will even mail the letters for you. Of course, people don't like getting e-mail solicitations about things that don't interest them, so the best bulk e-mailings will be targeted at specific groups of people who have a high probability of interest in what you're selling. You can obtain targeted e-mail lists from Internet bulk e-mail firms, from trade associations you may be associated with, or you can create them yourself using special programs designed to extract all the addresses from messages posted to discussion groups.

The key advantages to e-mail are that

- It's very fast, often arriving within seconds after you send it.
- It costs you nothing except your monthly Net account fee.
- It can be aimed at specific individuals or groups of individuals.

(See Chapter 4 for information on e-mail marketing strategies.)

Web sites

For many Net newcomers, the World Wide Web *is* the Internet. And while the Web is only one of several key services offered on the Net, it's true that the Net has become extremely Web centric. There are several reasons for this.

- The Web is the simplest, most flexible means of accessing and displaying information on the Net, and it's where most Net-surfers spend most of their time.
- Nearly all of the hottest new Net technologies, such as virtual reality, animation, modular programming tools such as Java, and Internet telephones and conferencing systems, are being developed for the Web.
- Web browser software has evolved so that it now incorporates other Net services. Netscape Navigator and Microsoft Internet Explorer not only let users surf the Web but also manage e-mail, participate in newsgroups, and transfer files.

Web sites make it easy for others to view lots of information about your products, ask questions, view photos or video (and even order products), and they're much more inviting visually than simple text advertisements or discussion group messages. Thousands of companies are now using Web sites to display product information like the following:

This is the *home page* for Guerrilla Marketing Online, the Web site for Guerrilla Marketing, viewed through Netscape Navigator version 3. The page's URL address is in the Location box near the top of the window. Each of the boldfaced, underlined phrases and small icons on this page is a *hypertext link* that calls up another page of information when you click on it. Just below the page title is a row of navigation links, each of which displays a different area or department of the Web site when clicked. At the bottom of the page are icons, which also link you to different areas of the site.

For example, clicking the Store icon at the lower right corner displays the site's store page, where visitors can order products online.

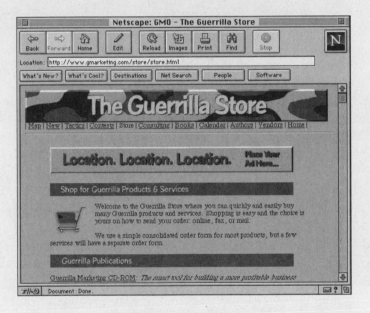

The Guerrilla Marketing Online home page also depicts an item you'll use yourself to promote your own Web site: a banner advertisement. Just below the row of navigation links at the top of the page, the banner ad for GoSite Internet Servers is a link that takes you to information about these Web servers. GoSite servers are rented Web servers for companies wanting to market on the Web, and since the Guerrilla Marketing Online site attracts a lot of Web marketers, placing a billboard here makes sense for GoSite's owners. You'll see lots of banner

---

VISIBILITY IS EVERYTHING

A Web site can display your company's product information, solicit feedback, and take orders, but it won't do any of these if your customers don't see it. With hundreds of thousands of Web sites out there in cyberspace, visibility is hard to get. It's essential to make your Web site's existence known to the people most likely to be interested in it.

Online services have What's New pages and pop-up advertisements that automatically direct visitors to a particular location, but a Web site is invisible unless you tell people how to reach it. As you'll see in Part II of this book, guerrillas use advertising, discussion groups, e-mail, conferences, electronic publishing, and publicity to promote their Web sites.

---

advertisements on popular Web sites as you surf the Web. *(See Chapter 6 for more information about banners.)*

In Chapter 5, you'll see how to design your Web site so that it delivers maximum marketing impact for your company in the most efficient and cost-effective manner.

Web directories and malls

Another way to market your business on the Web is to list it in a Web business directory. You can list your company by business category, display your electronic contact information (Web site or e-mail address), and in many cases include a 50- or 100-word description of your business. Generally, it doesn't cost anything to list your company in Web directories.

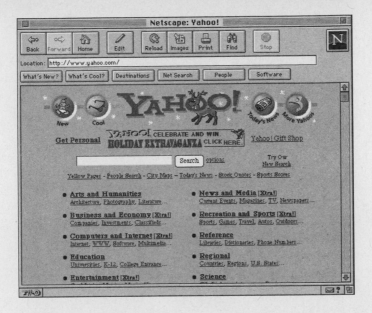

This is the home page of Yahoo, one of the most popular directory sites on the Web. You can search through the directory for a particular business by name, or you can search for keywords related to the services or products a business offers. If you prefer, you can display a certain category of businesses and then browse through the names shown there. *(See Chapter 5 for more details about marketing with Web sites.)*

Web shopping malls

A variation on the basic directory theme is a Web shopping mall, which lists only businesses that have something to sell. One of the most popular Net malls is the Internet Mall, as shown on page 35.

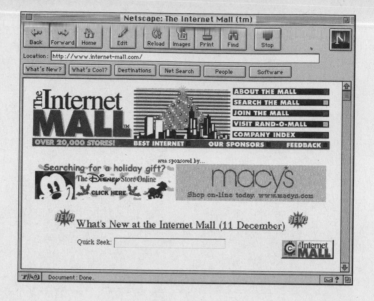

This mall began as a listing of business descriptions that was distributed via an e-mailing list, but now it's a Web site that hosts descriptions
of more than 20,000 companies as well as hypertext links to each company's site or e-mailbox. (When you click a Web link to an e-mail
address, you'll see a window where you can enter the message you want
to send, and then you click a button to send it.)

Like most Web directories, the Internet Mall accepts listings for free,
as long as your business sells something and accepts orders online.
However, it excludes multilevel marketing schemes and other get-rich
types of businesses. Most shopping malls will also host your company's
Web pages for an additional cost.

General-interest malls like the Internet Mall expand your visibility by
placing your company description and Web or e-mail link in another
location in cyberspace. However, these malls often list dozens, hundreds, or even thousands of businesses, and they may not draw many
people who are interested in your particular business.

There are also topic-specific or regional geographic malls that can
filter prospective customers much more effectively. There are regional
malls for places like Maui, Hawaii, and for cities like Palo Alto, California, or Sedona, Arizona, and there are topic-specific malls focused on
industries such as real estate, financial planning, and automotive prod-

ucts, to name a few. It usually costs money to locate in a regional or topic-specific mall, but it can be worth it. By listing your company in a mall whose subject automatically draws the hottest prospects to your business, you'll have a head start on online sales.

For example, Sedona, Arizona, hosts several million visitors a year from all over the world, and the Sedona Online mall attracts visitors from all over the world as well. It costs $50 a month or more to locate in this mall, but for a Sedona-based business, being listed here creates instant visibility with people who could well be planning a visit to the city soon.

If you're serious about getting as much visibility for your business as possible on the Net, you should be listed in as many Web directories as you can find. *(See Chapter 6 for more about advertising in Web directories.)*

Newsgroups

Newsgroups are the special interest groups of the Net. There are currently more than 20,000 such groups on just about any topic you could name.

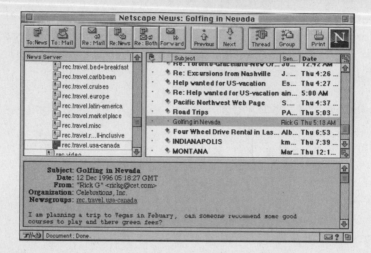

This is the rec.travel.usa-canada newsgroup as viewed with Netscape Navigator version 3. This newsgroup is devoted to travel in the United States and Canada, and it hosts messages relating to that topic. At the upper left corner is the list of available newsgroups (the specific selection depends on which groups your ISP subscribes to). In the list, the rec.travel.usa-canada group is selected, so we see a list of the messages in that group in the list at the upper right corner.

The icons and buttons around the list of subjects vary depending on the type of newsreader software you're using to view a newsgroup, but the list of subjects looks the same. Newsgroups can list thousands of messages stretching back for months or years, and the newsreader software allows you to limit the selection by viewing only messages posted since a certain date, or only messages that you haven't already read.

Once you select a subject name and open it, you see the text of the message itself. In the preceding example, the message titled Golfing in Nevada has been selected in the list at the right, and the message itself appears below.

Again, the newsreader you use may look different, but the features are the same. You can jump to the previous message, move to the next message, send a response to this message, or post a new message on a different subject.

A response differs from a new message in that it's attached to the existing message. A group of responses to an original message is called a *thread.* Typically, messages in a newsgroup are displayed in chronological order, but you can zero in on a particular thread of messages and view only the messages in that thread.

Participating in newsgroups is an easy way to focus on a group of people with a particular interest. You can find out what they're saying about the subject in general, what problems or needs they have, what they're saying about your competition, and even what they're saying about you. You can conduct market research about new products or promotions, and you can offer useful information that will help build your reputation and ultimately bring customers to your door.

Most newsgroups frown on blatant commercial announcements, but guerrillas know how to get their messages across without violating a group's etiquette. One key is to use a *signature* (or .sig) at the bottom of each message you post, identifying you and your business and explaining how to reach you online. *(For tips on signatures, see "Your signature" on p. 76. See Chapter 7 for more information about newsgroup marketing strategies.)*

Mailing lists

There are more than 20,000 mailing lists on the Net, and that number is sure to rise. Some lists are very specific and are sent only to a group of hand-picked recipients, while others are more general and have thousands of readers. In terms of marketing, mailing lists are a type of discussion group, and you use the same techniques in them that you use in a newsgroup or forum.

Mailing lists are groups of people who all read each other's mail. Any mail addressed to the list's address is sent to every subscriber of the list. There are three main advantages to mailing lists over other types of discussion groups.

- Anyone with e-mail access to the Net can participate in a mailing list. Forums on online services can only be accessed by subscribers of that service, and it's possible that a newsgroup won't be available to all of your potential online prospects. But everyone on the Net can get e-mail.
- When you subscribe to a mailing list, the messages come right to your mailbox. You don't have to access a particular discussion group and then scan through messages to keep up.

- You can set up a mailing list of your own fairly easily. You can do the whole thing yourself using shareware or freeware list management programs if you have a Windows, Windows NT, or Unix-based server connected to the Net. If you don't have such a server, many ISPs can set up a mailing list for you for less than $100.

Most mailing lists frown on blatantly commercial announcements, but as with discussion groups, participants often use signatures at the ends of their messages to promote their businesses. And it's not uncommon to see mailing list participants offering advice on a subject close to their own business, thereby encouraging requests for business by direct e-mail response.

To find out which mailing lists are out there, you can:

- search for mailing lists with a Web search utility
- participate in newsgroups that match your interests and watch for mentions of particular mailing lists on the same topics, or post a message asking if anyone knows of some
- check a "list of lists" maintained by someone on the Net *(See Appendix.)*

Once you subscribe to a mailing list, you receive copies of all the mail posted to that list. Each message looks exactly like an e-mail message *(see Chapter 4)*. Depending on how active the list is, that could be one or two messages a day or dozens a day. Some particularly active lists have a Digest option, in which all the day's messages are compiled into one document and sent to you that way.

In any event, joining a mailing list means paying attention to your electronic mailbox on a daily basis to check for new messages you've received. *(See Chapters 4 and 7 for more on using mailing lists for maximum marketing impact.)*

FTP servers

If you don't want to spend the time setting up and maintaining a Web site, you can publish information on the Net by storing it on a different type of server. Along with Web servers, FTP, Gopher, and WAIS servers can all present information on the Net. We won't consider Gopher and WAIS servers as marketing vehicles in this book, however, because the Web has eclipsed them as the simplest and most popular way to present text on the Net. While you may not want to store marketing information on a Gopher or WAIS server, however, there's lots of useful information you might want to locate on them. *(See Chapter 15 for more information.)*

FTP servers store files. By using an FTP server, you can place a graphic file, a program, or a video or sound file on the Net so that anyone can access it — all you have to do is publish the file's address. Most ISPs maintain FTP servers, and you can store files on them for free.

An FTP server is a computer that can be located by an FTP searching utility such as Archie or Anarchie. These servers can't display graphics, but you can list information in various files and directories to provide product information, order forms, and free information. When you access an FTP server, you see a list of files or directories like the following:

```
========= ftp.acns.nwu.edu:pub/newswatcher =========

  Name                        Size   Date     Zone  Host                 Path
□ helpers                       -   9/26/94    1   ftp.acns.nwu.edu  pub/newswatcher/h
□ inn-xpat-patch.txt           1k  10/10/94    1   ftp.acns.nwu.edu  pub/newswatcher/i
□ ms-word-format-docs           -  10/1/94     1   ftp.acns.nwu.edu  pub/newswatcher/m
□ newswatcher-20b14.sea.hqx  426k  10/1/94     1   ftp.acns.nwu.edu  pub/newswatcher/n
□ old-release-notes             -  10/10/94    1   ftp.acns.nwu.edu  pub/newswatcher/o
□ readme.txt                   2k  10/10/94    1   ftp.acns.nwu.edu  pub/newswatcher/r
□ release-notes-20b14.txt     12k  10/10/94    1   ftp.acns.nwu.edu  pub/newswatcher/r
□ source-20b14.sea.hqx       534k  10/1/94     1   ftp.acns.nwu.edu  pub/newswatcher/s
□ user-doc-20b14.sea.hqx     103k  10/1/94     1   ftp.acns.nwu.edu  pub/newswatcher/u
□ user-doc-20d17.sea.hqx      77k   7/3/94     1   ftp.acns.nwu.edu  pub/newswatcher/u
```

Here, the server name is ftp.acns.nwu.edu, and we've used the Anarchie utility to view the contents of the newswatcher directory on this server. This server offers a newsgroup reader program called Newswatcher, along with related files. You can view the list of files in any directory by double-clicking on the folder icon. To see what's in any individual file or to get a copy of the Newswatcher program itself, simply transfer, or download, it to your own computer and open it up there.

ONLINE SERVICES

In many ways, online services represent the richest marketing opportunities for the electronic guerrilla. Although even the largest online service is fairly small compared with the total online marketplace, you'll find a high concentration of high-quality customers on these services.

ONLINE SERVICES VERSUS THE NET

Some analysts say that online services are dinosaurs. After all, the World Wide Web offers superior graphics, sounds, and even video, and it's just about as easy to use as an online service. Also, Internet access through an ISP can be cheaper than a subscription to an online service.

There's no doubt that the Net has hurt the online services business. Apple Computer shut down its eWorld service in 1996, and Microsoft, which had planned to open Microsoft Network as an online service, decided instead to become an ISP and locate its services on the Web. Both Prodigy and CompuServe, the other two of the "Big Three" services, experienced declines in subscriptions between 1994 and 1996.

But don't count the online services out just yet. America Online now boasts more than 7 million subscribers, and it has an "unlimited access" rate that's as cheap as it is at many of the larger ISPs. In addition, AOL and the other online services still offer access to specialized sources of information — business databases, for example — that you can't get over the Net.

Our guess is that online services will never completely disappear, because they give Net newcomers what they want in the easiest possible way. Just as people buy magazines because they want a certain selection of news or information on a particular topic in a particular package, they will continue subscribing to online services because they like a service's look, feel, and its collection of services and information.

Here are some of the factors that make online services promising places to market your company.

1. The services are consumer-oriented. Online services cater to consumers with shopping, games, special-interest forums, and other services. People who join online services want these types of service, so your promotion or ad won't come as a shock, as it might in some Internet locations or bulletin boards where users frown on blatant commercial activity. Shopping has always been a major attraction for online subscribers.

2. Online services have built-in mechanisms for marketing your wares, including classified ads, billboards, and shopping malls. The marketing staff at each service will help you set up an electronic storefront or promotion. Online services have menus and icons that make it easy to notice and locate shopping or other services, so the chances of your attracting subscribers to your store are better than they are on the Internet.

3. Each online service has dozens of discussion groups that help you focus your marketing attack on audiences who are already interested in your product. And, unlike Internet newsgroups, these discussion groups include other features you can use as marketing weapons, such as libraries where you can publish articles and chat rooms where you can hold online conferences.

Marketing on the online services

Jump onto any online service and you'll find marketing in the picture from the very first screen you see when you sign on to the very last screen you see when you sign off.

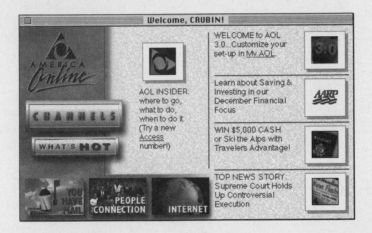

This Welcome screen automatically appears whenever you connect to America Online. Notice the icons and text promoting the AARP forum and a Traveler's Advantage contest at the right. Promotional messages like these appear on all the major online services. CompuServe's What's New window lists nearly two dozen such promotions each day. The specific promotions change daily or weekly, and you can arrange for your new storefront, *forum,* or any special promotions or contests you run to be listed here. *(See Chapter 6 for details.)*

Classified ads

Classified ads are a tried-and-true method of marketing at low cost, and some ads are free on online services. On America Online, for example, the entrance to the classified ad section looks like this:

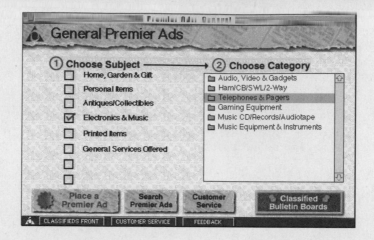

AOL offers Premier ads, which cost from $10 to $20 per month, as well as ads on its Classified Bulletin Boards, which are free. Premier ads can be searched for by the ad name or by a word or phrase in the ad text, and they offer other extras such as prominent headlines, built-in hypertext links to an e-mail address or Web site, and more prominent placement in a list of ads in their category. Here's the Telephones & Pagers category of Premier ads:

Each ad has a title or subject line. Unlike with newspaper ads, readers can't see all the text of an online classified as they browse the section; your ad title must prompt them to open up your ad and read

on. In addition to a general classified ads area, online services may
have topic-specific classifieds as in some of their forums (see *Forums
below*).

Here's a specific ad for a pager service:

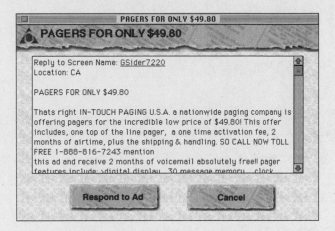

Notice the larger, boldface headline here, and the hypertext link
you can click to respond to the ad. In contrast, the free Bulletin Board
ads are just plain text without special headlines or hyperlinks. You save
money using Bulletin Board ads in this case, but your ad must compete with a far higher number of other ads for the reader's attention.
On a recent visit to the General Merchandise section of AOL's Bulletin Board ads, for example, there were more than 8,000 classified
ads in 32 separate categories. (*See Chapter 6 for more on using classified ads.*)

Forums

Forums, also called special interest groups (*SIGs*) or *Roundtables,* are
the clubhouses of online services. Most services have at least fifty forums
in a wide variety of topics. On page 46 is an example from America
Online.

The Aviation forum's main screen contains buttons that take you to the forum's chat rooms and information center. The scrolling list below the buttons lists other forum departments, such as file libraries. There's also a classified ad section specifically for aviation-related items. Notice that this forum hosts regular chat sessions. In this example, there's a Learn To Fly conference on this day at 9 P.M. Eastern time.

This forum is actually a collection of even more specific forums. There are message boards on such topics as military aviation, commercial aviation, and air shows. Many online forums are just as detailed and specific, so you can target customers with great precision. For example, if you have a great product for ultralight aircraft, just zero in on that area and its message board to hobnob with other ultralight enthusiasts and build your company or product's image.

Another feature of this forum is a billboard ad in the lower left corner. Clicking on this button displays information about a special message board for Stoddard Hamilton aircraft kits, as well as information about the Stoddard Hamilton company and its products *(see "Billboards, buttons, and banners" below).*

Forums are an excellent way to build public awareness of your company and give you invaluable feedback and competitive intelligence. *(See Chapter 7 for details.)*

Billboards, buttons, and banners

Online services also offer advertising in the form of billboards, buttons, and banners, which are interactive buttons or screens that pop up on specific screens throughout the service. For example, here's the main entrance to the Wheels forum on America Online:

Here, you can see three buttons at the bottom of the screen that advertise AutoVantage auto buying service, American Express, and Starbucks coffee. Clicking one of these buttons will display more information about the company or product. For example, clicking the Starbucks button displays information about the company's gift sampler products, and you can order them right on the spot if you like. Prodigy offers similar buttons on its pages.

Other billboards on online services pop up when you log on. Here's one from America Online:

Billboards like this let you grab the user's undivided attention, but they're expensive. You can spend anywhere from $5,000 to more than $50,000 a month for billboards. *(See Chapter 6 for more information.)*

Shopping malls

Electronic shopping malls host storefronts for dozens of vendors. Depending on the online service and your budget, you can put up your own storefront or participate in an online catalog. With a storefront, you can offer product information, online ordering, and photos of your products. Here's the shopping area from America Online:

As you can see, certain individual stores have paid extra for buttons right on the main shopping area page, while others are listed within categories accessed by clicking the buttons at the top. For example, if you click the AOL Member Zone button, one of the locations inside is the America Online Store. Let's go inside:

Each category of products has a separate listing, and clicking on a category reveals the products in it. For example, if you're interested in AOL-logo items, just click on the AOL Logo Shop listing to reveal a selection of logo merchandise, like this:

Here, you can choose from hats, shirts, and other items. Once you select a particular item, you can see a picture and more information about it, and then specify the size and quantity you would like. As you order items, they're added to your Shopping Cart.

```
┌─────────────────────────────────────────────────────────────┐
│  SHOPPING CART                                                │
│  Double-Click on cart entry to review item.                   │
│  ┌──────────────────────────────────────────────────────┐    │
│  │ (1)     AOL Gray Logo T-Shirt              $18.17     │⇧│  │
│  │ (1)     AOL Logo Denim Shirt               $43.87     │ │  │
│  │ (1)     AOL Black Twill Baseball Cap       $19.82     │ │  │
│  │                                                      │⇩│  │
│  └──────────────────────────────────────────────────────┘    │
│       Extra Charges May Apply. Please Refer to Individual Store Policies.│
│       (3) Items for: ($81.86)                                 │
│                                                               │
│         [Checkout] [Review Item] [Back to Shopping]           │
│       [Remove Item from Cart] [Remove ALL Items from Cart] [ ? ]│
└─────────────────────────────────────────────────────────────┘
```

You can view the contents of your Shopping Cart at any time and remove or add items to them before you actually place your order. When you click the Checkout button, you're asked for your shipping address. You don't have to supply credit card information, because this information is already on file for your AOL account.

The America Online Store is one of several dozen on America Online, and each has its own screens and ordering setup. America Online's is pretty fancy, but you can be successful with a far less elegant look to your store. Each online service lets you set up stores like this. *(See Chapter 5 for more information on strategies and techniques.)*

Online conferences

If you have some expertise that may be of interest to lots of online subscribers, you may be able to schedule a special online conference. Conferences related to specific forums are promoted on the forum's opening screen, and there's usually a schedule of conferences you can access within each forum. *(For an example of conferences promoted on AOL's Aviation Forum, see p. 46.)* If you're a really big celebrity, you can schedule a conference in the main auditorium of an online service, and it will be promoted on the service's welcome or opening screen, so all users can see the notice when they log on.

In a conference, an expert on a particular topic enters a chat room at a certain time, and you're invited to join him or her there to ask questions. Everyone in the conference sees all the comments or questions as they scroll down the screen, each preceded by the person's name or conference *"handle."* Here's how it looked during a chat session Charles did on the Guerrilla Marketing forum on AOL. (His handle here is CRUBIN.)

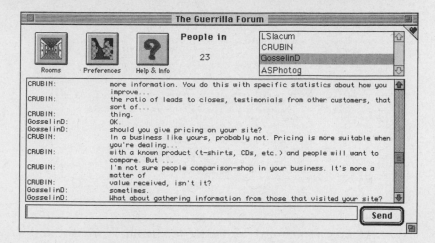

Here, you can see who is in the conference audience. Questions and replies are in the main part of the screen. Forums on online services are always looking for experts who can hold online conferences. *(See Chapter 9 for more information.)*

BULLETIN BOARDS

Compared with the Net and online services, bulletin board systems are very small slices of the online marketplace. Most BBSs have 1,000 or fewer regular subscribers, although some have more. The largest bulletin boards in the country boast more than 150,000 users.

But what you lose in numbers on most BBSs you gain in devotion. Many BBS subscribers are more active participants than their cousins on the Net or online services, so your chances of reaching any of them during a given day are better. Bulletin boards are also topic- or geography-specific, allowing you to focus on users in a particular subject area or city. Although the majority of BBSs are devoted to distributing shareware, games, pornography, or supporting adult chat lines, there are some in every part of the country that handle other topics such as religion, fishing, medicine, finance, bird-watching, screenwriting, scuba diving, space exploration, law, careers, reptiles, and ecology.

To get an idea of what sorts of things you can do on a BBS, let's look at the example on page 52.

```
Caller number     :  0,797,?81       | Your total calls :  1
You are on node#  :  105             | Security level   :  5
Subscription left: (never subscribed)| Your last call   :  Tuesday 10/04/94
Your uploads      :  0 files         | Your downloads   :  0 files
Download limit    :  1,000,000/day   | Used today       :  0 bytes
-------------------------- >>Demo Mode - Some Limits<< --------------------------
Exec-PC   T O P   M E N U
<F>iles ......... File Collection MENU
<M>essages ...... Message System - Conference MENU
<I>nternet ...... Access to Full Internet Superhighway
<K> QWK Mail .... Access QWK Mail - The off-line mail reader
<S>ubscribe ..... Exec-PC Membership and Renewal sign-up for full access
<R>ead mail ..... Display messages addressed to me
<D>oors ......... Doors MENU - Run PC Catalog, games, chat, more...
<W>ho ........... Show me who is on the system right now
<L>ist-user ..... Find names of subscribers to Exec-PC
<U>ser Settings . Setup MENU - Change my password, address, prompts, etc.
<A>nsi/color .... Turn on/off color and graphics from BBS
<B>ulletins ..... Information about this BBS
<H>elp .......... HELP on the most often asked questions for this BBS
<?>help ......... HELP with this menu
<G>oodbye ....... Log off of Exec-PC      <X>pert ....... Toggles short menus
(52 minutes left) TOP Menu <?=HELP> -> _
```

This is the *top menu* from Exec-PC in New Berlin, Wisconsin, one of the largest BBSs in the country. As you can see, it has a variety of services, including a library of files, a mail and conferencing system, Internet access, games, and a help system. This is a fairly representative sample of the kinds of services available on a BBS.

If you don't find one or more BBSs whose subscribers match your target market, you can always start one of your own. The lists of BBSs in the United States are littered with boards that have been set up by companies to support and market their own products. However, it's far simpler to set up a Web site to accomplish the same goals. More and more, today's BBSs are run as miniature online services by individuals who use them to earn money by selling subscriptions and advertising. *(See Chapter 8 for more information about how to market on BBS systems.)*

PART II

Strategies for Online Battles

4
E-mail and Mailing Lists

Electronic mail (e-mail) is as essential to online commerce as the telephone and paper mail are to offline commerce, so our in-depth discussion of guerrilla marketing strategies for the online market begins here.

As you've already seen, there are many different ways to market your business in the online world, but even if your online connection is limited to e-mail, you can do a remarkable amount of electronic business. You can:

- send promotional messages to individuals
- build your identity on mailing lists
- send product information
- accept orders
- offer customer support

This chapter gives an overview of e-mail and provides tips and techniques for using e-mail for maximum marketing impact.

ABOUT E-MAIL

Basically, e-mail is the electronic equivalent of paper mail. You compose a message and address it to the recipient, and the message is delivered to the recipient's mailbox. The recipient can check his or her mailbox at any time, read the message, and then save it, reply to it, forward it to somebody else, or toss it out.

The main difference between e-mail and paper mail is that messages are delivered in seconds or hours instead of days or weeks. Also, the computer gives you lots of automated features that make it much easier to manage than paper mail.

Using e-mail

In order to use e-mail, you need an online account through an ISP, online service, or BBS. The service you choose should have an *Internet mail gateway* that allows you to send mail to anyone else on the Internet, instead of only to people on the particular service you're using. Every ISP, all of the major online services, and many BBSs provide this type of mail service, but, as mentioned in Chapter 2, you may want to ask about or test several services for yourself until you find one that has a mail system you feel comfortable using.

Composing mail

With a mail account set up, you now have access to the 30 million or so other people on the Net who have e-mail addresses. Your job will be to reach the ones who are interested in buying your product or service, who have already bought your product or service, or who can recommend your product or service to someone else. The process begins when you compose a message. To do this, enter the mail function of your online service or BBS or start the mail program you're using on your computer.

To see how mail works, we'll look at the mail function on America Online. Most other mail programs have similar features, although the mail forms won't look the same.

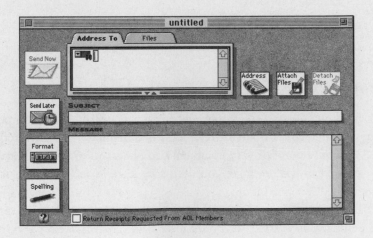

The upper box on the message screen (which contains the Address To box) is called the message's *header*. The header contains the information your mail system (or *mailer*) needs to properly handle your message.

The To: box, where you type the address or addresses of the person(s) to whom you want to send mail, can contain as many addresses as you like, but it must contain at least one.

- If you're sending only to someone on the same online service as you, you need enter only their user name on that service. For example, if you're on America Online and you want to send mail to Guerrilla Marketing's mailbox, the To: box address would read GM INTL.
- If you're sending to someone across the Internet, you need to enter their full Internet address. For example, if Guerrilla Marketing wanted to send a message to someone named Bob Jones on Netcom, the To: box address would read, bjones@netcom.com.

As you work with e-mail, you'll build a list of addresses for people you contact all the time. You can add these to your *address book* and then quickly look up an address and copy it to your message header. In the preceding example, you display the address book by clicking on the Address icon at the right.

Most mailer programs allow you to compile a list or group of address-ees under one group name (or *alias*) and then send to everyone in that group by simply putting the group's name in the To: box.

E-mail also allows you to send carbon copies (Cc:) and blind carbon copies (Bcc:). In some cases, these options are shown below the To: box. On AOL, you click on the To: icon in the Address To box and you can select a Cc: or Bcc: if you like. A carbon copy address shows up in the message's header when it's delivered, while a blind carbon copy address doesn't, so you can send a copy to someone without others knowing you've sent it.

The Files tab behind the Address To tab displays a list of any files you've attached to this message. If you're attaching a file to your message (perhaps sending a proposal or a price list), you click the Attach Files button at the right and then select the name of the file from a list that shows the contents of your disk. That file's name then shows up in the Files list. If you're sending mail to someone on the same online service, you can attach formatted program files, graphics, or any other binary file; to send a file across the Internet, you may have to convert the file to a text format that the Internet's mail communication protocol will accept. Most mail programs will convert attached files automatically. If you've attached a file and want to remove it, just click the Detach Files button and select the file name.

The Subject box displays your message's subject line (a message can't be delivered without a subject). The proper address ensures that your message reaches its proper destination(s), but a good subject line is crucial if you want your message to be read. Some of your recipients will be wading through dozens or even hundreds of mail messages a day. Your subject line must work like the title of a book or magazine article so that readers will want to read the message itself.

The Message box contains the actual message you're sending. Simply type text into the box or paste it in from another document.

It's tempting to use the same formatting conventions you use with postal mail. However, as *"Reading mail"* on p. 61 indicates, the sender's name and address, the date and time of the mailing, and the recipient's name and address are automatically attached to every e-mail message, so you can leave these out of the body of the message. It seems weird to just start typing the message itself without so much as a "Dear John," but you'll get used to it.

On the other hand, your signature at the end can be an important marketing tool that includes not only your name and company name, but also a promotional message. *(See "Your signature" on p. 76.)*

The Format button displays an icon bar that lets you either choose the font, style, and size of text in your message or include hypertext links in it. For example, you might include a hypertext link to your company's Web site in an e-mail message; anyone interested in more information can simply click the link to connect to your Web site.

The Spelling button activates a spelling checker that checks your message for spelling errors.

The Return Receipt box lets you request a receipt that tells you when the message is actually read by its recipient. When the message is read, you'll receive a mail message telling when this occurred. The Return Receipt function works when you send mail within an online service or BBS but not when you send mail across the Net.

Saving mail

At any time after you begin creating a new message, you can save the message to your disk. You must type a name for the new file when you save the message; do not use the same name as the message's subject. We recommend saving early and often. There's nothing worse than getting halfway through a fabulous marketing message when you're called away by a customer in the store, and you forget you were work-

TEXT IS STILL BEST

The Attach Files feature of e-mail is particularly useful when you want to send a word processor file, spreadsheet file, program file, or graphic to someone else. You may have a nice brochure in an Adobe Acrobat file and want to attach it to your e-mail sales pitch, for example. But be careful when attaching files to e-mail messages.

Lots of people who use e-mail never use the Attach Files feature and don't know how to retrieve or open an attached file when they receive one. Furthermore, not all mail systems can properly receive and decode files attached to e-mail messages.

If you're sending mail to someone you know and you've successfully attached files in the past, then it's no problem. But if you're sending mail (a brochure, for example) to new prospects or people you don't know, don't attach a file to your mail message. Instead, copy the contents of the file into the message itself. Since e-mail messages are limited to text only, you won't be able to send graphics inside a message, but at least you'll be sure your recipient can read the message.

ing on the message, and the janitor comes by and shuts off the computer. Save any messages in progress, and save finished messages when you're done.

Sending mail

Once you've completed the header and body, click the Send Now or Send Later button to send the message. On America Online, the Send Now button works only if you're currently connected. If you're not currently connected, click the Send Later button and the message is saved for transmission the next time you are connected.

Most mail programs let you specify the exact time you want a message sent, so you can have it sent automatically the next time you connect, or you can have the program connect for you at a particular time and send the message then. It's useful to preset a time for sending messages when you use a service that is particularly busy during certain times of the day, or when you have a message that shouldn't be delivered before a certain day or time.

Checking your electronic mailbox

Each time you connect with your service provider, you can check for new mail you've received, send mail you wrote since you last connected,

DELIVERY PROBLEMS?

E-mail is remarkably reliable, but sometimes it doesn't go through. Delivery problems are most likely to happen when you send mail across one or more Net gateways rather than when you send a message to someone at your ISP or online service. If the delivery system is working properly and the mail was undeliverable because you used a nonexistent address, you'll receive a message that says your mail couldn't be delivered.

If the delivery problem is due to a glitch with a Net gateway or the computer that should be receiving the mail, you may not be notified. If you suspect that your mail didn't go through, however, you could try sending a message to "postmaster@network name," stating the time you sent your message and its subject and asking if the message was delivered. (Fill in the network name shown here with the actual one.) This message will go to the person responsible for the mail system at the network where you sent the message. If this overworked person has time to check on the delivery for you, you may get either a reply asking you to resend your original message or confirmation that your original message didn't go through.

and then read, reply, forward, save, or delete any new mail. You'll either be notified by a beep, a flashing menu bar, or a blinking icon when you have mail waiting, or the mail program will simply open your in box and show you the new mail there.

Let's see what it's like to receive mail on America Online. When you check your electronic mailbox, you see a window like this one:

The list shows messages in your in box in the order in which they were received. You can see the receive date, sender address, and subject line for each of the messages waiting here. To read a message, select it and click or double-click the Read button. *See "Reading mail" below.* Once you've read a message, you usually see a check mark or other symbol next to its title in the in-box list, so you'll know in the future that you've already read this message.

The Status button displays a box of information about each message, such as the exact receive time, the addressee name, and whether or not it has been read.

If you read a message and you don't want the "already read" symbol to appear by its name in your in box, you can select the message name and click the Keep As New button.

The Ignore button tells your in box to check the item as if you've read it even though you haven't opened it.

To delete a message, select its name in your in box and click the Delete button.

The Auto AOL . . . button lets you set up preferences for what happens when you perform timed, automatic connections to AOL, such as sending mail, receiving mail, and downloading files attached to mail.

Reading mail

When you select a message and give the command to read it, the message then opens in a window like this:

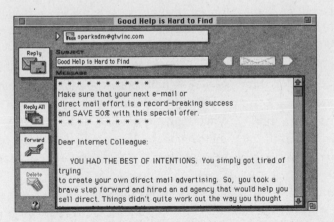

Notice that the header information at the top shows the sender's address and the subject. You can see any cc: recipients by clicking the triangle icon to the left of the sender's address.

In this particular example, the text of part of the message wraps in an odd place on one line. You can make it "unwrap" by making the window itself wider. You can also scroll the window to read the rest of the message. Oddly wrapped lines may be caused by extra line breaks in the author's document. *(See "The well-mannered message" on p. 73.)*

The buttons at the left show you the options for dealing with this message while it's open.

The Reply button displays a new mail message window with the header already filled out, like this:

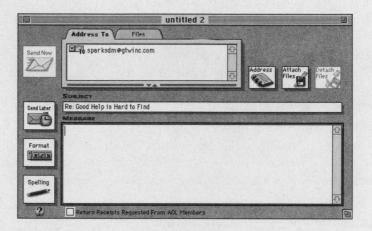

The mail program automatically puts the original sender's address in the Address To box of this new message for your reply, and it fills out the subject line as well.

The Reply All button creates a new message, but instead of automatically addressing it only to the original sender, it adds the addresses of everyone who received the mail (that is, any addresses in the original message's cc: window). When replying to mail, make sure you send it only to the person you want to send it to. It's a common mistake to reply to everyone who got the message when you really just want to respond to the author.

The Forward button lets you forward the message to someone else. When you click this icon, you get a new message form with the previous message copied into the body and space above the forwarded message for you to type a note about why you're forwarding it. You also need to fill in the new message's header with the e-mail addresses where you want the message forwarded. The subject line of this new message is

---

SAVE YOUR MAIL

If you have an account with an online service, it's important to save incoming mail to your disk, because every service provider stores messages in your in box for only a specific period of time — a week, two weeks, or a month, perhaps — and then automatically deletes them. To make sure important messages are saved for posterity, save them to your own disk. If you use an ISP account and run a mail program from your own PC's disk, incoming messages are automatically saved to your disk as you receive them.

---

usually filled in automatically with "FWD:" followed by the old message's subject.

The Delete button deletes the message from your mailbox. Once you click it, the message is deleted and you'll be returned to the mailbox list so that you can deal with other messages.

Other important mail features

The functions just described are the bare essentials of any e-mail system. Here are some other features that will help you use mail most effectively in your marketing effort.

Formatting. The best mail programs today let you apply formatting attributes to your messages, such as changing the font, font size, text alignment, or text color. Enhancements like this can make your messages much more effective.

Printing. Every mail program gives you a way to print your messages. Some require you to save the message to your own disk first (which you should do anyway so that during printing you don't incur service or phone charges).

Automated sending and receiving. Your computer can issue the commands to send and retrieve messages much more quickly than you can, and it can do these things when you're not around. If you have a dial-up connection, you should be able to set your computer to automatically dial your service provider, send any messages you composed earlier, retrieve any messages waiting in your in box, and then disconnect. This automated mail handling lets you make sure your mail is checked often. You can set a program to check your mailbox several times a day, every day, if you like. It also allows you to send and receive mail during late-night hours when your office is otherwise closed, and it takes care of the nuts and bolts of mail delivery while you're working on other things. The only thing you have to do is make sure your computer and modem are on during the times you've set up for mail transmissions.

Group message management. This gives you options for selecting or arranging the contents of your in box. Some mail programs are quite sophisticated at this; others are rather poor. At the least, you should be able to select a group of messages in your in box and save or delete them all at once. In addition, some programs give you easier options for saving your mail in different folders or directories as well as sorting your in box listing in different ways — by date, sender address, or subject, for example.

Quoting. Use this when you reply to a message. You quote all or part of the message to which you're replying so that the reader has a frame of reference. For example:

```
On November 1, you wrote:

>I'm sure there must be a way to reform campaign spending.I'm preparing a
>new bill for the next legislative session.

I agree about the need for reform, but asking Congress to do it is like
asking the fox to voluntarily leave the henhouse.
```

The two lines preceded by > symbols are a quote from a previous message, and the response to it appears on the two lines below. Quoting is a standard practice when replying to e-mail, and the better mail programs let you do this with ease. They either quote the entire message you're replying to automatically (you then go into your reply message and delete parts of the quotation that aren't relevant to your response) or they allow you to select parts of the previous message and then add quote symbols like those above when you paste the selection into your reply message. If your mail program doesn't offer an automated quoting feature, you'll spend extra time identifying quotes yourself.

Filtering. This allows you to reject certain e-mail messages automatically. The best mail programs let you set up filters that refuse to accept incoming mail based on the sender's address or a key word or phrase in the subject line. For example, you could set up a filter to automatically reject any messages that had MAKE BIG MONEY NOW in the subject line, or that come from an address which you know only sends out crass get-rich-quick advertising. With a filter in place, you won't even have to deal with messages like this in your in box, because they'll never be placed there.

Of course, you have to be careful when filtering out mail this way. Any filters you set up must be very specific so that you don't end up rejecting mail that could have meant business.

ABOUT MAILBOTS

If your Net connection is through an ISP, one simple way to distribute product or company information to those who request it via e-mail is to use a mailbot, or *mail reflector*, which is a program that receives e-mail messages and then automatically sends a form letter in response to each message. Most ISPs can set up a mailbot program for less than $50; you can sometimes do it yourself.

For example, suppose you have a file that describes your consulting services, and you don't want to be bothered with having to send it manually to everyone who requests it. A mailbot would have its own e-mail address and automatically send your file in response to any mail it receives.

Sometimes mailbots respond to certain commands that must be included in the subject line or body of an e-mail message, but others simply send out a file in response to every message they receive. If you have only one information file to distribute, then a single-function mailbot with a one-track mind is all you need. In this case, your promotional mailings might contain the phrase "For more information, e-mail info@galacksy.com," where info@galacksy.com is the mailbot's address.

On the other hand, if you have several different pieces of information to distribute, your mailbot can be a multifunction one that sends different files in response to different commands. For example, your promotions might ask people to send various commands in their message subject lines or bodies to get different files, as in:

MESSAGE BODY CONTAINS	MAILBOT SENDS
send background	general info about your company
send prices	a price list
send prodinfo	product information

Once you've set up a mailbot program, you can always change the files it sends so that they include the most current information. For more about mailbots, ask your ISP.

ABOUT MAILING LISTS

Mailing lists are groups of people who discuss a common topic by sending e-mail to one particular mail address. Usually, the messages (or postings) are compiled by a special *mailing list manager* program at the common address, which automatically distributes every incoming message to all members of the list.

So, for example, if you were interested in shareware programs, you could subscribe to the Shareware-Dispatch mailing list, and then all mail sent to that address by the list's members would be forwarded to you. Whenever you had something to add to the discussion, you would send a message to the Shareware-Dispatch list address, and the message would be automatically sent to all of the list's subscribers.

Some mailing lists are unmoderated, which means all mail sent to them is automatically redistributed to all list members. But most lists are moderated, which means somebody actually reads all the messages sent to the list address and reserves the right to edit or refuse to post them.

Lists can also be open or closed. An open list can be subscribed to by anyone; a closed list has specific requirements for membership. For example, a list might focus on African archaeology, and your request for a subscription may be approved or denied depending on your qualifications to discuss that topic.

Finding out about lists

Usually, you'll hear about a particular list you may want to join by participating in newsgroups on the same topic. For example, if you sell stereo equipment and you participate in the newsgroup rec.audio.high-end, you may come across the name and address of a mailing list on the same topic.

However, you can also search indexes of mailing lists on the Net. For the *Listserv* and Listproc mailing list manager programs (the two most popular at this time), there are several indexes available on the Web that show the names and addresses of every list that uses each manager program. You can often search these indexes by keyword to see all available lists on a particular topic. For example, to find one of more than 9,000 mailing lists that use the Listserv program, you can use a Web browser to view the site at http://www.lsoft.com. This site is maintained by the people who sell the Listserv program.

Another way to locate lists of mailing lists is to click the Search button in your Web browser and then search for "Mailing Lists" or for the name of a particular list manager program.

Subscribing to a list

Anyone with an e-mail address reachable over the Net can subscribe to a mailing list. To do this, you need to know the mailing list name, the address of the mailing list's manager program, and the command you use to subscribe to the mailing list.

When you see a list name that looks promising, you'll probably want to send for more information about it. Some lists keep their information (and past messages) on Web sites; others have a mailbot address you send to for information. The information file about the list will tell you what topics the list covers, whether or not it's moderated, and how to subscribe.

When you subscribe to any list, be sure to save the list's information file or confirmation message, as these contain all-important information about how to drop your subscription in the future and how to use other options available for that list. For example, some lists make available an index of all messages ever posted to them, so you can search a message archive for messages on a particular topic. Some moderated lists have a Digest function that lets you receive all the list's traffic for a day or so in one e-mail package, rather than finding lots of individual messages from that list in your box every day.

Participating in a list

To participate in a list, subscribe to it and "lurk" there for a couple of weeks — just read the other messages posted to the list until you get a feel for the topics being discussed and the level of tolerance the list's members have for promotional information. Once you're satisfied that you understand the local etiquette, you can begin active participation. There are three ways to do this:

- Respond to a previous post when you feel you have something to add to the discussion.
- Post some new information that would be valuable for other list members.
- Suggest a new topic of conversation or ask a question related to the general subject of the list.

Make sure to send your message to the list address and not to the list manager program's address. *(For more tips on how to say what you want to say in the most effective way, see "Marketing with e-mail" on p. 69.)*

Starting your own list

The reason there are 20,000 or so mailing lists on the Net is that you can always further subdivide topics of conversation. Someone may have started out with a list on automobiles, for example, once upon a time, only to see it generate dozens of lists about autos from different countries, auto repairs, auto racing, and so on. If after scanning the Net for lists on a particular subject, you find them all too general, you may want to start one of your own. The more tightly you can focus a group of people around a specific topic, the better your chances of ending up with a group of hot prospects for your business. You don't need anyone's permission to start a list, but you do need three things:

1. an e-mail address to which you want the mail sent
2. access to a list manager program or the willingness to process the list's mail yourself
3. the willingness and Net contacts to promote the list so that others will join it

You also need to decide whether you want to moderate the list.

To meet the first two requirements, first check with your Net access provider. Most ISPs can help you access and run a list manager program to establish your list, or they can direct you to someone who can. There are several widely used mailing list manager programs, including Listserv, Listproc, Mailbase, Majordomo, and Procmail. Your ISP should give you access to one of these. If you're running your own Net-connected BBS, you can even set up a list manager program on a PC to manage a list on your own.

If you want to run a list with a small number of subscribers, you can do it yourself without a list manager program using the group mailing function of your mail program. For example, you can set up a CompuServe account for the list address, create a mail group called List for the list's members, then read all the incoming messages yourself and remail them to the List group. Of course, if your subscriber base gets too big or the list has a lot of traffic, it will require a lot of effort to maintain the list. But if you can apply the ultimate test of guerrilla marketing (profits) and the activity generates more money than it costs, then why not?

If you do set up your own list, make sure to prepare a list description that explains the list topic, whether it's moderated or not, how to subscribe and unsubscribe, and any other list manager options. Another important item to include is a statement saying that, as the list owner, you reserve the right to remove any subscriber from the list. That way, you'll be covered if you get a subscriber who spews a lot of off-topic garbage and you want to feel okay about booting him or her off the list.

MARKETING WITH E-MAIL

E-mail is so fast and convenient that you'll soon feel like firing off dozens of messages, but your marketing success demands a more cautious approach. Every aspect of e-mail has its marketing possibilities and pitfalls, including:

- subject lines
- message bodies
- signatures
- your address
- e-mail targeting
- your ability to respond quickly to the interest your mail generates

Let's look at some strategies for making the most of this messaging medium.

E-mail isn't paper mail

Aside from the method of delivery, the main difference between e-mail and paper mail is this: With paper mail, the sender pays for delivery, but with e-mail, the recipient usually pays something for delivery, even if it's only the time they must spend to receive your message and throw it away. There's so much to do online that time is a very precious commodity, and the time your mail recipients take to read or toss your e-mail is time they can't spend doing other things.

E-mail also has the feel of a direct appeal. It's much more like getting a phone call or a knock on the door than like opening a mailbox and sorting through letters. E-mail is more personal than forums or newsgroups or even mailing lists where the mail is being broadcast to many people at once. Somehow, receiving unwanted e-mail is like hitting your own personal pothole on the information highway.

Ideally, the e-mail you send for marketing online will be so useful, informative, or entertaining that the recipients will be glad to have gotten it. If you can't be sure that this is so (and you can't), the next best thing is to make sure your messages are as efficient as possible — don't bore people, and don't take up any more of their time than necessary.

From the first word in the subject line to the last letter of your signature, everything you put in every message you send either contributes to or detracts from your overall marketing message. The look of each message is just as important as the look of your store, the way your employees dress, or the type of phone greeting your employees give out. It's your job to make sure that every aspect of your e-mail contributes to your success.

A few words about online expression

The most important tools you'll have for getting your message across are the letters and symbols on your computer keyboard. Most of the people who frequent the online marketplace can see and transmit only these keyboard or text characters, so you're limited to words and standard typewriter symbols when it comes to expressing yourself.

Of course, anyone who's spent more than a few minutes online realizes that everyone else labors under the same limitations, and each of us in business seeks an attention-getting advantage. But when writing anything online, whether it's an e-mail message or subject line, a newsgroup or forum posting, or the name of your online store or departments inside it, you should follow some conventions of expression to avoid putting people off. Just as there are signage and architectural conventions you should follow when decorating a storefront (such as not painting your storefront bright red with yellow spots if you're in a neighborhood of stately brick and slate façades), there are stylistic conventions you should follow when expressing yourself online.

Follow normal rules of capitalization. Using all capital letters or asterisks is the online equivalent of shouting. Most people resent it — it's like standing in front of your store and yelling at people passing by. And if you think using all lowercase letters will make your subject line stand out, it won't. Don't overdo it with emphatic symbols like exclamation points or dollar signs, and don't get too carried away with fancy fonts, different font sizes, or text colors. Dressing up your messages with strange capitalization, extra punctuation, or needless formatting is a poor substitute for effective writing.

Use emoticons. Since we're not all professional writers, it can be hard to convey emotions like anger, sadness, or laughter, but netizens have come up with a whole range of *emoticons* or *smileys*, combinations of text characters that look like facial expressions when viewed sideways. For example:

Smiling   :=)

Frowning   :=(

Winking   ;=)

There are several books that define hundreds of smileys, although you need to know only a few basic ones like those just shown above to cover most situations. If you forget the smiley for a particular emotion, you can always express it as a word inside brackets, such as [grin]. As you cruise the online world, you'll see lots of examples of these and you should become familiar with them.

Use acronyms. There are several acronyms in use online that shrink common expressions to a few letters to save typing, screen space, and most important, the reader's time. Learn these and use them. Here are a few examples:

IMHO — In my humble opinion

FWIW — For what it's worth

BTW — By the way

ROTFL — Rolling on the floor laughing

FAQ — Frequently asked questions (There are thousands of FAQ files that answer obvious questions about various Net services, newsgroups, or other features for newcomers.)

RTFM — Read the f——ing manual (A common response to dumb questions that are answered in a FAQ or online instruction file.)

Spell and punctuate everything correctly. Why make grade-school mistakes that will turn off 20 percent of your potential readers? Misspelled words label you as a nonprofessional who can't take the time or lacks the intelligence to do things right. And if your messages reflect this, prospects may think your products or services will, too. If you're not sure about the spelling and punctuation of your messages, get someone to proofread them.

The subject line is your message's front door

The subject line and your name as the sender are the envelope of your e-mail message. They're all your recipients will see when they receive your mail, and they alone must carry the burden of getting someone to actually open your message and read it. Remember, your recipient may be skimming through dozens of messages along with yours, so your subject line should stand out. A good subject line should clearly explain what the message is about and provide a reason to open the message. If you're mailing to an online service, the subject line should accomplish these things in 32 characters or less.

The 32-character limit is imposed by the e-mail medium. Those receiving your messages on online services could well be using mailer software that shows no more than 32 characters of a message's subject line (ISP mailers allow up to 80 characters). As a result, any subject descriptions that begin after the 32nd character might be invisible. If you must use a longer subject line, make sure that the line works well if only the first 32 characters are showing.

The subject should give a compelling reason for the reader to open the message. The best reason is that the information inside is something the reader requested. For example, if you're responding to a request for information about your product or business, the subject might read, "Book Catalog You Requested" or "RE: Your Info Request."

If your message is a first-time contact, then it should mention a subject you know the reader is interested in, or it should refer to a message the recipient previously sent (for example, "RE: Your Comment On Toys" or "Free Dollhouse Plans").

If your message is a "cold contact" and doesn't relate to a previous message you or the recipient sent, you can boost the power of your subject lines with these words from the guerrilla's vocabulary:

you	now	why	proven
money	secrets	yes	guarantee
save	results	benefits	announcing
new	health	love	how

free	easy	discovery	fast
sale	safety	secret	insider

Of course, since the main reason many people cruise the information highway is to get free information, we would also add the following:

info	information	news
intelligence	report	bulletin

Important as they are in the battle for your reader's attention, most online marketers practically ignore subject lines. Frequently, we receive marketing messages that have vague or hyperbolic subject lines like this:

Gear Sale

Howdy!

Make $1,000 a Week!

Just Checking In

Here are some much more effective examples:

Free Tax Bulletin

Home Pricing Report

Futures Trading Secrets

Below-Wholesale Computers

Subject lines shouldn't be taken lightly. Try out some potential subject lines on your friends, associates, or staff. Show subject lines around without the message they'll go with, and ask people which one makes them most likely to want to read what's behind it. Eventually you'll become a pro at crafting subject lines, but get some help and objective advice in the beginning.

The well-mannered message

Having a great subject line on a long, boring, confusing, or sloppily written message is like putting a gold-plated front door on a garbage pit. In fact, since you've managed to entice readers into opening your message (and spending a few more of those online pennies of their time), they'll resent it if your message is disappointing. Here are some key guidelines for messages that sell:

> **CHECK SUBJECTS IN REPLIES**
>
> Most people give very little thought to the subject lines they use in
> e-mail. When you reply to a message, be sure to check the subject
> line in your outgoing message. Remember, when you reply to a mes-
> sage, your mail program automatically uses the same subject line
> from the previous message and puts RE: in front of it. Therefore, if
> you reply to a message with no subject line, your message's subject
> line will read, "RE: ——."

Keep it short and to the point. If you can't say what you need to say
in one page (well, okay, two at the most), then you're not sure what you
want to say. This rule applies to promotional messages, not to substan-
tive ones that thoroughly describe your products or services. The initial
contact with an online prospect should be brief and inviting. If it leaves
prospects with a few questions, they'll ask them and you'll have an
opportunity to explain in detail and at greater length just what it is you're
offering. Here's an example:

CD Values
*Atomic CDs has the lowest prices on the Net on thousands of CD
music titles. From Rock and Roll to Classical selections, you'll find
just the right gift for yourself or that special someone. We cut prices
to the bone! Some examples:*

	Their price	Our price
Beach Boys — Pet Sounds	$11.99	$9.99
Horowitz — Favorite Sonatas	$15.99	$13.29
Thelonius Monk — Standards	$12.99	$10.59
Beatles — White Album	$14.99	$12.89

*Visit our Web store at www.atomic-cd.com for the tunes you want at
prices you can't pass up!*

This message gets right to the point and offers specific examples of its
primary claim that its prices are lower than those of its competitors. The
message selling Internet direct mail advertising shown on p. 61 is an
example of one that rambles on quite a bit before getting to the point.
Supply enough information to interest the reader. On the other

hand, don't be so overly concerned with brevity that you don't really explain what you're offering. For example:

Ad Specialties
Advertising specialties are the best promotional value for your dollar, and we have hundreds of products to choose from. E-mail info@adsco.com for our free catalog.

In this case, the message makes the unsupported claim that ad specialties are the best promotional value, and it doesn't give any examples of the kinds of products being offered. Further, it assumes every reader knows what an advertising specialty is, and that is a dangerous assumption.

Don't apologize. Don't start a message by apologizing for intruding into the person's e-mailbox. If you have confidence in your product, demonstrate it by describing it in a positive way, not by starting out on the defensive.

Check the format. There's nothing more annoying than trying to read a message with odd line breaks, short lines, or numerous extraneous characters. Sometimes your mailer and online service may add line breaks or extra characters as it transmits your message, but you can try to anticipate these problems and avoid them by following these suggestions.

- Format your messages so that each line is between 60 and 80 characters long, which is the length of a line in a typical word processing document.
- Make sure paragraphs are separated with a blank line between them so that they don't run together (any indents or tabs you use may be eliminated in transmission).
- Avoid centered or justified alignment, as these formatting options may not survive a trip across the Net.
- Avoid special formatting characters, which are often unique to the computer system you're using and won't survive Net travel either.
- Use underline characters to indicate underlining or italics.

Your mail program may let you apply boldface, underlined, or italic styles to type, but these may not travel intact across the Net. On page 76 we show how it looked when we sent a formatted message from the Eudora program via an ISP to an America Online mailbox.

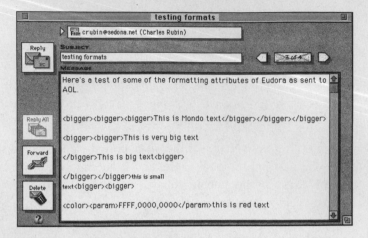

To italicize something like a book or magazine article title, enclose it in quotation marks, or put a single underline character before and after the title, like this: "See Jay Levinson's _Guerrilla Marketing_ for more information."

- Proofread the text thoroughly before you send it, to make sure there aren't any last-minute typos or problems that will interfere with the quality of your message. After all, this one message may be your only chance to reach a particular prospect.

Your signature

You can end your e-mail message with a "Sincerely yours, Jane Doe," just as you would with paper mail. But if this is all you do, you're missing a big marketing opportunity. It has become an accepted norm for people to add a sig, or signature, a business-card-like block of information below their sign-off. The sigs can provide your business name, contact information, and even a brief identity slogan in one convenient place. You can also use your sigs in newsgroup or forum postings where more blatant forms of marketing are frowned upon.

Here's a vertically oriented sig that spells out the person's name, company, postal address, phone, fax, and e-mail address:

```
-------------------------------
Adam Bunting
ARB Mattress Company
460 Menkin Place
Drowse, Virginia 20150

Phone  (703) 555-9247
Fax    (703) 555-4560
E-mail bedrest@arb.com


-------------------------------
```

Notice the dashed lines on either end of the sig that act like the visual edges of this electronic business card. The only problem with this sig is that it wastes screen space. Remember: the more lines you use, the longer it takes to read and transmit your sig, so the sig should be as space-efficient as possible. You won't be getting off on the right foot if your sig shows you to be an ignorant waster of precious online bandwidth. Further, many newsgroups and mailing lists frown on sigs that are blatant wasters of screen space. Six lines is considered a safe maximum, but above that you risk being labeled as a bandwidth hog. The previous sig could just as easily have been squeezed into four lines if the information was arranged horizontally. For example:

```
------------------------------------------------------------
Chris Terman, Financial Aid Advisor: chris@clarity.com
Clarity College Funding Service: For info, info@clarity.com
Quality Scholarship Search Services for USA Students
PO Box 1002, Globe, AZ    85711   (602) 555-7155
------------------------------------------------------------
```

This sig crams a lot of information into four lines. It even adds information about the nature of the service and the e-mail address of a mailbot program that automatically sends information. Still, this seems a little crowded and hard to read. How about:

```
_____
Robin Shadegg: The Shadegg Corp.   | shadegg@mphisto.com
    Strategic Planning for          |
    Marketing Development           | Voice: 206-555-6477
8203 - 39th Street                  | Fax: 206-555-6553
Spokane, Washington 98115           | Home: 206-555-6551
_____
```

This sig combines a lot of information in a visually appealing layout. The only problems we see here are the vertical dashes and the indenting of the company's identity statement. As you can see, the vertical lines don't quite line up (they would on some computers, but not on others), and the indenting could be thrown off in the same way. It would depend on the type of computer being used to read the message. You should make your sig format "translation-proof."

In lieu of a business identity statement like the one just shown, some cybernauts like to include a quotation that expresses their company's mission or their outlook on life or business:

```
------------------------------------------
   Adult Literacy Consultants
   415-555-8271  info@readme.com

"Knowledge will forever govern ignorance...."
          -James Madison
------------------------------------------
```

Again, notice the mailbot address in this sig. Also, the person's name isn't included in the sig itself, because it was used in a sign-off line located between the sig and the end of the message body. Finally, some internauts like to use ASCII graphics (little pictures made up of symbols or letters from the keyboard):

```
=============BROADWAY INDOOR PLANT CO.=================oo====
=============1124 Division St., Chicago, IL 60611=================oooo===
============Phone: 513-555-8977 * FAX: 312-555-4560============oooooooo==
===========www.bigcity.com * E-Mail: info@bigcity.com============[[]]====
```

ASCII graphics can be a good way to make your sig stand out visually, but you have to be careful with them. The problems of spacing and alignment that you can have when your message is viewed on different types of computer systems make it difficult to come up with a graphic that looks the way you want it to look on every computer where it might be viewed. Here's how to minimize problems with ASCII graphics.

- Don't use special keyboard symbols that may not be available on the computers where your sig is received.
- Don't use more than one blank space between any two characters, because extra spaces are usually deleted from e-mail when it's transmitted.

MULTIPLE SIGS FOR MULTIPLE USES

Don't think of a sig as something you create just once and then forget. Use different sigs for maximum marketing effect in different situations. If you're in the furniture business, for example, you might have one sig that highlights your expertise in bedding, another that promotes your decorating services, and a third that stresses your financing or free deliveries. If you're planning to do an online conference in an investors' forum, create a sig that promotes the conference date and time and use that sig on messages you post to the forum in the week or two preceding your appearance. If you're promoting a new feature on your Web site, plug that in to your sig for a while. And finally, create one or more personal sigs you can use when corresponding with friends or longtime customers.

The best mail programs will let you store an unlimited number of sigs and then choose the one you want from a menu as you create each message. However, if your mail program doesn't support multiple sigs, just create the sigs in an e-mail message, save the message in your e-mail outbox, and then open the message and copy the appropriate sig from it each time you create a new message.

- Don't use tabs, indents, or other alignment controls, because these may not travel well over the Net.

However you choose to format your sig, you should definitely come up with one or more of them. The sig doesn't have to be fancy; it just has to provide your name, company name, and at least your e-mail address in a compact format so that your correspondents can refer to it again easily.

Your address

Whether your mailbox is on an online service or you have access through an ISP, use an address that helps promote your business. If you're on an online service, use your company name or an evocative word as the mailbox name, such as gladrags@aol.com for a clothing store or literati@prodigy.com for a bookstore. If you have access through an ISP, you can go further and request your own domain name so that it appears to all outsiders as if you have your own corporate network. For example, your bookstore might have the domain literati.com, and it could have one or a dozen different mailboxes such as sales@literati.com or info@literati.com.

Domain name service is available from most ISPs. It costs about $100 per year in most cases.

Provide useful content

People on the Net are usually looking for useful information — they're not just hanging around in cyberspace looking for people to talk to (if they are, they're in chat rooms doing that). Whether you're sending mail to one individual or to a list, or posting to a newsgroup, make sure your messages have a high *signal-to-noise ratio*, which means that useful content outweighs meaningless blather. This is the ultimate test of any good message.

Stay on the topic. You probably wouldn't appreciate having to get up from *Monday Night Football* to take a call from a solicitor peddling accident insurance, and most people don't like being intruded upon with messages on topics they have no interest in (or no interest in at that time or in that context). The main reason spam attacks — mass e-mailings or newsgroup postings of messages — don't work is that they're off the topic for 99.5 percent of the people they reach. The reason well-written messages to targeted markets *do* work is that they're on the topic — you're adding information to a discussion others are already involved with.

Obviously, you're anxious to tell the online world about your business, but you have to accept the reality that most of them just won't care. Of course, this general apathy won't matter because you can make plenty of money by reaching those who do care. The best way to make sure you stay on the topic is to use e-mail only to respond to queries from others or to post relevant and useful information on mailing lists.

Provide information, not hype. Quote objective sources or cite objective findings rather than expecting people to take your word for it. Use statistics. If your service saves people 40 percent over another service, explain how and why. Try your best to put out messages that others will consider to be information rather than an intrusion.

Use word-of-mouth marketing

Word-of-mouth advertising is the best kind because it involves one friend telling another about something they found useful. The built-in forwarding function in every mail program makes word-of-mouth advertising spread even more quickly. Since it's so fast and simple to forward a message to someone else, it would be great if people to whom you sent promotional messages or product information would forward them to others they knew were interested.

Some forwarding happens automatically. Friends on the Net are constantly forwarding information to one another or posting something they thought was particularly interesting or useful to a mailing list or newsgroup where they felt it would be appreciated. However, just as you might ask your in-store customers to recommend friends who might be interested in your products or services, you can come right out and ask your e-mail customers to forward your information to others who might be interested. And the beautiful thing about e-mail is that the information will be forwarded from friend to friend, associate to associate, rather than from seller to prospect.

You don't have to hit anyone over the head with the idea of forwarding your messages, but a brief "If you found this information helpful, feel free to pass it on" at the end of your mail could expand your marketing efforts with no extra effort from you.

Save messages to save hours of effort

After you've spent hours, days, or weeks coming up with a dynamite subject line, a killer message, and a sig that will live forever in your prospects' memories, it would be a real waste if you used them only once. E-mail is a fast and efficient medium, but it's even faster and more efficient when you can pull prewritten messages and sigs from your arsenal of marketing weapons and fire them off at will.

As you create messages and sigs, save them with descriptive names in directories or folders on your computer. As your marketing attack advances, you'll find yourself expanding the library with new messages, but a message you wrote weeks or months ago may be just the thing for a new prospect, or it can quickly be modified to suit a new marketing task.

If you develop a series of sigs for different purposes, create a directory for them and save them with descriptive names so that you don't have to open them all up and read them each time to decide which one you want to use.

And along with your library of e-mail classics, save any customized messages you send to specific individuals or mailing lists so you can refer to them if you need to. For example, if you send a promotional message to a particular mailing list, save it with the name of the list you sent it to and the date so that you can find it again easily. That way, when someone responds with "Regarding your message of November 20," you'll have a better chance of knowing what they're talking about. Many mail programs have an option you can set to automatically save each message you send.

Test messages before broadcasting them

You wouldn't put out a radio, TV, or newspaper ad without running it by a few friends or employees first, so don't make this mistake with e-mail you're sending to a group. Before you send the message, have others you know and trust read it and make sure the message hits the bull's-eye. Your first message is your best chance to establish your online identity (and it may be your only chance with many prospects), so don't blow it.

Customize messages to test markets

As you craft e-mail messages for different markets, you can test which message or which market is responding the best by asking respondents to include different code numbers or key words in the subject line of their information requests. For example, if you mail to both a high-end audio mailing list and a professional audio mailing list, your messages could tell people to ask for high-end amplifier information or professional amplifier information. Comparing the number of messages using each phrase will show which of the two messages worked better for you.

If you're using a mailbot to dish out your product information, you can still track which markets are best by programming the mailbot to send the same document in response to two or more different messages (for example, "send high-end amp info" or "send pro amp info"). The mailbot will keep track of how many messages it responds to, and you'll have a quick gauge of which market is working the best.

Build a mailing list and use it

The best source of future sales is people who have already bought or shown interest in your product. When you receive requests for information or orders, save the customer names and e-mail addresses, and make a note about what the customer bought or asked about. You can use the same computer you need to go online to set up a simple database of customer information. This way, you can create mailing lists that let you make the most of the information you gain from your marketing efforts.

For example, you could set up a simple database file with one field for the e-mail address, another for the person's name, a third for the date of the last contact, and a fourth for a note about what the person bought or asked for information about. If you used uniform code words to describe various customer interests in the notes field, you could later select records based on different interests. For example, if you sell books, your notes field could contain genre information such as romance, general fiction, mystery, and cooking. Then if you have a spring sale on cookbooks, you could target just that part of your list with an e-mailing.

E-mail makes it easy to gather customer information, because the person's mail address is included in the header of any message you receive. You can simply copy the address information right into your database file and then fill out the rest of each database record by hand. Once you've set up a simple database in which to store the information, the real strategy comes in choosing which types of addresses to use. In selecting your addresses for mailing, there are three categories of prospects:

1. People who have bought from you in the past.
2. People who have requested more information from you in the past.
3. Everybody else who might be interested (newsgroup or mailing list members, for example).

For categories 1 and 2, it's appropriate to send special notices every few months, just to keep in touch, especially if you're offering either something special for a limited time or something that isn't part of your regular marketing effort. This could be in the nature of a "thank you" or "preferred customer" offering or simply a brief update on what's new with your business. For category 3, your goal is to elicit inquiries for more information so that you can convert more people into category 2 prospects.

Once you've begun a relationship with someone, be sure to maintain it with an occasional new contact. Remember, you're fighting for share of mind with dozens of other companies and thousands of other information sources on the Net, so you need to take the initiative once in a while.

One thing each targeted message should contain is an offer to drop people from the list. Some people just won't want to receive your mailings, especially if they're paying a special Internet receive fee to get the message delivered to an online service. A sentence at the end of the message offering to drop people from your mailing list lets them know that you're sensitive to their concerns about unsolicited mailings. This is

WHAT ABOUT BULK E-MAIL?

If you've had an e-mail account on AOL or another of the big online services, you've probably received lots of unsolicited messages from people selling bulk e-mail services. These outfits promise to mail your message to thousands, tens of thousands, or hundreds of thousands of people for a remarkably low charge — usually less than $50 per mailing.

The Net's tolerance of bulk e-mail has grown a little over the years as the whole marketplace has become far more commercial. Most individuals on the Net would prefer not to have to wade through dozens of junk mail messages every week, but bulk e-mail is a very cheap, fast, and efficient way to get a marketing message out to a lot of people, so it's probably here to stay.

But just as guerrillas in the offline world look for the most focused mailing lists when sending out promotions, you should do the same in the online world. Don't buy a list because it will reach lots of people; look for e-mailing services or programs that will help you reach the people you want to reach. For example, there's a program distributed on the Web called Floodgate that will extract e-mail addresses from participants in Internet newsgroups. If you're participating in a group whose members seem likely prospects for your business, using a program like this will produce a focused mailing list for you.

(For more information about Floodgate, use a Web browser to search for "Floodgate" on the Web. See Chapter 15 for more information about searching.)

much better than saying nothing and waiting for people to flame you for intruding into their mailboxes.

THE TOP TWELVE E-MAIL STRATEGIES

In summary, here are the top twelve e-mail strategies for the online guerrilla.

1. Compose and read mail offline.   Don't try to write new messages or responses to ones you've received while you're connected. You're much more likely to write an effective message, correctly spelled and formatted, if you have the leisure to compose and review it offline.

2. Use an effective subject line.   You may not get the chance to explain further in your message if the prospect won't open it.

3. Pay attention to the message's style and clarity.   You wouldn't dress like a slob at the office; don't dress your messages like slobs on the Net.

4. Use an effective signature.   Everyone appreciates having a business card, and your signature is your electronic business card.

5. Use an evocative address.   Choose a screen name, user name, or domain name that helps promote your business.

6. Keep messages short.   Don't waste people's time. If they want more information, they'll ask for it and you can then take more time to explain things.

7. Provide useful information.   There's a big difference between hype and information, and your readers know it.

8. Create an e-mail library.   As you develop successful messages and signatures, save them and reuse them. Also, save all your outgoing messages so that you'll know what you said where and when.

9. Stay on the topic.   If you're participating in a mailing list, don't contribute unless you have something interesting to say that's related to the topic.

10. Test messages.   Try out your messages with individuals before sending them to the masses.

11. Test markets.   Use slightly different response mechanisms to test the pull from different markets.

12. Build and use a mailing list.   Stay in regular contact with former customers or prospects to keep your identity fresh in their minds.

5

Electronic Storefronts

An electronic storefront is a place in cyberspace where you present information about your company, products, or services. A storefront is in a specific location: a Web site, or a store on an online service or bulletin board system. Anyone who knows how to navigate to your store can get information about your company at any time.

We usually think of storefronts as places where we sell products, but a storefront on the Net is any location where you can publish information about your company for others to view at any time. You can publish product descriptions and prices and take orders online if you like, but you can also offer general data about your company, articles about using your products or services, or other types of information.

Guerrillas use electronic storefronts to expand their virtual selling space, offering their products and services to thousands of self-targeted people they wouldn't otherwise reach. If you sell lots of different items, a storefront is the most efficient way to tell prospects about them. Companies now offer books, software, music, flowers, food, clothing, cars, luggage, jewelry, airline tickets, securities, and many other types of merchandise online. A neighborhood bookstore in Berkeley, California, can gain an international marketing presence via the Net or an online service. An art gallery in New York can sell posters in Australia. It's much less expensive to put up a catalog of products on the Web than it is to print a catalog and mail it to thousands of people, and you can take orders twenty-four hours a day.

There are tens of thousands of electronic storefronts on the Web, on the Net, on online services, and on bulletin board systems. They run the gamut from a single Web page that provides basic company information and lists an 800 phone number to a full-blown catalog on the Web, on an online service, or on a bulletin board system. In this chapter, we'll look at the ins and outs of planning, locating, setting up, operating, and promoting an electronic storefront that matches your budget and your overall marketing plan. You'll learn how to choose the right storefront location, how to design it, and how to bring customers into it.

PLANNING AN ELECTRONIC STOREFRONT

One of the greatest mistakes online storekeepers make is to treat a storefront as a glorified advertisement, a static weapon in their marketing arsenal that needs only to be created, set up, and then forgotten. But the real guerrillas know that online stores are opportunities to build ongoing relationships with customers, a place where you attract a community of people who are interested in topics related to your business. Your online store should be so inviting and informative that your customers would get an online account just to visit it, and it should be a place they'll want to return to again and again. So before you consider specific options for setting up and running an online store, think in more general terms about why you want to have an online store to begin with.

Know your goals

Ideally, your online store should dovetail perfectly with your other marketing strategies and should reflect your business identity. The first question to ask yourself is, "Why do you want to have an online storefront?" Don't rush onto the Web just because everyone else is doing it. Think about exactly what you hope to accomplish with your store so that you can do what it takes to reach your goal. There are several different reasons why you might want to have an online store.

Establish a foothold in cyberspace. Online commerce has nowhere to go but up, but it will be several years before electronic sales begin to approach any of the forms of offline business sales. You may want to set up a store now simply to gain experience in electronic sales and marketing so that you'll know exactly what you're doing by the time the online market really takes off.

Reach new customers. Putting up a Web site or online service store lets you reach new customers you're probably not reaching now. Many U.S. firms have gained their first sales in Europe, Latin America, or Asia by setting up on the Web.

Reduce advertising and communication costs. It's far less expensive to distribute information via an online storefront than through direct mail or telemarketing. Many firms post all their corporate information, press releases, and financial results on the Web to save millions in printing and postage costs.

Reduce selling costs. By posting a catalog of products online and taking orders electronically, you can create a self-service sales mechanism that reduces your costs for salespeople.

Distribute product samples. You can publish and distribute video clips, formatted brochures, software, book or magazine excerpts, or samples of written reports or consultations. These samples will help convince customers of the value of your products or services, and you'll save the cost of mailing them.

Offer better customer service. With a storefront you can allow customers to get any type of information they might need about your products or services twenty-four hours a day. Customers can check their account status or check on the progress of an order, for example.

Improve communication with customers. With e-mail connections through your store, you can put customers in direct communication with the people in your company best qualified to handle their questions. You can set up e-mailboxes for customer service, sales, press information, and other departments, and you can eliminate a lot of phone calls or e-mail messages by anticipating your customers' information needs and posting the information in your store.

Establish an online community of customers. Your store can include a discussion area where your customers and employees can share information about using your products or services.

Enhance your company's image. Many companies set up Web sites simply to enhance their reputations as modern, progressive firms.

You may well have more than one of these goals for your store, but it's important to know what your goals are so that you can focus on achieving them.

Know your online advantage

Your store must have an online advantage, or it won't have much chance of success. The simple fact that your store is online doesn't automatically make it more useful or attractive to your customers. Essentially, people go online because they can get information more conveniently than they can from other sources. Either the information is more up-to-date, or a few clicks of a mouse bring far more of it than they could get in any other way. When planning your store, think about why people might want to visit your online store rather than doing business with you in other ways, and make sure your store gives them reasons to visit.

In most cases, your online advantage will be that your store offers more information or more convenience. Customers who might only be able to phone in orders during business hours can enter them online in the middle of the night. Or the answers to questions a customer might have (such as product specifications, or ideas about how to use or care for a product) can be found in your online store. Your store might also offer direct e-mail connections to specific people in your company who can best help different types of customers.

And don't forget the power of the computer in seeking an online advantage. Many sites have search capabilities, so visitors can search for products or information by topic names. Some real estate sites include mortgage loan calculators. Your site might let customers move around in a 3-D environment or view furniture or clothing in different colors or sizes.

To find your store's online advantage, think about how the store could make life easier for your customers, and deliver the specific information or services that will accomplish that goal.

Select and organize information

Useful information is the magnet that attracts online visitors. When planning what information you'll put on your storefront, go beyond strictly sales-oriented things like product descriptions, a company description, and employee resumes. Think about your customers and about the kind of information that might appeal to them. For example, if you sell hiking and camping supplies, you could post information about recommended hikes or camping trips, cold-weather camping advice, weather reports, fishing reports, and many other types of information. If you have a financial management service, post articles about economic conditions or investment planning.

As you come up with different kinds of information to place in your store, make sure the information is organized logically. The home page should provide the site's name, purpose, contents, and departments and make it easy to get to any of them by clicking a link or button. Each department should have its own contents page if there's lots of information there, and each page within a department should have a link or button that quickly takes the visitor back to the department contents page, to other department contents pages, or to the store's opening screen, or home page. A quick look around at other stores will show you lots of ways to make it easy for visitors to navigate within your store. *(For more information on storefronts, see "Designing your storefront" on p. 103.)*

Plan for orders and shipping

If you're going to sell merchandise online, plan in advance how you'll accept orders. Will you accept CODs, credit cards, or purchase order numbers? Will you ask people to fax or phone verification of their purchase? If you'll be selling overseas, will you accept international credit cards such as JCB or EuroCard? Remember, your storefront may have an international clientele, and the more payment options you offer your customers, the easier it will be to buy from you.

You may begin receiving orders the first day you open your storefront, so establish your credit card accounts in advance so that you'll be able to process them immediately. If you don't have an established offline business, you may find it difficult to obtain a credit card merchant account, so don't wait until the last minute to find out. And if you're worried about hackers stealing credit card information from your storefront, make sure your ISP or online service allows encrypted transfers of sensitive financial information.

Also, find out exactly how you will receive the orders. Typically, orders from online stores are sent to your e-mailbox as they come in, which means that you'll have to check your e-mailbox regularly if you want to provide prompt service.

Finally, work out shipping options in advance. Ideally, you want to be able to get products to your customers as quickly as possible, but over-night or two-day delivery will be very expensive when you're shipping overseas. Offer your customers a range of shipping options so that they have control over how fast they receive an item: a customer in Singapore who really wants your product in two days may be willing to pay the extra shipping costs.

Plan for the store's evolution

Unlike an advertising campaign or store layout that you may live with for months or years, your online storefront must change regularly if you want to attract repeat visitors. There are so many Web sites and online service storefronts to visit that people will visit yours only once unless they know that something new and interesting will be added regularly.

When planning your store, don't just plan the initial layout and contents; plan for its evolution over time. Your store should have at least one feature that changes every week, such as News of the Week, Tip of the Week, or Recipe of the Week. This feature should be prominently announced on your home page so that first-time visitors immediately know that there will be something new every week.

CHOOSING AN ELECTRONIC STOREFRONT

Once you've planned the basic purpose for and contents of your store, you'll have to decide whether you want to set up a Web site, a store in an online service, or a bulletin board system. The best way to evaluate your store options is to surf the Web, online services, and bulletin boards and see what's out there. This will give you ideas about how your store might look and about where you might want to locate it. To make the final decision, ask yourself these basic questions:

How much time do you have?

Each of the options for setting up shop online requires a certain amount of time. You're already spending time learning what the various options are, but you'll have to spend more time to implement them.

A Web site. This will involve researching the market for Web space to get an idea about pricing and find the best deal, designing the site (how information is organized on various screens), preparing the information and uploading it to the Web server, and promoting and maintaining the site. You can use a consultant to design the Web site and find a server for you to reduce your time spent, but doing so also increases the cost of creating the site.

A store on an online service. Choosing this option means researching the costs of various plans on the major online services and designing the store's content. Online services have their own production staffs that will help you in designing the store and setting it up on the service's computer. You'll also have less work to do to promote the store, because the service has built-in advertising and promotion mechanisms.

A store on a bulletin board system. This will require you to set up a PC with bulletin board software, connect one or more telephone lines to it, and use the bulletin board software to set up your storefront. Once

SHOULD YOU USE A CONSULTANT?

The simplest way to create a storefront is to hire a consultant or Web designer to handle the whole thing for you. The consultant will sit down with you, analyze your marketing needs, and help you determine the best type of storefront to have, and will then research the best option and help you set it up. (If you choose to set up shop on an online service, you'll be assigned a consultant by the service.) All you'll have to do is sit in on some meetings and provide the information you want to make available in the store when the construction gets under way.

But if using a consultant costs you less time and effort, it costs money, and it also makes you dependent on someone else whenever you want to make changes to your store. This can mean delays in making changes you need to make if you can't reach the consultant right away.

A half-step between these two alternatives is to use a consultant as needed. You might use the consultant to locate the cheapest or best ISP for your storefront or for help in creating the basic design or setting it up on the server. You would handle the actual work of creating the store's individual screens and working with the ISP to maintain it.

To get an idea of how much time you'll need for each of these options, find some storefronts you like and contact their owners. Most owners are glad to talk about their experiences if you're in an unrelated business.

the store is up and running, you'll have to maintain the equipment yourself. You can also find a consultant to handle most of the setup for you. *(See Chapter 8 for more information.)*

What are you selling to whom?

The best location for a service business might not be the same as the best location for a consumer goods business.

If you're in a service business, you may not want a storefront at all. Your online marketing efforts might best be handled through e-mail and participation in forums, mailing lists, and newsgroups. On the other hand, having an online storefront would give you a place to offer free information, and that would help build awareness of your services. If you're an accountant or financial consultant, your online store might offer free information about budgeting, retirement planning, or other topics as a way to attract new customers.

If you're selling industrial supplies, you may do best on a focused online service like IndustryNet, which connects buyers and sellers of material for industrial companies. *(See Appendix for more information.)*

If you're selling cosmetics, you might opt for an online service with a high percentage of female subscribers.

You can get demographic information about any online service by simply asking for it. If you're planning on establishing a Web site, you can draw customers from specific newsgroups or mailing lists that focus on topics related to your business.

How much traffic do you expect?

Your location should fully support the kind of traffic you hope to get, or it should be easily expandable to support an increase in traffic. If you expect 10,000 people a day to access your store, make sure your storefront's technology can handle it. There's nothing worse than enticing customers to your store and then having them find the door locked. If in your wildest dreams you expect perhaps 100 people a day to browse your site, you can live with a slower setup.

To get an idea how many visitors per day you can expect, ask operators of other stores about their traffic. The most popular sites on the Web get more than 100,000 visitors per day, but these are Web directories like Yahoo. A typical store is doing very well if it gets 5,000 visitors a month, although the most popular stores (www.amazon.com, for example) do much better than that.

What makes a store fast? The type of telephone connection to the Net, the type of server hardware you're using, and the amount of other traffic moving through the same link.

A Net connection can occur over everything from a dial-up connection and a modem operating at 9,600 bits per second (bps) to a *T1, T2, T3,* or *T4 line.* A T1 line delivers data at 1.5 million bits (megabits) per second. A T2 line works at up to 6.3 megabits per second, a T3 transmits at up to 45 megabits per second, and a T4 line screams along at 274 megabits per second. There are also fractional T1 lines that use only part of a T1 channel and operate at 128,000 bits per second and up.

The server that presents your store on the Web can be anything from a $1,500 PC to a $60,000 high-speed *Unix workstation.* You should check with your ISP to find out whether it's using servers at the faster or slower end of the range.

HITS VERSUS VISITS

Server traffic, or traffic into your online store, is measured on the Web as *hits*, or individual requests for files from that site. Your ISP maintains a *server log*, a log of traffic to your site, and you may be elated to discover at the end of one month that your total hit count is in the thousands. But the ratio of hits to actual human visitors is about 10 to 1.

Requests for files can come not only from human visitors, but from other computers that routinely scan the Web to create indexes of sites for online directories.

Also, a typical Web page is made up of several files (one text file plus a couple of graphic files, for example). When a person clicks a link to display your home page, the server that hosts your Web site must transfer several files to present the text and graphics that make up that page. Therefore, one person viewing one page of your Web site might easily generate several hits.

Even with the fastest server and the fastest connection, access to your server can be slowed by other traffic using the same part of the data highway. For example, you may rent space on a server and share the same connection and hardware with a dozen other stores. That's fine if each store has only a few dozen hits per day, but it can mean that browsers have slow access or are blocked from entry when the server gets too busy.

And even if your ISP has a fast connection to the Net, the actual speed of that connection is affected by other traffic. We've seen storefronts connected to the Net via a T1 line that were slower than storefronts connected via a 56,000-bit-per-second line, all because the T1 connection was in a part of the Net that had a lot of other traffic.

If you're expecting thousands of hits per day, make sure your service contract with your ISP guarantees you a certain minimum level of service to your site. Find out how many hits per day the ISP says it can support on your site, how many simultaneous hits it can support, and how many other stores are sharing the same equipment. Ask for references to other businesses sharing the same equipment or using the same Net or online mall, and find out if they've had problems with customers gaining access.

If you're in an online service's shopping mall, the service should provide all the access you need, and reliability shouldn't be much of a problem.

How much can you spend?

Any expenses associated with your electronic storefront are considered marketing expenses, since you're using an online presence to boost your other marketing efforts. An online storefront must fit within your overall marketing budget, and the costs of running such a store can vary widely. Here are some expenses to consider.

Server space. If you set up in an online service, you may have to spend $20,000 on store design and maintenance. If you rent Web space, you'll spend from $20 a month up to $250 a month or so.

Production costs. After you've arranged for the physical storefront, you have to stock it. This includes gathering the information you want to display, organizing the information into screens or pages, designing a menu and navigation system (although online services provide a standard system), formatting your information for display in the store, and producing any graphics you want to provide.

Maintenance Once the store is up and running, you'll have to pay someone to monitor its activity, make regular changes to its look or information content, and process orders if you're taking them online.

STOREFRONTS ON THE WEB

Now that we've covered some of the issues in choosing a storefront, let's look more closely at each type of store. There are many different ways to create an online storefront, but the most popular way is to create a Web site. A Web site usually includes several *pages*, each of which may contain text files and graphic files. When you navigate to a Web site, you see the site's home page.

Web sites frequently have one or more *scripts* stored with them as well. Scripts are programs that automatically perform chores such as adding visitor names to a registration file, tallying up the total charges in an order, or allowing visitors to search a Web site for a particular item by keyword.

To set up a storefront on the Web, you need a Web server (or space on one) that's connected to the Net, and the storefront itself — the collection of files that explains your company, products, or services.

Most ISP accounts include Web server space, so for a simple Web site, the monthly "rent" for your electronic Web storefront may be included in your $20-a-month account fee. You can do the store's design yourself as well, either by modifying existing Web pages that you see and like or by creating them with one of the Web page authoring programs available. On the other hand, large companies spend tens of thousands of dollars setting up and maintaining elaborate Web sites created by professional designers and run on expensive servers.

There are three basic steps in creating a Web site:

- Deciding what your site will offer
- Deciding who will create the site
- Deciding where the site will be located

Envisioning your Web site

The first step in deciding what sort of Web site you want is to surf the Web yourself and look at other storefronts out there. Look at lots of sites, especially those from businesses like yours. Dig into each site, looking at several of its pages and making notes to yourself about things you like or don't like about them. Use your browser's Bookmark feature to mark sites you really like so that you can find them again quickly in the future. As you look around, you'll get ideas about how your own store should be organized, how many individual pages it will contain, what sorts of graphics it will have, what kind of ordering system works the best, and so on.

Once you've got some general ideas about what you'd like in a site, make an outline showing how your site will be set up. Start with the home page and list the different departments you'll want. Make notes about any graphics, navigation buttons, or other features the page will have as well. Try to decide the approximate size of any graphics. For

ORDERING SYSTEMS

If you plan to sell more than a handful of items directly from your storefront, you'll want to implement an ordering system that automates the process as much as possible for your customers. Ordering systems, or shopping cart systems, allow visitors to select items as they browse through your store and have them automatically added to an order form. To complete the order, visitors must only verify the items and the quantity and choose a shipping option. The order total is automatically calculated.

Shopping cart systems cost from about $500 to $2,500, but many ISPs have licensed a system for their customers' use and will allow you to use it as part of your monthly storefront rental fee.

If you have only a few items, you can create an order form that lists each item, but your customers will have to fill in the quantity and order total themselves. Systems like this make shopping more difficult for your customers and should be used only if you expect to sell just one or two items per order.

example, do you want the home page to be a graphic *image map* where visitors click in various places of an image to view different departments, or do you want simple graphics such as colored bullets or divider lines? Do the same thing for each of the pages in your various departments. Finally, think about special features you'll want in your site, such as a visitor counter, an ordering system, a discussion group, or a registration page that collects the name and e-mail address of each visitor.

Building your Web site

When you're finished, your next step is to decide how you'll create the site. You can do it all yourself, or you can pay for various levels of assistance. For example, you may be able to do the basic page design yourself but need help with creating scripts or implementing an ordering system. On the other hand, you may want a Web designer to do the entire site for you.

The least expensive method is to build a Web site yourself. You can use a Web-creation program such as Microsoft FrontPage, Adobe PageMill, or Claris HomePage. These programs cost about $100 and allow you to create pages, organize them in a site, and add text and

WEB PUBLISHING OPTIONS

The Web has become such a force in the computing world that there are many ways to get your information onto it. Microsoft and most other major software companies have built-in utilities in most of their word processors and desktop publishing programs that will turn any document into an HTML-compatible Web page. Microsoft's Web Publishing Wizard (available with Word, Publisher, or other Office 97 products) will not only convert a page to HTML, but actually helps you upload that page to your ISP's Web server. Since Web-conversion capabilities are included with any of the newer word processors, spreadsheets, or desktop publishing programs, you can get this capability at no extra cost.

However, Web conversion utilities will simply make your text and graphics visible on the Web. They don't let you add special features such as frames, discussion groups, or searching capability to your Web pages, and they don't let you organize a series of pages into a storefront site. To truly create and manage a full-featured Web site on your own, you'll need a Web-creation tool like Microsoft FrontPage 97, Adobe PageMill, or Claris HomePage.

graphics to them very easily without having to learn much or anything at all about HTML, the programming language that specifies the format and behavior of Web pages. As you finish each page, you save it as a file, and you can open that file with your browser to see how the page will look to others on the Web.

If you don't want to spend the money on a page-creation program, buy or borrow a book about using the HTML language, and within a week or so you can learn how to create simple Web pages from scratch. All you need is a word processing program to create HTML pages. Every Web page file is simply a text file, but it contains special HTML instructions that specify formatting, graphics, and other features. Here's an example.

```
<IMG
SRC="gifs/header.gif".
ALT="Guerrilla Marketing Online".
WIDTH="499".
HEIGHT="53"
BORDER="0".
VSPACE="0".
HSPACE="0"><BR>

<FONT SIZE="2">|.<A HREF="map.html">Map</A>.|.<A HREF="new/new.html">New</A>.|.<A.
HREF="tactics/tactics.html">Tactics</A>.|.<A
HREF="contests/contests.html">Contests</A>.|.<A HREF="store/store.html">.
Store</A>.|.<A HREF="consulting/consulting.html">Consulting</A>.|.<A.
HREF="books/books.html">Books</A>.<A HREF=
"calendar/calendar.html">Calendar</A>.|
<A
HREF="authors/authors.html">Authors</A>.|
<A
HREF="vendors/vendors.html">Vendors</A>.|
Home.|.</FONT><HR SIZE="4">
```

This is part of the HTML code from the Guerrilla Marketing Online home page. All the HTML instructions are inside the < and > brackets.

With a page-creation program or an HTML programming guide, you can put together a basic Web site within a few days. Thousands and thousands of the Web sites you'll see on the Net are created just this way. But if you want your store to have an elaborate ordering system or other special features that require custom scripts or an advanced level of programming expertise, you'll probably have to find a Web designer to help you create the site. *(For more details about designing a Web site, see "Designing your Storefront" on p. 103.)*

Getting a location

There are three basic choices you have in locating a Web site. You can use space on a server with the same ISP with which you have your e-mail account, you can use a different ISP for your Web site, or you can set up your own server.

The most common situation is to use the free space you get as part of your account with the ISP who supplies your e-mail address. Most ISPs include anywhere from 1 to 5 megabytes of Web server space with a basic dial-in account. If you can design a store yourself, you may need only an ISP to provide space on one of its Web servers.

In many cases, 1 to 5 megabytes is a lot of space. The text portion of a typical Web page usually runs from 25 to 100 kilobytes. Small, simple graphics (lines or bullets, for example) are less than 15 kilobytes each, and you need to store only one file for each graphic you use, even if you use the graphic more than once. For example, to display five colored

FINDING A WEB SITE DESIGNER

There are plenty of Web site designers out there, from high school and college kids doing it as a sideline to full-scale design firms with staffs of artists and programmers. You can spend anywhere from a few hundred dollars to tens of thousands of dollars on Web site design. Your pocketbook will help you decide on who to use for design help, but here are some other ways to find the right designer.

Ask your ISP for help. If have an online account, ask your ISP for help with your site's design, or ask for references to other designers. Some of the largest ISPs have whole sets of design tools you can use to build a site yourself. For example, AOL's PrimeHost Web hosting service has user-friendly design tools and a shopping cart system you can use.

Locate designers of sites you admire. If you spot a site on the Web that you particularly like, find out who designed it by contacting the site's *Webmaster*, or administrator. (The e-mail address is usually located at the bottom of the home page.)

Decide what you want in your site first, and then make sure the designer can handle it. For example, some people calling themselves Web experts may not know how to implement a Web-based discussion group or a shopping cart ordering system.

Don't worry about the designer's location. Thanks to the magic of e-mail and FTP, it doesn't matter where your Web site designer (or the ISP that hosts your Web site, for that matter) is located. Don't be afraid to check out designers located across the country from you. You can transfer any files to them electronically, and their design talent and pricing matters a lot more than whether they're located within driving distance from your office.

dividing lines on a page (or on any of the pages in a site, for that matter), you need only one graphic file that contains that line: you simply refer to the same file each time you want it to appear.

If you want your site to contain larger, more complex graphics or sound or video files, then you may need to rent more space from an ISP. Server space is very inexpensive, and you should be able to get all you need for $100 a month or so. However, if you're shopping for space at different ISPs, there are other factors to consider beyond price.

Server performance. You can have the greatest site in the world, but it won't do you any good if nobody can access it. If your site is sharing space on a server with dozens or hundreds of other Web sites, you'll want to make sure that the ISP's server and that server's connection to the Net are robust enough to handle lots of traffic. Web server software runs on everything from discount-store PCs to technical workstations costing more than $60,000. Make sure your service contract guarantees a minimum amount of data transferred per day from your site, or a certain minimum number of visitors handled per day.

Server reliability. Even the most expensive server needs maintenance. Make sure the ISP you choose maintains its servers and Internet connections regularly and during non-peak hours. For example, you wouldn't want an ISP that shuts down its servers for memory upgrades or other maintenance during normal business hours.

In-house expertise. Some ISPs specialize in setting up Web sites for small businesses and have technicians who can assist you in creating ordering systems and other complex scripts. Some ISPs include such programming work in the price of server space, but they charge more than $100 per month for the space. Still, it may be worth paying more for space if you need a lot of technical help. Ask any prospective ISPs for references to other companies they host on their servers, and then contact people at those companies to ask about their experiences.

The third alternative to locating a Web site is to do it yourself, setting up your own Web server and maintaining a continuous connection to the Net. This makes sense for companies large enough to have their own Information Systems (IS) departments, because they already employ people whose job it is to know about servers and Internet connections. But it probably doesn't make sense to a guerrilla, unless you want to get into the ISP and Web design business yourself.

STOREFRONTS ON AN ONLINE SERVICE

When you locate in an online service, you put up a storefront in the service's shopping area or mall. Your store appears as a name on a list or menu, or as an icon in the shopping area (see "Web shopping malls" on p. 35). When customers select that listing or icon, they're taken into your store to see selections of merchandise or services.

Why choose an online service?

Locating in an online service has both good and bad points. Some stores come and go within months in an online mall, while others make money year after year. Here are the basic advantages to choosing an online service as your store's location.

Production services. Online services like AOL, CompuServe, and Prodigy will "build" your electronic storefront for you. These services have a standard storefront look — all you do is supply the text and graphics you want to display. The process takes a month or two, and the cost is included in the store's rental fee.

A captive subscriber base. Online services funnel large, well-heeled groups of subscribers to your store. If you set up on the Net instead, you'll have to do more to attract them yourself.

Visibility. The shopping mall is a main feature of every online service, so subscribers can find it (and your store) easily. And you can get even more visibility by renting buttons, banners, or billboards to advertise your store. *(See Chapter 6.)*

Promotion. As part of your store agreement, you get a grand opening notice on the service's welcome screen. Every subscriber will see a message about your new store for a week or more. Depending on the service, you may also get other promotional help, such as your own store icon on the service's shopping mall's entrance screen for a period of time.

Simplified ordering. Online services have each subscriber's credit card information on file, and they have well-established ordering systems that are standard for every store. Subscribers can order from you without having to type in their credit card numbers, and these ordering systems are perceived as being more secure than similar systems on the Web because they're maintained within the online service.

The major drawback to having a store in an online mall is the cost. For example, the least expensive option for having a store in CompuServe's mall is $20,000 per year plus 2 percent of sales made through the store. Other options go as high as $100,000 per year, and other major online services have similar rate structures. You have to move a lot of product to make such a store pay. Recent statistics on CompuServe's shopping area reported that only 4 percent of people browsing in the mall actually bought something.

But 4 percent is a better rate of return than most direct-mail campaigns, and when the mall has thousands of shoppers per day, 4 percent can be plenty. Penny Wise Office Products in Edmonton, Maryland, has had stores on CompuServe, America Online, and GEnie since 1991. Although the company has a multimillion-dollar direct-mail business, its online stores and bulletin board service now account for about 20 percent of its orders.

Online services also give you less control over the information your store presents and how it looks. The online service's own computer technology limits your presentation: If you want to include pictures of your merchandise, your options for showing pictures are limited to the method by which the online service can deliver them. In some online malls, it can take a minute or more to transfer one graphical image to a shopper who wants to see it. Your store agreement may also place a limit on the number of products you can list, the number and type of graphics you can use, and the number of changes you can make to the store in any month or year.

To explore shopping malls on online services further, get a trial account on each of the major services and browse their shopping areas. Each service's mall has its own personality; one may appeal to you more than the others. Each service also has a different group of subscribers, and one service may have more hot prospects for your business than another. To find out more about the demographics, the cost, and the procedure for setting up a store in any online service, contact a marketing representative at the service. *(See Appendix for phone numbers and addresses.)*

DESIGNING YOUR STOREFRONT

Once you've determined your store's location and basic contents, you can turn to the store's design, its look and feel. The look of your store on a given type of server is dictated by the image you want your company to have, the type of merchandise you're selling, and the people to whom you hope to sell it. Here are some basic principles to keep in mind as you create your store.

Design for accessibility

Your store is useless if it doesn't deliver your information to your customers as quickly and simply as possible. If you've chosen a location for your store, you've already made a decision that affects the method and ease with which customers can reach it. But the design can also affect the speed with which your site delivers information.

Make it fast. Any time spent waiting online can seem like an eternity, so design your store for maximum presentation speed. This means using

Information that can be transmitted quickly. Avoid using too many large graphics. Any graphic that takes longer than 3 seconds to transfer — typically graphic files larger than 30 kilobytes — should be optional, not mandatory. For example, the following home page took us more than one minute to load because the dealership name and introductory paragraph are graphic files rather than text.

If the dealership name and introductory text was stored as text rather than as a graphic, this page would load in about 10 seconds. When designing pages with graphics on them, think about how you can use text formatting commands to add visual appeal without resorting to large graphics, especially with less important elements on the page. Here's an example.

This page still has a nice graphic at the top, but the department names are shown as text links with small graphic bullets next to them. Also, the logo is a low-resolution drawing in three colors, rather than a photo-quality picture of a house. You can make your pages load more quickly by limiting the number of colors you use or by using lower-resolution images instead of high-resolution images.

If you really want your site to have lots of high-resolution graphics, another option is to offer visitors a choice of high-resolution and low-resolution versions of your site. Here's a notice that appears when you navigate to a site devoted to freelance writers and artists:

> Link to Freelance Online's home page
> Graphics-rich: high modem speeds click here
> Minimum graphics: low modem speeds click here

Visitors who care only about the text on the site can view a faster version of it by clicking the bottom link.

As it is with graphics, so it should be with your text. Be as concise as

WHY IS THE WEB SO SLOW?

The World Wide Web is often called the World Wide Wait these days because it seems to take forever to move from one site to the next. Basically, the Web is a victim of its own popularity and the inability of technology to keep up with the explosion of traffic. There are several factors that can influence your browsing speed.

Slow dial-up connections. You may have a 33.6 kilobit-per-second modem, but due to local line noise, your actual connection speed may be much slower. Non-dial-up connection options such as digital (ISDN) phone service, cable modem links, and satellite downlinks give you much faster access, but at higher prices.

Slow servers. The server that stores the Web pages you're trying to view is very slow, or it's linked to the Web via a lower-speed (T1) connection rather than a faster one (T3, for example).

Busy servers. The server that stores the Web pages you're trying to view is fast and has a fast Net connection, but it's very busy processing lots of requests from lots of people. If the server is *too* busy, you'll see a message that says the server is too busy to respond to your request.

Hub and router problems. A hub or router — one of the hardware devices that links various portions of the Internet — that sits between your ISP and the server you're trying to reach is out of order or simply overloaded. If you get a message that says a site can't be found and you know you've entered the right URL, this is most likely the problem.

possible with your department names and descriptions. Use short para graphs rather than long ones. Subheadings in your information give people visual bookmarks to use as they scan your text.

Finally, divide your store's information into screen-size chunks whenever possible. Smaller pages load much more quickly, and it's faster to load and view short pages than to wait for long pages to load and then have to scroll endlessly down them.

Make it easy. Shoppers can become frustrated when they have to take too many steps to view your information. Make every piece of information you offer as directly accessible as possible. Rather than having three options on your top menu or home page with each option leading to two more options, put all six options on the top menu or home page so that people can proceed to them more directly.

Also, use a consistent design on each page, and offer navigation buttons at the bottom of the page so that visitors can easily jump to different departments on the site. Some designers use graphics to create navigation buttons, but text buttons work just fine — and again, they load more quickly. Here's an example:

Sauces & Salsas | Gifts of Fire | Specials | Clearance
Non-Edibles | Contest | About Us
Ordering Info | Order

Make it clear. One way to steer customers wrong is to use ambiguous or misleading names for menu options or buttons in your store or to cram information together so that it's hard to read. For example, put your price list under "Prices," not under "Sales."

If you have a Web site and you're using graphics, make sure the pages make sense without the graphics. Some Web surfers turn off the graphic-loading feature of their browsers so that pages will load more quickly. If your page includes text that describes it as well as graphics, visitors will know what you have to offer whether they're looking at your graphics or not.

Real Estate 10
Your Arizona Internet Connection

A Little About Real Estate 10

Real Estate Vocabulary

Contacting Real Estate 10

Real Estate 10's Arizona Property and Home Search

This page makes perfect sense without the graphics loaded. Don't force a customer to spend a minute or more downloading graphics just to figure out what you're selling. Lots of customers won't wait that long.

Also, beware of getting so caught up in making your store look cool or unusual that it becomes unreadable. We've seen some pages with really awful color schemes — yellow text on a black background, for example — that are so cool you can get eyestrain trying to read them.

Design for customer involvement

There are many examples of poorly designed stores on the Net right now, menus or Web pages that just sit there and wait for the customer to start exploring. But the best guerrilla-owned storefronts use computer technology to add value to the presentation. Your design can use the equivalent of in-store signs, banners, lights, and sirens to draw customers further inside.

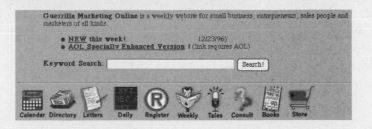

On the Guerrilla Marketing home page in the preceding figure, the Daily (stock ticker) icon and Weekly (newspaper) icons at the bottom of the page are both animated, and the What's New line contains a message ("Happy Holidays!" in this case) that blinks on and off. Used judiciously, effects like this can add snap to your pages without getting in the way of your message.

Add something new regularly. Every online service uses welcome messages that change daily. CompuServe's What's New window greets members every time they connect. AOL's Welcome screen lists half a dozen items that change daily. Your storefront should have something new and exciting every time a customer returns to it. On the Guerrilla Marketing Online Web site, for example, we offer new marketing tips every day via e-mail, and new marketing articles and success stories each week.

Think up evocative names for store functions. The 7-Up company boosted its sales tremendously by coming up with "The Uncola" as a new name for its product. You can make shopping fun and engaging for your customers by using evocative names for the options in your store. Instead of a *Place Order* button, you could name the button *I Want This*. The online world is impersonal enough without your adding to it with boring generic names for your store's departments and options. The Amazon Books site (www.amazon.com) does a good job of creating a rich, evocative experience with the language it uses for its departments:

HOT THIS WEEK:
Keeping up with Oprah these days isn't easy, but books can help. Read Jane Hamilton's **The Book of Ruth** (Oprah's book club pick) and **Make the Connection** with her personal trainer Bob Greene. Also to warm you on these chilly December nights: **The English Patient**, Michael Crichton's **Airframe**, Margaret Atwood's **Alias Grace**, **The Digital Estate**.

AMAZON.COM NOTES...
Travel writer and historian Sunny Delaney was born December 31, 1968. This last day of the year also marks the birthdays of Spanish writer Jose Maria Gironella (1917), and Essayist Holbrook Jackson (1910). Artist Henri Matisse was born on this day in 1869. Have you made your New Year's resolutions yet?

WANNA PLAY?
What songs make you sob? What would you do if you were as rich as Bill Gates? What's your favorite movie adapted from a novel? How about your favorite sexy movie? Check out the tearjerkin' tunes of choice, the financial plans, fiction-to-film picks, and movies that get our readers' motors running.

AMAZON.COM CHATS WITH...
Bill Gates about his take on the Internet revolution and The Road Ahead, Lawrence Schiller on O.J. Simpson and the tragedy of a divided America, James Ellroy about the literary search for his mother's killer, Peter Hoeg on the art of chaos, and Randall Stross about the Microsoft v. Netscape Internet war.

Another example of a site that uses language very effectively to create a rich atmosphere is the Ragú Sauce site at www.eat.com.

Avoid visual boredom. You shouldn't bombard customers with unwanted and unnecessary graphics, but every site needs some visual appeal. Still, using text formatting options alone, you can avoid large, gray blocks of text. Here's an example:

Mo Hotta-Mo Betta®

"The world headquarters of hot."

The Los Angeles Times, May 9, 1991

Sauces & Salsas	Gifts of Fire
A sampling of sauces & salsas from the Mo Hotta-Mo Betta Catalog.	We've got the right gift for any hot food lover and any occasion.
Specials	**Clearance**
Some of our newer hot specials.	Discontinued merchandise available at a 40% discount.
Non-Edibles	**Contest**
Hot merchandise you can't eat.	Information about our current contest.
About Us	**Order Information**
A brief word about Mo Hotta-Mo Betta.	Information about ordering over the web, by phone, e-mail, snail-mail, or internationally.

For a catalog or more information, please contact us:

This site's designer arranged text in columns and used a different color for the department names. It's not fancy, but it delivers the information quickly.

Provide free information. Your product descriptions and prices are information, but customers want more than price lists. Add value to your store by offering free information about related topics that will help sell your merchandise. Food sites should offer recipes, for example. Auto-related sites should feature articles about maintenance and purchase options. One online jewelry store offers a guide to jewelry cleaning and care.

Design for buying comfort

Effective marketing is a circle that begins with your message and ends with a satisfied customer. Your online storefront is a ghost that exists only in cyberspace until your customer completes a satisfactory transaction. Customers act as if the store does exist, of course, but they won't really feel comfortable with that assumption until a satisfactory transaction has taken place. It's like buying from a mail-order firm that you've never heard of before — you're a little anxious until that sweater, tie, or commemorative Elvis plate actually arrives at your door.

Design your store and its merchandise to soothe your customers' concerns about the permanence and stability of your business. There are several ways to do this.

Offer a guarantee. Every mail-order firm worth its stamps guarantees satisfaction. There are few services you can offer that will provide more comfort for your customers.

Display your physical address and phone information. If your on-line store is a branch of a physical store someplace, your customers will feel a lot better knowing that. They'll be more comfortable buying from a company that has an actual building than from someone who's simply Net-selling from their kitchen table.

Host a feedback area. Design a message area for customer questions and comments, or make it clear that you welcome feedback. Buying and selling is always a two-way transaction, and guerrillas always encourage a dialogue that gives the customer more of a stake in the sale. As you collect and respond to questions in your feedback area, pull out the ones that are frequently asked and compile them into a *FAQ* (frequently asked questions) file customers can browse. This will add to your information offering and cut down on the number of times you have to answer the same questions.

Use a nonthreatening order process. People hate thinking they're locked into something, and a poorly designed ordering process can give them acute claustrophobia. Make sure the ordering process is logical, and offer an easy-to-use Cancel function on the order screen so that customers know they can change their minds.

[Add This Book to your Shopping Basket] (You can always remove it later…)

On the Amazon book site, this button appears at the bottom of the page each time you view information about a particular book. Click the button to add the book to your shopping basket. (Notice that it says that you can always change your mind: this puts the customer at ease.)

Later in the process, Amazon explains its secure server option.

Amazon.com Books

Use the secure server.

We'd like to use the Netscape Secure Commerce Server to satisfy your request. The Netscape Secure Commerce Server works with most browsers, including Internet Explorer. It encrypts information, keeping it private and protected. This technology makes it safe to transmit your credit card number over the Internet. (But you don't have to--you can always call in your credit card number **after** you've completed our online order form.)

If you get an error message when you try to use the secure server, it may be because you've run smack-dab into a firewall! Ouch! Ask your system administrator to reconfigure it. (You can say that the port for Secure HTTP, 443, needs to be opened up.)

You can still send us your order or view your account. We'll use our standard server to fulfill your request. (This is the server you're already using.) You may transmit your credit card number using this server. It won't be encrypted. Again, you can always call in your credit card number after you've completed our online order form if you prefer not to transmit the number online.

Use the standard server if you've received an error message.

This screen explains the safety of using a secure server to transfer credit card information, but also makes it clear that customers can phone in their card information if they like. With this notice, Amazon anticipates and soothes any customer jitters about placing an online order.

Finally, the order form itself has the same way of anticipating and dealing with problems. In the following example, Amazon again tells customers they can supply credit card information by phone if they like, directs customers to scroll to the bottom of the page if they have questions about the form, and alerts them to the dangers of making typos when entering their e-mail address in question 1.

Finalizing Your Order is Easy

You can place your order online without transmitting your credit card over the Internet! However, you must first complete the online ordering forms. If you have questions about this form, please scroll down the page for more information, along with our toll-free number.

VISA   MasterCard   NOVUS   AMERICAN EXPRESS Cards

1. What is your e-mail address?

Note: One small typo here, and we won't be able to communicate with you about your order.

My e-mail address is [   ]

Please check your e-mail address carefully!

2. What method of payment do you intend to use?

○ Credit Card (Visa, MasterCard, Discover, or American Express only) (why this is safe)
○ Check or Money Order (why this takes longer)

3. Is this your first order from Amazon.com Books?

It would be a shame to have your sales derailed by a confusing or unfriendly ordering process. Make sure your store does everything it can to anticipate visitor concerns and questions and to give your customers as much flexibility as possible for placing an order, supplying financial information, or choosing shipping options.

Get some design help. If you use a consultant to help design your store, make sure you get one who has experience with computer interface design and (if it's a Web site) graphics design. A Web page layout can benefit from the same graphics savvy used by an experienced magazine or advertising designer. Any storefront's navigation system will be better if its design is influenced by someone who knows how to make computers easy to use. Ask your ISP, presence provider, or consultant about these types of experience. If nobody on your store construction team has it, find someone who does. If you see a storefront design you particularly like while surfing the Net, contact the owner and find out who helped build it — they can probably do an equally good job for you.

Test your design. Before you go public with your storefront, test the design by accessing the store from different kinds of computers. What looks great on one computer system may not look so great on another. Host a pre-opening period for your friends and associates. Invite them to browse your store and offer any comments or suggestions about its appearance and operation. It's much better to discover and eliminate problems this way than to let your customers be guinea pigs.

If possible, ask people to try accessing your store at different times of the day or days of the week so that you can check out the speed of your ISP's Net connection. If the connection is consistently slow for several days at different times, your ISP is probably to blame.

One way to turn such testing into a promotion of its own is to offer significant discounts or free gifts for testing the service by asking early browsers to record their addresses and names in your feedback area or send them to your e-mailbox.

OPERATING YOUR ELECTRONIC STOREFRONT

Once your store is up and running, your manner of operating it will greatly contribute to your success or failure. Customers demand service, and prompt, professional service is the only way to establish your credibility. Remember, customers are entrusting their digital bits and bytes to the black hole of cyberspace until you respond and reassure them that there's an actual human being on the other side of the screen, so you should be as prompt and reassuring as possible. There are several ways to show your attentiveness.

Check for queries and orders frequently. Your level of store traffic will determine just how frequent "frequently" is, but never let twenty-four hours lapse without checking your store for orders or queries. In the first few weeks of operation and after any new promotional efforts, check your store every two hours.

Respond quickly. The more quickly you can respond to orders and queries, the more impressed your customers will be and the more quickly they'll come to trust you. Nobody likes doing business with someone whose business is just a part-time hobby. Your attentiveness to your store will convince customers that you're in the business full-time — even if you're not. Unless you're delivering merchandise within a day, send a confirmation message for each order so that the buyer knows the order was received and that the goods are on their way.

Check your own service. You can't fix a problem if you don't know you have it, so act like one of your own customers once in a while to make sure your store is working properly. Browse around your store frequently and display its various departments. Send in an order yourself now and then. Try this at different times of the day and night and on different days to determine whether there are any access problems.

Check out the competition. Check out some of the other online vendors, particularly those in the same type of business as yours, and see what they're doing. They may be trying promotions or store designs you hadn't considered.

Make frequent changes. Guerrillas change their physical stores' signage, displays, and sales approaches constantly to keep them fresh and inviting. The same goes for your online store. Add new information to your store at least once a week. Offer new, nonproduct information regularly and draw customers' attention to it. Come up with a tip of the day or week for your business, news or trends related to your products, or a quote of the day or week for the general enlightenment of mankind.

The time to encourage the next visit is during the current one. Make your store the kind of place where people know they'll see something new every time they stop by. As you now know, netizens are information hounds, and if your store becomes known as a place where new, useful information appears frequently, they'll become regular visitors.

PROMOTING YOUR STOREFRONT

If all you do is open up an electronic storefront and wait for customers to come in and buy, you could be waiting until your bank balance sinks beneath the waves. Here are some practical tactics for increasing your store's traffic.

Plan an opening. Treat your online store like an offline store, and plan a specific opening day promotion. Hold a grand opening event such as a contest or special discounts to generate interest in the store. Well before the store's opening day, you should create press releases to announce the grand opening events, and have a list of magazines, newspapers, or other media outlets where you'll send the press releases. *(See Chapter 15 for more information.)*

Make it visible. If your store is located in an online chopping mall, make sure the store name and description are easy to see. A lot of mall directories span more than one screen. If possible, get your name on the top menu or home page, or at the top of the mall department where you are listed. If your store is on the Web, place listings about it or links to it on as many other sites and directories as possible. Submit your site's URL to places like the Yahoo, Infoseek, and Alta Vista directories. Search for more specific directories related to your business, and make sure you're listed in those, too. A store all by itself is like a book in a library that nobody knows about — people may end up finding it, but only by chance. Each new directory listing about your Web site magnifies its visibility.

Spread the word. Every day you go online, make a point of promoting your business, not only in replies to queries at your store, but in newsgroups, forums, or mailing lists related to your business. *(See Chapter 7 for more information.)* Use a signature on your e-mail messages and discussion group postings that promotes your store. Post classified ads in the free areas of forums related to your business, or to online services

---

BOOSTING YOUR SEARCH VISIBILITY

Ideally, you want your site to be one of the first ones listed when someone uses a Web search engine to locate sites related to your business. Most search engines prioritize a list of pages they find by the exactness of the match for the word being searched, the number of times that word appears on each Web page, and the position of those words on the page (closer to the top is better). With these realities in mind, here are a couple of strategies to make your Web site more visible to search engines.

Use multiple keywords. Think of every possible word that someone might use to describe your business, products, or services, and make sure all of those words appear on your home page. You don't have to include the words as visible text — you can include them as comments to the HTML code that makes up the page, hide them behind graphics, or format them in the same color text as your page's background so that they're invisible, and the search engine will find them just as well.

Repeat the most important keywords. Repeat the most likely and descriptive words several times on your page. Rather than listing "business financing" once as part of your home page's visible text, for example, include the words half a dozen times as invisible text near the top of the page.

---

that allow free ads. *(See Chapter 6.)* Don't rely on directory listings alone to promote your site — seek out your customers and go after them.

Ask for referrals. When you respond to customer inquiries, ask them to pass along the information to anyone else who might appreciate it. If your information is useful, people will share it.

Seek fusion marketing partners. Make fusion marketing arrangements with other stores that complement yours. If you sell sportswear, make a fusion arrangement with a store that sells sporting goods: you get a link or a notice about your store on the sporting goods store's site, and they get a link or a notice on your site.

Offer to exchange informational articles with other stores if each of you has something the other could use. People reading your article in another store will see you as an expert on the subject. For example, if you're an ergonomics consultant, your paper on proper furniture adjustments could enhance the information area of an office supplies dealer and win business for you at the same time.

Host a conference or write an article. If you're an active member of a forum, host a conference on a topic that showcases your expertise. *(See Chapter 9 for more information.)*

Hold contests. Come up with a crazy contest that relates to your business, and offer a significant prize for the winner. Put the contest information in your store to attract people, and promote the contest in newsgroups, forums, and via online services when appropriate. For example, CompuServe's What's New window has a Special Events/Contests item that always lists any contests its members or merchants have under way.

Plan to revive interest. Most online store owners report a plunge in interest in their sites a few weeks after the initial store announcement. Everyone checks the site out when it's new, but many never return. Plan a promotion or contest for the second month of your store's life to pull shoppers back in, and announce this upcoming event when your store opens. This way, people who visit the store during its early days will have a reason to come back a few weeks later. If your store opens in September, announce a Halloween contest or Thanksgiving promotion.

Promote your store offline. Tell your other customers about your new online presence. Put up a PC in your store and invite customers to see your online store. Mention your online store in your print ads and brochures, and give customers a reason to visit it (such as the free

information they'll find there). List your Web address on your stationery. If you're in a small town, your online store may even be newsworthy for the local TV station or newspaper. *(See Chapter 15 for more
information.)*

Follow up. The best time to improve your reputation and plant seeds
for future sales is when the customer is basking in the glow of satisfaction from the last purchase. After the order is shipped and has had time
to arrive or after your service is delivered, follow up with a note thanking
the buyer for his or her business. Follow-up notes tell people you care
about their satisfaction and not just their money.

Be patient. Most online storefronts ramp up slowly. You may spend
weeks or months attracting nothing but tire-kickers before you start
making consistent sales. When you set up a storefront, commit yourself
to at least a year's operation. Remember, there are millions of people
online, and despite your best promotional efforts it may take time for
many of them to learn of your store. Also, the Net is changing rapidly,
and more people have better access to it all the time. Waiting a year will
give you a chance to expose your store to a larger and larger pool of
prospects as the months go by.

SEVEN STRATEGIES FOR ELECTRONIC STOREFRONTS

In summary, these are the seven top guerrilla strategies for choosing and
operating an electronic storefront.

1. Choose the right location.   Choose a storefront technology and a
location that balances the needs of your budget, your desire for the
broadest online market access, and the type of product you sell. The
store should be:

- easy to find for as many customers as possible
- capable of displaying your products as well as possible
- able to handle the traffic you anticipate
- within your budgets for time and money

2. Make the store attractive, fun, and easy to navigate.   It's a mistake
to think that people will flock to your store just for the thrill of shopping online. Your store competes with other online stores as well as with
print catalogs and physical stores. It should be inviting, attractive, fun,
and easy to browse in. It should have an online advantage, adding value

or convenience that shoppers can't get when they're away from the computer.

- Work with your consultant or designer to put as much excitement as possible into your store design, from its name to the names of departments or options.
- Make the store easy to navigate.
- Add new information frequently.
- Present the information in small, screen-sized chunks rather than having product descriptions spread across several screens. Use evocative descriptions that help readers visualize what your products or services can do for them.
- Offer regular customers a special discount for shopping online.

3. Make the store an information source.   Give shoppers some free, useful information about topics related to your products or services, and offer something new regularly. Hardware stores sell most of their products in the course of helping a home owner solve a problem or learn about some aspect of home repair. If your store becomes a reliable source of information, people will buy and they'll keep coming back.

4. Reassure customers about your permanence.   Do all you can to allay customer fears about buying online.

- If you have a physical address, display it in your online store and invite people to visit.
- Offer a 100 percent satisfaction guarantee on your merchandise.
- Explain your ordering and refund policy clearly.
- Give people a way to ask questions and get them answered promptly.
- Design a clear order form that gives customers the chance to cancel.

5. Pay attention.   Once you've attracted customers, the key to satisfying them is service. Pay close attention to your store's activity.

- Check your store mailbox, feedback area, or ordering system at least every two hours so that you can respond to customer requests as quickly as possible.
- Shop the store yourself at different times and on different days to make sure it's working properly.
- Ask friends with different types of computer or Net navigation software to visit the store and report any problems.

6. Tell the World.   Promotion is vital in the online marketplace, because your store is invisible unless people know about it.

- Use e-mail and discussion group signatures that include your store name and its address.
- Participate in newsgroups and mailing lists whose topics are related to your business, and build a reputation as a good source of information.
- Establish fusion marketing relationships with other store owners.
- Use promotional tools such as advertisements, What's New announcements, contests, and directory listings to spread your store's name around and invite people into it.

7. Follow up.   Build a relationship with your customers that goes beyond one sale, and don't stop trying to improve your store.

- Follow up each sale with a thank you note via e-mail, and ask people to tell friends about your products or services.
- Prepare monthly or quarterly mailings of store news and send them to your customer list.
- Stay abreast of Net or online service developments and add any new services to your marketing arsenal.
- Continue surfing the online marketplace yourself, watching for ideas you can incorporate into your store to make it better.

6
Advertising

Day in and day out, advertising is the number-one way for you to promote your business. With advertising, you can put your message in front of the public whenever you want, as long as you can afford it. In the physical world, you can place ads on anything from billboards, transit benches, buses, and taxis to newspapers, magazines, and television. In the online marketplace, you can place ads on Web sites, forums, newsgroups, mailing lists, and in classified ad areas.

Advertising should be part of every guerrilla's online marketing arsenal because it contributes to your visibility. Remember, your business is invisible online unless people happen by your storefront or see your company name somewhere else. Advertising helps you spread the word about your business throughout cyberspace.

The four main advertising media in the online market are classified ads, graphical ads, sponsorship notices, and directory listings.

CLASSIFIED ADS

Classified ads are the oldest and most widely used form of online advertising. Most online services and some BBSs have classified ad sections where, just as in a newspaper, you can place a brief ad about your business. Online services have both paid and free classified ads. On the Net, you can post free classified ads in Web directories, and several newsgroups are essentially collections of classified ads. Classified ads are easy to create and post, so they're an excellent way to get your message out quickly, and at guerrilla prices.

In a classified ad, you're putting your message before an audience that is already shopping, so you have a leg up on gaining the reader's interest. Many people browse online classifieds just as they browse the backs of newspapers and magazines. Some people are looking for a particular product or service, and others are just window shopping. But classified advertising works, which is why it has made the transition virtually intact from the printed world to the online marketplace. In fact, if you have only one product or service, your classified ad campaign can be your main method of promotion.

Online classified ads can serve two purposes:

- to promote other online presences you have, such as advertising your online store or soliciting subscriptions for your online newsletter
- to serve as the main method by which you sell a particular product or service

Online classified ads are almost as old as online services and bulletin boards. Legions of business consultants, multilevel marketers, and all sorts of retailers have used them for years to sell products effectively.

How classified ads work

In the online world a classified advertising section is a type of discussion group or bulletin board. However, the bulletin board's messages are blatant ads rather than contributions to a discussion about a particular topic. An online classified ad section contains a list of messages, each of which has a title. When you browse the section, you scan the titles and then select a particular title to read the message behind it. The details of posting and reading ads are different, depending on whether your ad is on an online service or BBS, on a Web site, or in a newsgroup.

Ads in online services or BBSs

The classified ad area of an online service or BBS has several subsections, just like the classified section in a newspaper or magazine. Here's the main directory of free classified ads, which are called Bulletin Board Ads, on America Online.

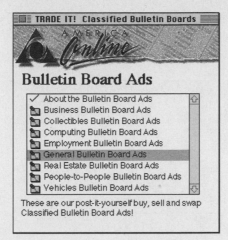

There are several different ad categories, each of which has its own subcategories. For example, the General Bulletin Board Ads category here has thirty-two subcategories, or topics under it:

```
┌─────────────────────────────────────────────────────────────┐
│                  General Merchandise Boards                    │
├─────────────────────────────────────────────────────────────┤
│   Here's where you can buy, sell, and trade general merchandise with other │
│   America Online members.                                      │
│                                                                │
│  Topics: 32              Total Posts: 8606     Created   Latest │
│  📁 Art & Craft Items              224         8/13/94   1/2/97 │
│  📁 Books/Mags NON-BUSINESS        244         8/13/94   1/2/97 │
│  📁 Bridal & Wedding               306         11/3/95   1/2/97 │
│  📁 Camera/Photography Equipment   282         2/27/95   1/2/97 │
│  📁 Catalogs                       234         8/12/95   1/2/97 │
│  📁 Children's Items               310         8/17/95   1/2/97 │
│                                                                │
│      Date of Last Visit:        12/17/96 6:08:30 PM            │
│                                                                │
│   [List      [Read 1st    [Find New]  [Find Since...] [Create Topic] [Help & Info] │
│    Messages]  Message]                                         │
└─────────────────────────────────────────────────────────────┘
```

There are a couple of hundred ads in each of the categories, and the listing also shows when the latest ad in each category was posted. Inside an ad category you see the listing of ads, like the following:

```
┌────────────────────────────────────────────────────────┐
│ ▣    ▤      Camera/Photography Equipment          ▤   ▣ │
│  ✎  Film cameras, lenses, lighting, darkroom, film, processing.  No video or │
│  🖳  digital cameras. REPLY BY EMAIL                     │
│                                                          │
│   Messages: 284                    Author      Latest    │
│  ┌──────────────────────────────────────────────────┬─┐ │
│  │ Rollei 2.8F, TLR                JMogu3      1/2/97 │▲│ │
│  │ Canon 100-300mm 5.6L            SndanceKid  1/2/97 │ │ │
│  │ Digital Video                   DGT INC     1/2/97 │ │ │
│  │ Computerize Your Photography    BOBOISTER   1/2/97 │ │ │
│  │ WTB MINOLTA 400si               PRIOR2      1/2/97 │▼│ │
│  └──────────────────────────────────────────────────┴─┘ │
│                                                          │
│        Date of Last Visit:     1/2/97 7:25:18 PM         │
│                                                          │
│              📄        📄        ⬇                       │
│             Read   Post Another  More                    │
│            Message   Message   Messages                  │
│                                                     ▣    │
└────────────────────────────────────────────────────────┘
```

Unlike printed classifieds, the ads here aren't sorted alphabetically by title. Instead, they appear on the list in the order in which they were placed. People who are attracted by your ad title and want to read on can select the ad and open it. Most online classified ads are short and to the point, like this one:

```
┌────────────────────────────────────────────────────────────┐
│ ▣  ▤  General Merchandise Boards  /Camera/Photography Equipment  ▤  ▣ │
│ ┌──────────────────────────────────────────────────────┬─┐ │
│ │ Subj:  Photo Image Scanning! $2                       │▲│ │
│ │ Date:  12/17/96 5:55:00 PM                            │ │ │
│ │ From:  Scans4Pics                                     │ │ │
│ │ Posted on:  America Online                            │ │ │
│ │                                                       │ │ │
│ │  4 Easy Steps For You To Take!                        │ │ │
│ │ 1. Enclose Photo(s)                                   │ │ │
│ │ 2. Enclose self-addressed stamped envelope if you want your photos back │ │ │
│ │ 3. Enclose Check,Money Order,or Cash for correct amount │ │ │
│ │ 4. Enclose your email address and mail it to the address below │▼│ │
│ └──────────────────────────────────────────────────────┴─┘ │
│                                                              │
│     ⬅            📄              ➡                           │
│  Previous        Add           Next                          │
│  Message       Message        Message                        │
│                                                         ▣    │
└──────────────────────────────────────────────────────────────┘
```

Typically, browsers expect ads to be brief. A lot of people like to browse the classified sections they find online, but they don't want to spend a lot of time reading any one ad.

This ad also makes it easy for customers to respond and get further information. AOL, CompuServe, and other online services have a convenient Reply button right in the window that displays the ad. If you post

WHY ADS MOVE ON LISTS

Your brand-new ad will appear at the top of the list in its category when you first post it, but when you check the ad area the next day, you'll probably have to scroll down the list to find it. As other ads are posted after yours, your ad moves down the list until it's no longer visible in the window.

In a busy ad area, your ad can move from the top of the list to two or three screens down the list within one day. It's best to keep your ad as close to the top of the list as possible — if you can stay on the first screenful of ad titles, you'll have automatic visibility.

To keep your ad near the top of the list all the time, repost it, or submit the same ad again. In most cases, you'll have to give a reposted ad a slightly different title — you may not be allowed to post two ads with the same title in the same category.

If your ad is in a busy area, plan to repost it every day.

to a bulletin board or a service without a Reply button in its ads, ask readers to phone, fax, or send e-mail.

As in printed media, classified ads in online services run for a specific amount of time. In free classified ad areas such as the one just shown, the life of any given ad depends on how active that particular ad area is and how much space is available for it on the online service's computer. You'll want to check an online classified area every few days to make sure your ad is still there.

Ads in forums

Along with the general classified ad areas on online services, you'll also find topic-specific ads inside many discussion groups or forums. For example, AOL's Business Strategies area has advertisements for marketing, advertising, accounting, and other business-related services. Ads in forums are usually free, and they're much more likely to be read by people very interested in what you have to offer. If you're on an online service, check out forums related to your business, and see if you can post classified ads there.

Paid classified ads

The free classified ad areas on online services and large bulletin board systems are crowded with ads, which reduces the chance that your particular ad will be seen. But most online services have paid classified ad space as well. Prodigy sells space for both consumer and business ads, for example, and America Online has a Premier Ad service where you can place ads in more than a dozen categories.

Paid classified ads cost from $5 per month up to about $25 a month, but they have some key advantages.

- You automatically have more visibility because you're not competing with the huge volume of ads in the free areas.
- You will probably get extra services in a paid ad. For example, AOL's Premier Ad service allows you extra text formatting options for ad titles and content screens (rather than just plain text), and it allows you to include hypertext links in your ads that can take readers directly to your storefront or Web site.
- You can purchase an ad for as little as a week or as long as a year and the service will maintain it in a visible position on the ad list.

Ads on the Web

Dozens of Web sites feature classified ads offering everything from autos to jobs to real estate to vacation packages. Some of these sites charge for ads, but most are free. Check out this page from the Yahoo directory:

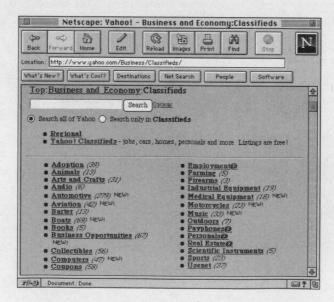

This is the main list of classified ad sites, listing hundreds of individual Web sites hosting classified ads in more than two dozen categories. Among these general categories, you'll find lists of sites that handle specific categories of merchandise. For example, here's the list for industrial equipment:

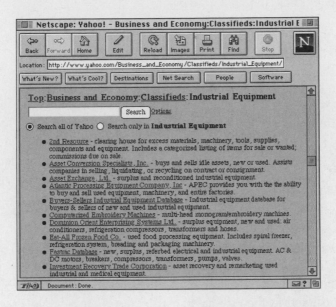

When you navigate to a specific ad site, you can post an ad there. Some sites are quite elaborate, hosting hundreds of ads in specific categories (regions or cities for real estate, or categories of industrial supplies, for example). It won't hurt to place your ad on more than one site, but if you're being selective, choose the sites that are well designed, easy to use, and easy to access. For example, look for sites that have well-defined ad categories, are easy to search, and are hosted on servers that deliver pages quickly.

Ads in newsgroups

Most newsgroups on the Net prohibit blatant advertising, but some groups are actually set up to contain nothing but ads. Other newsgroups have primarily given themselves over to ads, whether or not the groups' original creators intended that to happen. These groups contain all or mostly commercial ads:

alt.business.misc

biz.misc

misc.entrepreneurs

alt.marketplace.computer

alt.marketplace.non-computer

Any newsgroup with "forsale" in its name is also devoted to ads, but these groups are usually restricted to ads by individuals selling items such as used stereos or ski equipment. If you're advertising in forsale groups, it's best to offer one or two specific pieces of merchandise.

There are lots of forsale groups. Some are geographically specific newsgroups like ca.forsale and nj.forsale, and others are groups focused on certain types of merchandise like computer equipment. Before you post an ad to a newsgroup, though, check the group's FAQ (Frequently Asked Questions) message to see if commercial ads are allowed. *(See Appendix for more information.)*

Classified advertising in newsgroups is different from advertising in online services or BBSs in three major ways:

1. You can place an ad for free.   There's no way the Net can charge you to post anything to a newsgroup. All you pay is the online time you spend posting the ad. Because newsgroups are free, the ad-related ones have more activity than fee-based classified sections on online services. Some of the ad-related newsgroups get dozens or hundreds of new postings every day. And while some online services only allow you to post a particular ad to one classified area, you can *cross-post* an ad to several newsgroups on the Net at the same time.

2. Newsgroup ads aren't classified.   The classified sections on online services are divided into different categories so you can choose a category to browse that will contain only ads for certain types of merchandise or services. Any given newsgroup is just one long list of ads, like this:

```
┌──────────────────────────────────────────────────────────────────┐
│ ▦                          nj.forsale                          ▦  │
├──────────────────────────────────────────────────────────────────┤
│ 130 articles, 130 unread                                          │
├──────────────────────────────────────────────────────────────────┤
│  -     Unknown            Complete 286 system for sale.         ▲  │
│  -     Mark J. Sarisky    Gear Sale                             ▓  │
│  -     Dr. Peter Forst…   ==> VIDEO PROCESSOR and VIDEO EDITOR for sale <==│
│  -     shah               PAL palmcorder for sale..                │
│  -     Unknown            Sun i386Dx forsale.                      │
│  -     Roger A. Quon      TICKET: Phila --> Detroit $100           │
│  -     Sang T. Lee        Re: FORSALE: HP Scanjet IIcx Color Scanner│
│  -     Jesse Bunch        Megatek X-Window Accelerator Cards For Sale Cheap!│
│  -     Abdellatif Marr…   ***repost:Dot matrix printers***         │
│  -     Alec Yin           Forsale: SNES games                     │
│  -     Joshua M. Burgin   For Sale - Desk + Shelving Unit         │
│  ▷  3  Jason H.           Basic 486 System for sale.              │
│  ▷  2  on belay           For Sale - Avalanche & K2 boards        │
│  -     Fred Falk          RECORD/CD Expo, Wayne, NJ 10/8          │
│  -     Norman Garfinkle   Sears Kenmore Stack Washer/Elec. Dryer for sale in N. NJ│
│  -     avinash.kachhy     Indian Festive Ornamental Ladies Dress for Sale│
│  -     131G40000-S.W.N…   NJ:  1986 IROC for sale                 │
│  -     say,h sabit        ONE WEEK VACATION RENTAL IN FLORIDA     │
│  -     Charles Lesburg    WTB: 19", 20" or 21" monitor for Mac Q700 ▼│
├──────────────────────────────────────────────────────────────────┤
│ ▟                                                              ▤  │
└──────────────────────────────────────────────────────────────────┘
```

As you can see, this group is a hodgepodge of ads for everything from vacation rentals to cars to clothing to computer equipment. Most people who post ads on forsale newsgroups cross-post, so this sort of chaos is normal. Some newsgroup titles help restrict the type of merchandise sold on that group (misc.forsale.computers.pc-clone is devoted to PC-compatible computers, for example), but once you view any newsgroup, you'll see one long list of ad titles.

The jumble of ads on any newsgroup makes it more difficult for anyone to locate your particular ad, and it makes it all the more important for your ad to have a position on the list and a title that will give it maximum visibility and pulling power. *(For more information see "Marketing with classified ads" on p. 128.)*

3. Ads on newsgroups usually last longer.   Newsgroups don't have the same time restrictions you'll find in a more formal online classified section. Ads can sometimes remain on a newsgroup for weeks or months.

As in an online service, the list of messages in a newsgroup is chronological, and when new messages are added to the group, your message moves down the list. Because of this, it's vital to check any ad every few days to make sure it still has good visibility. Unlike with online services, you can post an ad with the same title over and over again on a newsgroup, if you like.

To get an idea of what's out there and who is posting what sorts of ads where, browse the newsgroups yourself. *(See Chapter 7 for more information about browsing newsgroups.)*

MARKETING WITH CLASSIFIED ADS

With thousands of ads in dozens of different places in cyberspace, you're competing fiercely with others for your readers' attention. Your product or service probably isn't unique, and even if it is, you'll still have to get readers interested enough to respond. Here are some ideas for creating classified ads that work.

The title

Your ad title may be the only chance you have to reach a prospect, so make it count. The title must stand out in a list of titles and make the reader want to know more.

- Use 32 characters or fewer if your ad is on an online service, because that's all the space your title will get. It would be a shame if the best part of your title was invisible to most readers.
- Use power words like the ones on pp. 72–73 to spark your readers' curiosity.
- Ask a question to position what you're selling as the solution to a problem, such as *Tired of tax problems?* or *Sore back?*
- Be as explicit as possible about what it is you're selling. In the list of examples on p. 73 one ad title reads *Gear Sale,* but *gear* could mean anything from transmission parts to hiking equipment to audio components.
- Use capital letters, asterisks, or other emphatic symbols to help key words in your ad title stand out visually from the others. As we explained on p. 70, capitals and emphatic symbols are the online equivalent of shouting. They shouldn't be used in normal e-mail or newsgroup messages, but classified ads are the exception.
- Test different ad titles on different classified areas or newsgroups to see which ones pull the best. For example, ask readers to reply to Dept. P for an ad on Prodigy, Dept. C for an ad on CompuServe, or Dept. B for an ad on the biz.misc newsgroup.

The message

If your ad title has motivated the reader to open your message, then the message should continue that momentum toward the sale. You can safely use two or even three screens' worth of space for your message, but be clear and concise in any case.

- Choose two or three main benefits of your product or service, and then explain each one in a sentence or two.
- Talk to the reader as if it's just the two of you, person to person. Use *you* instead of *people*, and give the message a conversational tone. For example, *Our experts can show you how to eliminate tax problems* sounds a lot better than *ABC Accountants is nationally recognized for its tax expertise.*
- Explain your company's advantage. Your company's competitive advantage — and it should have one or you won't be in business long — is the reason the customer should do business with you. Make sure the customer knows about it, whatever it is.
- Give the reader an extra incentive to respond by offering something free — a list of tips for gardening, your two-page report on tax news, or a discount on the first order of office supplies.
- Be sure to include your e-mail address, server address, phone or fax number, or postal address so that people can respond.
- Use different response codes or key words in different ads so that you'll know which ad is pulling the best. For example, you could ask people to send for your free *Tax Guide* in one message and your free *Tax Report* in another.
- Proofread your message and let others read it before you post it. Your employees or coworkers may point out problems with your copy that you, as the author, have missed.

Check the ad's position

Monitor the ad area or newsgroup daily to see how quickly your ad changes position, and then post a new ad when yours is more than two screens from the top of the list. Don't overdo it, though. There's a difference between posting often enough to maintain your visibility and hogging so much space that other advertisers resent you.

Check for replies

You can't respond quickly to customer inquiries if you don't know they're inquiring. Check your classified ad and your response address regularly. If you post an ad on a newsgroup or in the classified ad area of a forum, check the newsgroup or forum at least daily for responses to your message.

Rather than sending e-mail to your mailbox or phoning for more information, some newsgroup or forum readers may use the Reply button in their newsreader software. The Reply button posts a new message in reply to your original one. You can tell when your message has replies, because a number appears next to it, like this:

```
-          Alec Yin            Forsale: SNES games
-          Joshua M. Burgin    For Sale - Desk + Shelving Unit
▷  3       Jason H.            Basic 486 System for sale.
▷  2       on belay            For Sale - Avalanche & K2 boards
-          Fred Falk           RECORD/CD Expo, Wayne, NJ 10/8
```

Here, the message posted by Jason H. has three replies attached to it.

Respond promptly

If your classified ad promises free information, make sure you've prepared the free information in advance and have it ready to send out quickly. The more quickly you respond to requests, the more readers will come to trust you. If your mailbox is through an ISP, set up a mailbot program that sends out free information automatically when people request it. *(For more information about mailbots, see "About Mailbots" on p. 65.)*

GRAPHICAL ADS

A graphical ad displays your promotional message as a button that readers can click to get more information. There are several types of graphical ads: buttons on Web sites, banners or buttons in online service forums, and billboards that pop up on online services.

Buttons and banners on the Web

Selling advertising space has become one of the major profit opportunities on the Web. Most Web sites will be happy to sell you space for a graphical button or banner that identifies your company, product, or service, and serves as a link readers can click to navigate to further information about it. Here's an example:

This banner appears on Yahoo's games directory page. The site being advertised offers games on the Net, and since thousands of people view this page each week, this banner provides excellent visibility for the advertiser and offers a quick way for readers to find out more by navigating to the Happy Puppy site.

Advertising rates for buttons and banners on the Web vary from $15 per month to more than $100,000 per month, depending on the size of the ad and the server's popularity. There are three different models for pricing: cost per thousand (CPM), click-through, and per-sale.

CPM is the advertising industry standard charge for space in print media. You pay so much for each 1,000 impressions, or pairs of eyes that see your ad. The CPM rate depends on the volume of traffic at the site and its ability to deliver a particular audience, just as it does in print magazines. When you're paying a CPM rate, you must have faith not only in the ad's location, but in your ad's ability to attract readers (since you pay for the space whether the ad works or not).

Click-through is a Web-specific pricing model based on the number of people who actually click on your button and navigate to your site. Your site's server log reports the domain address of each visitor, so you can easily count the number of visitors coming to your site from a button's location. With a click-through rate, you pay only when people are interested enough in your ad to find out more.

Per-sale rates allow you to pay only when your ad actually results in a sale. This is the best possible type of rate, since you don't risk anything. It's difficult to find sites willing to offer per-sale rates, but as the competition for Web advertisers grows, this option may become more common.

FREE BUTTON SPACE

Guerrillas get even better deals by trading products or services. If you're in the stereo business and you want a button on an audiophile Web site, for example, you might trade a stereo receiver (for a contest held on the site) for a month's worth of button space. And don't think in terms of just one button space: think about ways to place button ads in every Web location where your prospective customers are likely to visit.

For a good beginning reference to trading advertising buttons on the Web, check out the Internet Link Exchange service at www.submit-it.com. When you sign up for this service, you agree to host buttons from other advertisers on your Web site in exchange for them doing the same for you, all for free.

The best deals for banner ads are on smaller sites that are closely related to your business. If you're an investment advisor, for example, you might shop for button space on an investment directory page, where your prospects are likely to visit.

Buttons on online services

A good way to get your message in front of likely prospects on online services is to buy button space on a particular forum related to your business. Here's an example:

At the entrance to the House & Home forum, we see ad buttons for a real estate firm, a home improvement firm, a mortgage company, and a school watchdog organization. You can buy forum-specific button space for as little as $50 per thousand impressions (CPM). By choosing the right forum, you can place your message before people most likely to be interested in it.

Button strategies

The presentation options for buttons, particularly on the Web, are increasing all the time. Today, you can offer static buttons that show one graphic only, or buttons that transform themselves two or three times as the viewer looks at them. An animated button attracts the viewer's eye much more easily than a static button, but a static button can work well if properly designed and placed. Here are some ideas:

Remember the button's purpose. The only purpose a button has is to get the viewer to click it. When designing a button, your only job is to get viewers interested enough to click it and get more information. *(For ideas about ad titles, see "Classified Ads" on p. 119 and apply these to the space limitations of a button.)*

Use a simple design. Even if you use an animated button, don't overload it with too many colors or graphics. The more complex a button is, the larger its graphic file and the longer it takes to appear on the viewer's screen. Don't clutter a button up so much that it's the last thing a viewer sees.

Design for the environment. If you're buying space in a place where there will be other buttons, try to find out in advance which other ad buttons your button will be grouped with, and choose colors or text that make your button stand out from the crowd. Also, choose colors and text that make your button stand out from the page background rather than blending into it. This may require using different color schemes for buttons in different locations, but it will be worth it.

Negotiate a location. People's eyes tend to gravitate to the upper right corner of a page or screen. Try to find out exactly where your button will be placed, and view the page before it's published on the Web or online service to see how it will look. If possible place your button at or near the upper right corner (ideally on the first screen the viewer sees). If your button must be at the bottom of a screen, try to place it at the right side rather than the left: the viewer's eye goes to the right more naturally.

Billboards on online services

Billboards are electronic notices that pop into view on your screen as you use a commercial online service or surf the Net. Unlike buttons, which have a fixed location on a certain screen, billboards pop up as the user navigates from one location to another, or appear randomly at the bottom of certain screens at different times. For example, a billboard might pop up when someone enters the online shopping area on CompuServe, logs onto America Online, or enters the Personal Finance area on Prodigy.

Here's a billboard that popped up as we entered the shopping area on AOL:

This billboard occupies the center of the screen and so has the viewer's undivided attention. In other cases, billboards either appear in the lower portion of the screen or cover the whole screen. Like banner ads, electronic billboards give your customers a chance to find out more about the product instantly, offering doorways to your online store or to a more detailed message in places where you wouldn't otherwise have them.

Billboard ads on online services have the advantage of grabbing the reader's attention as no button can, but you don't have much control over which reader's attention is being grabbed. Your billboard ad for travel services might pop up when an eleven-year-old is logging onto AOL. The other drawback to billboards is the cost: you'll spend from $5,000 up to gain this kind of attention on a major online service,

THINK QUALITY, NOT QUANTITY

When paying for advertising space, aim for precision: try to place your ads in the locations where the highest percentage of people seeing them will be likely prospects. You can reach tens of thousands of people by advertising on Yahoo or on Netscape's home page, but you'll be paying a lot of money to reach an audience largely composed of people who won't be interested in what you're offering.

It's much better to spend less money to reach a smaller audience with a higher percentage of hot prospects. Rather than thinking about ad expenses as paying to reach people, guerrillas think about making the most of their money by reaching the highest possible percentage of likely customers.

although your contract may include a certain number of billboards like these if you rent storefront space on an online service.

SPONSORSHIP NOTICES

Graphical ads on the Web and on online services are the hottest advertising area now, but that doesn't mean you should rule out good old text. Sponsorship notices and other text messages are less expensive to place and less expensive to produce, but they can work as well as graphics. The challenge is to place the text in exactly the right location. Let's look at a couple of options.

What's New, welcome, and sign-off messages

Every major online service has a welcome or log-on screen that includes promotional messages. CompuServe has a separate window containing What's New items. America Online and Prodigy announce new items on their welcome screens. There's no extra charge for these notices. *(For an example of the America Online Welcome screen see p. 43.)*

When you open a new store in the online mall in an online service, a notice about your store appears on the What's New portion of the welcome screen. And when you make a major change to your store or offer a new and exciting service or contest, you should be able to place a message about it on the welcome screen as well. Your online mall marketing representative can help you place your promotional messages on the welcome screen.

On Prodigy and America Online, the sign-off or goodbye screens can also contain promotions, like this:

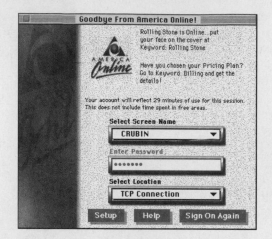

This screen lists a promotion for *Rolling Stone* magazine online, but AOL's sign-off frequently promotes online conferences, too. If you were planning to hold an online conference to promote your business (*see Chapter 9*), this would be a good place to get some free advertising for that event.

Sponsorship notices

If you know of a popular mailing list discussion that is sent out in digest form (all the day's messages are combined into one message mailed daily), approach the list's owner about a sponsorship notice. A sponsorship notice is paid space that identifies you as the list's sponsor that week or month and appears at the beginning of each message digest sent out by the list's owner. Here's an example:

```
Internet Marketing Discussion List

Digest #0714

To UNSUBSCRIBE send any text to the email address IM-UNSUB@I-M.COM
If you can't get off the list and want to, PLEASE email <glenn@i-m.com>

-------------------------------------------------------------------
This week's sponsors:
DirectChoice - One-to-one marketing on the web. <http://www.directchoice.com>
* HTML:THE DEFINITIVE GUIDE, http://www.ora.com/www/item/html.html *
-------------------------------------------------------------------
```

This sponsorship notice cost $250 for a week's exposure on this marketing-related mailing list. With about 4,000 subscribers receiving at least one digest every day, that's very good exposure to some very good prospects for the price.

Along with mailing lists, look for electronic newsletters distributed weekly or monthly where you might be able to buy a sponsorship notice or text advertisement.

DIRECTORY LISTINGS

The Web has dozens of directories that list thousands of sites, and these directories are some of the most popular destinations for Web surfers. You can usually add your business's URL to Web directories for free, so you should be listed in as many of them as possible. Here's Guerrilla Marketing Online's listing on Yahoo:

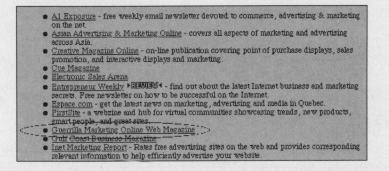

Anyone searching Yahoo for "Guerrilla Marketing" will find this link, and they can click on it to go directly to the Guerrilla Marketing Online Web site.

Getting listed in a directory

Every free directory has a simple form you fill out so that you can add your listing to it. Before you fill out the form, however, think about how you want your listing to appear, and prepare the description in advance. You'll need your company name, your e-mail address and Web address, of course, but you'll also need:

Keywords under which your URL will be listed. You'll be asked to list three or more keywords or categories under which your business can be found by someone searching for it. For example, your architecture firm might use keywords like "design," "architects," and "space planning." Browse through the portion of the directory where you think you'll want to be listed to get an idea of the keywords you'll want to use when submitting your listing.

A description of your business in fifty words or less. This should be a clear, evocative paragraph that says what you do and makes people want to know more.

You can submit listings to the major directories yourself, or you can pay a Net visibility firm to do it for you. Some companies charge $50 to $100 to list you in dozens of different directories, and they guarantee that your listings will appear within a few days. However, there's a free service called Submit-It that will post your listing to several directories at once. You'll find the Submit-It site at www.submit-it.com. *(See Appendix for individual directory options.)*

SEVEN STRATEGIES FOR ONLINE ADVERTISING

Anybody can post a classified ad or rent ad space, but only a guerrilla will make the most of it. These seven key strategies make the difference:

1. Use a strong title.   Whether you're writing a classified ad title, the copy for a button, or the heading of a billboard, use a short, enticing title that fires the readers' curiosity and encourages them to take the next step.

2. Use people talk.   Ad and billboard messages should talk to a specific person, not to the masses. Write copy that mirrors what you'd say to someone if you were talking in person.

3. Use power words.   Check out the list of power words on pp. 72–73 and use them in ad or billboard titles and message copy. They work.

4. Make it easy to respond.   If the online service offers a quick button that takes readers to an order or reply form, use it. If not, use e-mail as the response mechanism rather than postal mail because your prospect is already connected to the computer and can send e-mail quickly and easily. Use a mailbot if you can.

5. Offer something free.   Give customers a tangible reason to respond to your message — a limited-time offer, a discount, or free information. Even if prospects are curious about your product or service, the offer of something free will help push them forward to the next step in the sale.

6. Check your ad regularly.   If you post a classified ad in an online service or newsgroup, check its position daily to make sure it's still in a good position to be read. Repost ads when they drop more than two screens down from the top of the list. If you post in a newsgroup or forum, make sure you check your message for any replies attached to it.

7. Code responses to track their effectiveness.   Use coded responses to test the effectiveness of different ads or billboards.

7

Discussion Groups

Two of the most important elements in a successful marketing campaign are visibility and credibility. Customers can't buy from you if they don't know who you are, and they won't buy from you if they don't trust you to deliver the goods. Participating in discussion groups — online service forums and Internet newsgroups — lets you communicate directly with the people most likely to be interested in your business, and it lets you do it in a way that gains your company both visibility and credibility. Better still, it costs you nothing but time.

Discussion-group marketing requires subtlety and tact. Rather than boasting about your product or service in an ad, you respond to messages posted by others or propose discussion subjects of your own. This may seem like a roundabout way to win customers, but it works, sometimes dramatically.

One netizen we know has an interest in futures trading. He also has some friends in the brokerage business. Surfing the Net one night, he stumbled upon a newsgroup related to futures investments. It was a relatively inactive group, with only seventeen posted messages at the time. One of the messages posed an investment question, and our friend posted a reply with a partial answer. Along with his partial answer, he mentioned a broker friend who would know the whole answer and added the broker's 800 number.

The next day the broker called to thank our friend, saying his phone had been ringing all morning with calls from people who had read that newsgroup posting. In two days the broker had twenty-three new account leads from that one posting; many of the callers ended up opening accounts.

This futures broker normally spends about $400 to produce a single new account lead, but thanks to a newsgroup posting he neither made nor encouraged, he gained a handful of leads for nothing. By marketing in discussion groups for yourself, you can do even better. Online guerrillas have told us that next to electronic mail, participating in discussion groups is the top tool for generating sales leads.

Your online marketing arsenal should definitely include discussion-group marketing. It takes time and patience to do it right, but it pays off. Besides, you can set specific goals and budget your time so that you get the results you want without spending more than a few minutes a day at it.

There are three types of discussion groups you'll likely find online: forums on online services, Internet newsgroups, and discussion groups on Web sites. Let's take a close look at how discussion groups work and how you can make the most of them.

ABOUT FORUMS

Forums are discussion groups located on commercial online services and some bulletin boards. Sometimes a forum is just one discussion area (scuba diving, for example), and sometimes it's a collection of areas on a handful of related topics. (A small business forum, for example, might include discussions of marketing, sales, and management.) In addition to discussion areas, forums often contain libraries of files posted by members and conference rooms where members can chat. Sometimes forums have their own classified ad areas as well.

To participate in a forum, you must be a subscriber to the online service or BBS that hosts it. The major online services have dozens, if not hundreds, of different forums. Often, a major area such as health or business will have half a dozen or more forums of its own. It may take some snooping around in an area related to your business before you discover all the forums hosted there and find one or more that are particularly suitable to your marketing needs. Let's look at an example.

Navigating in a forum

The Business Strategies forum on America Online shows how a forum works. It's up to each forum's administrator to design a forum, but this one shows the major features you'll find. The main forum screen is shown at the top of page 142.

This forum offers chat rooms, message boards, software libraries, and a list of topic-specific features. Clicking any icon or double-clicking any list option takes you to that area.

Our Chat Rooms! shows you a list of the forum's chat rooms. Forum visitors can use these rooms to chat with each other at any time, but the rooms are also used for electronic meetings at specific times, where an expert on a particular subject answers questions. For example, this forum might invite an expert on direct-mail advertising to hold a conference on that subject at a certain time. At the appointed time, dozens of members will enter the conference room to listen to the expert field questions from the conference's moderator or to pose questions themselves. *(See Chapter 9 for more on online conferences.)*

Message Boards takes you to a list of this forum's message boards. This particular forum has more than a dozen different discussion areas:

```
┌──────────────────── Message Boards ─────────────────────┐
│ 🏦 Message Boards                                         │
│ ┌──────────────────────────────────────────────────────┐│
│ │ 🗂 Advertising, Sales & Marketing                    ▲││
│ │ 🗂 Classified Ads                                     ││
│ │ 🗂 Coffee Break Messages                              ││
│ │ 🗂 Consultant's Corner Messages                       ││
│ │ 🗂 DTP, WP & Office Services                           ││
│ │ 🗂 Home Business Message Board                         ││
│ │ 🗂 International Business                              ││
│ │ 🗂 Multi Level Marketing Boards                       ││
│ │ 🗂 Newsletter Publishing                              ││
│ │ 🗂 Small Business Issues 1                            ▼││
│ └──────────────────────────────────────────────────────┘│
│          [ Open ]              [ More ]                   │
└───────────────────────────────────────────────────────────┘
```

Inside each area is a list of different message topics, like this:

Each of the thirty-seven different topics listed here contains more than one hundred messages. If you're a regular visitor to this area, you can list only the new messages that have been posted since your last visit, or messages that you haven't read before (New messages). Here's the list of messages in the Direct Marketing Discussions topic:

Since messages are shown in the order posted, you have to scroll to the bottom of this list to see the most recent ones. Each message is shown with a title, the author's name, and the date it was posted. Any replies to a message are shown directly below the message. To read any message online, just open the message board and select the message you want to read. The message opens in a window like this:

```
╔════════════════════════════════════════════════════════╗
║  ▦▦▦   Adverts, Sales & Marketing  /Direct Marketing Discussions  ▦▦▦  ║
╠════════════════════════════════════════════════════════╣
║ ┌──────────────────────────────────────────────────┬──┐ ║
║ │ Subj:  Telemarketing Syst                        │▲ │ ║
║ │ Date:  2/15/97 9:28:16 PM                        │  │ ║
║ │ From:  MrlouBus                                  │  │ ║
║ │ Posted on:  America Online                       │  │ ║
║ │                                                  │  │ ║
║ │ Does anyone know of a good incoming telemarketing│  │ ║
║ │ operation that does business in the Northeast? I │  │ ║
║ │ have a client interested in setting up a         │  │ ║
║ │ customer order center, and the company sells     │  │ ║
║ │ mostly to customers in the Northeast. They want  │  │ ║
║ │ telemarketers who are familiar with and can      │  │ ║
║ │ understand accents from Maine, Massachusetts, and│  │ ║
║ │ New York. If anyone                              │▼ │ ║
║ └──────────────────────────────────────────────────┴──┘ ║
║                                                          ║
║    ┌─────┐              ┌─────┐              ┌─────┐      ║
║    │  ⇦  │              │  🗎  │              │  ⇨  │      ║
║    └─────┘              └─────┘              └─────┘      ║
║    Previous              Add                 Next         ║
║    Message             Message             Message        ║
╚════════════════════════════════════════════════════════╝
```

The title bar of the message window shows which message board it is from. The header inside the message shows the topic name, who posted the message, and when and where it was posted. You can click buttons at the bottom to skip to the previous or next message or to add a reply to this message. If you click the Add Message icon, for example, a blank message form appears, and you can type your response. The message is then added to this message board. To post a message on a new topic, return to the Advertising, Sales, & Marketing topics list and create a new topic there.

Download Libraries shows you a list of the forum's software libraries, like this:

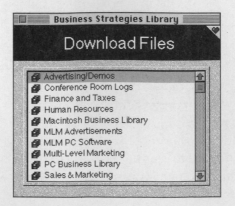

You can open any library to see a list of its files and download them to your own computer. For example, here's the list of files in the Sales & Marketing library:

UpId	Subject	Count	Download
12/14/96	BIG IDEAS: Propel Sales	88	1/2/97
12/14/96	MILLION DOLLAR SALES LETTER	99	1/2/97
12/14/96	MARKETING QUICK STUDY	51	1/2/97
12/4/96	Sharing Recipes With Customers	50	1/1/97
11/26/96	Customer Appreciation - Ornam...	120	1/1/97
11/22/96	Free Direct Response Newsletter	241	1/2/97
11/16/96	Medical Claims Analysis	51	12/30/96
11/11/96	Holiday Marketing Ideas	261	1/1/97
11/11/96	Big Ideas: Why Do Buyers Buy?	161	1/2/97
11/5/96	8 Ways to Great Service on In...	76	1/2/97

Sales & Marketing

Read Description   Download Now   Download Later   Upload   List More Files

To find out more about any file, simply select its name and click the Read Description button to see a short text description of the file. You can download a file immediately or have it downloaded at a later time. To add a file to the library, click the Upload button to select the file you want to add and to write a short description of it. The List More Files button scrolls the list down one screen. (There's also a scroll bar at the right edge of this window, but it's not shown in our example.)

On some business-related forums, one library may be devoted to product announcements, resumes, or company information. This would be a good place to introduce your business to the forum's visitors. In other libraries, you can upload articles related to your business as a way to improve your online credibility. *(See Chapter 9 for more information.)*

Starting your own forum

If you spend most of your online time on a particular service that doesn't have a forum relating to your business, you might want to start one. To create a new forum, come up with a plan that states the purpose of the forum and its main features (message boards, libraries, conferencing, ads, or whatever), and then propose the forum to the online service's management. The service's management will probably have a specific proposal process you go through to pitch a new forum. Most online services welcome new forum ideas, since the variety of discussion groups on a service is one of its major drawing cards.

GET TO KNOW THE FORUM LEADERS

Many forums host a variety of discussion groups, chat rooms, libraries, and other resources, and you can spend a lot of time poking into one thing or another before you get an overall sense of how the forum runs and what sorts of marketing activities are permitted there. A much faster way to get up to speed is to find the forum administrator or leader and ask specific questions.

Every forum has at least one (and often several) leaders who can tell you where to upload marketing-related information about your business (or whether such information is permitted at all). You can also ask the leader(s) which discussion groups will most likely focus on topics of interest to you, and whether or not your area of expertise would make a good topic for an online conference.

Also, by staying in touch with the forum leader(s), you'll know in advance when new message boards, libraries, or regular chat sessions are being planned.

The trick to proposing a new forum is to make it specific enough to draw potential customers for your business, yet general enough to draw a significant portion of the online service's subscriber base. If you sell woodworking tools, you might propose a woodworking forum, but that would probably be too specific for an online service's subscribers at large. However, a handcrafts forum might be general enough, and you could have a woodworking message area where you can gain credibility by answering questions. You might also include a woodworking library and start it off by posting your own articles about carving techniques or advice on how to choose tools.

Running your own online forum gives you more freedom to post your company information (since you make the forum rules), but it also means spending time online every day to monitor the forum's activity and make changes as needed. Like an electronic storefront, your forum should continually offer something new to its members (aside from posted messages) to keep the browsers and members coming back.

ABOUT NEWSGROUPS

A newsgroup is the Net's version of a forum. It's a place where a group of people post and read messages on a particular topic. Unlike forums, newsgroups support only messages, not libraries or conferencing.

But despite this limitation, newsgroups offer a lot of marketing leverage. Nobody has to subscribe to an online service or BBS to join a newsgroup. Your potential audience includes anyone who has access to the Internet and who is interested in the newsgroup's topic. Many newsgroups are followed by thousands of people around the world. And once you have access to the Net, it doesn't cost you a dime to participate in as many newsgroups as you like.

How to access newsgroups

In order to access any newsgroup, you use a newsreader, a program that can access and read the contents of newsgroups. Web browsers like Netscape Navigator or Microsoft Internet Explorer have the ability to participate in newsgroups, and there are also programs designed solely for reading newsgroups, such as NewsWatcher, tin, or rn. Online services offer newsgroup access, too.

Every Internet service provider subscribes to a selection of newsgroups, but there are thousands of newsgroups, and no ISP offers access to them all. In order to access any particular newsgroup, your ISP must subscribe to it.

To find out which newsgroups you can access, use your newsreader program to display a list of those available on your system. (If you're on an online service, go to the service's Internet area and use the function to read newsgroups.) If you hear about a newsgroup that might help you promote your business but your ISP doesn't subscribe to it, you may be able to get it by asking your ISP's administrators to subscribe to it.

SEARCHING NEWSGROUPS ON THE WEB

Newsreader software is fine, but now you can access newsgroups directly from a Web site called Deja News (www.dejanews.com). This site lets you search all newsgroups for messages that contain certain keywords. Deja News displays a list of all the individual messages that match your search criteria, including the message's subject, author, date posted, and the name of the newsgroup where it was posted. When you view the list, buttons at the top of the screen let you open messages, reply to them, or send an e-mail note to the author.

With its powerful searching capabilities, Deja News is a perfect tool for the guerrilla marketer, because it lets you quickly find and read all the messages that relate to the subject you have in mind, no matter which newsgroup they were posted to. It can save you hours of browsing with a typical newsreader.

Newsgroup names and categories

There are several types of newsgroups on the Net, but the largest collection of groups is called *Usenet*. The majority of newsgroups on Usenet are organized in different categories, or *hierarchies*. The prefix of a group's name indicates the newsgroup hierarchy. Some of the largest Usenet hierarchies are:

alt (alternative topics)

biz (business)

comp (computers)

misc (miscellaneous topics)

news (news and discussions about Usenet itself)

rec (recreation)

sci (science)

soc (social topics)

talk (controversial topics)

The suffix of the group's name indicates its subject. For example, news.announce.newgroups contains announcements of new Usenet groups that have been formed, and misc.entrepreneurs focuses on entrepreneurship.

Initially, newsgroups covered general topics that were not specific to location. But as the number of ISPs has skyrocketed, many of them have started groups that carry news or announcements for the cities in which they're located. For example, newsgroups devoted to news about specific places often have names like bay.general, which covers general announcements in the San Francisco Bay Area. Your local ISP probably won't subscribe to all the local-topic newsgroups, as there are hundreds of them.

Joining a newsgroup

Assuming your ISP provides access to the newsgroup you want, joining a group is simple. You just go to your online service's Internet area and display the list of newsgroups, or direct your ISP's newsreader software to list all the available newsgroups. (This usually happens when you start up the newsreader anyway.)

For example, when you choose the Netscape Newsgroups command in Netscape Navigator, the newsreader automatically opens and displays the list of groups carried by your ISP, like this:

You can choose either to show the names of all the groups to which your ISP subscribes (as in the preceding figure) or only the names of the groups you have chosen to view. Since it takes a minute or more to read and display the names of all the groups, you might want your newsreader set to show only subscribed, or active, groups. Your newsreader window might look different from this, since there are many different newsreader programs. *(For an example from a different newsreader, see p. 127.)*

Once you see the list of groups, you can view the contents of any group by selecting it. When there's a collection of newsgroups organized under a hierarchy, the list shows the hierarchy name and the number of groups in it.

When you find an interesting group, you use a command in your newsreader to subscribe to it. Once you've subscribed, your newsreader program knows that you always want it to retrieve any new articles that have been posted to that group since you last viewed it. If you decide not to continue your involvement with a newsgroup, simply cancel your subscription.

Reading and replying to messages

As in a forum, a newsgroup's messages appear as topics in a list.

Newsreaders usually give you a choice of displaying either all the group's messages or only those you haven't read. When a newsgroup contains hundreds or thousands of messages, it's faster to display only the unread messages. Often, you can tell by a message's title that you don't want to read it. In this case, you can use a command in the newsreader to mark the message as read even if you didn't actually read it.

In most cases, you'll be able to download any new messages to your computer so that you can read them offline at your leisure.

You can read any message by selecting it. Whenever you read a message, it's automatically marked as having been read (in our examples, messages that have been read are no longer shown in boldface).

A message can have one or more replies attached to it. When you have a message open, you can reply to it by choosing a Reply command in your newsreader and then typing your message. If you reply to a message, your reply is posted to the board and can be read by anyone else. If your reply is personal, you can send a message to the original author's e-mail address so that only he or she can read it.

Finding out about newsgroups

There are thousands of newsgroups on the Net, and your newsreader software will probably provide access to most of them. Only a few of these groups will be suitable for your marketing purposes, though. The trick is to discover which groups they are.

One way to find out what's going on in these groups is by trial and error. Browse the list of newsgroups displayed by your newsreader, open up any that look interesting, and read a few messages on it to see if it's a group you might want to participate in regularly. If it looks potentially interesting, subscribe to the group and monitor its activity for a couple of weeks.

Your newsreader software will also notify you about any new groups that appear on the Net. New groups appear every week (if not every day). Most newsreaders automatically display a separate list of groups that have appeared since you last browsed the newsgroup list. You should check any new groups that look interesting, since it's easier to build a reputation on a newsgroup if you are active in it from its beginning.

Another way to find out about newsgroups is by reading an Internet magazine or consulting a directory like *The Internet Yellow Pages*. Directories list newsgroup names and subjects. Internet-related magazines often have articles about new or interesting newsgroups as well.

Finally, you can check the news.announce.newgroups newsgroup on the Net itself for messages announcing groups that have been recently formed.

STARTING A NEWSGROUP

If you can't find a group that suits your marketing purposes, start one of your own. A newsgroup doesn't exist on only one host computer system, and you don't need permission to create one. Many ISPs sponsor newsgroups about the Net or about their services in particular. Software companies like Oracle and computer companies like Digital Equipment Corporation host newsgroups of their own to offer product information and advice. You can do the same.

A newsgroup exists in the storage space provided by every ISP that subscribes to it. New postings to the group are transmitted over the Net and are received by all ISPs subscribing to that group. So a newsgroup's existence and its leadership are determined by the number of ISPs who subscribe to that particular group, and by the number of people connected through those various ISPs who participate in that group.

To create a Usenet newsgroup, just have your ISP or a consultant set the group up on your ISP's news server. You then announce that the group exists and invite people to participate. Once the group exists, you announce the new group by placing a notice in news.announce.newgroups and any other place that seems appropriate. Since your new group won't automatically gain subscriptions from different ISPs, you should promote it by posting announcements to related newsgroups and mailing lists. The more people you can interest in joining your newsgroup, the more they'll request their ISPs to subscribe to that group, and the more ISPs will join.

So, for example, you could set up alt.oldfords to further your reputation as a source of information about restoring antique Ford cars (and thereby attract customers to your parts business). You would certainly want to announce the new group in groups such as alt.autos.antique and alt.autos.rod-n-custom. As members of these groups ask their ISPs to subscribe to alt.oldfords, your group will develop a following.

WEB SITE DISCUSSION GROUPS

The third type of discussion group is based on a Web site. Hosting a discussion on your company's Web site is one of the best ways to maintain a flow of fresh information through the site and to attract a

WHICH DISCUSSION SHOULD YOU START?

The easiest type of discussion to start is a Web site discussion. Some of the inexpensive Web page creation programs have options that practically create a discussion area for you automatically, and you can have your discussion area up and running in a day or two. A Web discussion gives visitors something extra to do on your Web site and keeps them returning.

However, all the message management that's built into newsgroups and forums is difficult to duplicate with current Web technology. For example, in a forum, visitors can easily sort and select messages by date, view only unread messages, and upload files.

Still, for most uses, the Web is the best location for a discussion. It's easy to use, and your visitors don't need a subscription to visit.

loyal community of visitors. For example, the computer book publisher Peachpit Press hosts discussion groups about several computer-related topics on its site at www.peachpit.com.

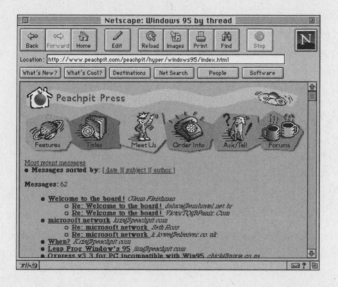

This particular discussion is about general PC-related topics. All the messages on this topic are listed in chronological order on one Web page. Each message's title is listed, and you click on the title to see the message. To post a message (or a reply to an existing message), you fill out a form located at the bottom of the group page.

Peachpit Press hosts discussions related to several topics covered in its line of books, including digital photo enhancement, Macintosh subjects, Windows 95, and others. Other book-related sites such as amazon.com host discussions where visitors can read and post book reviews or general messages about books and authors.

MARKETING IN DISCUSSION GROUPS

It's not hard to figure out the basic procedures for posting and reading messages in discussion groups. With a little research you can find the right groups in which to bolster your online reputation. But actually building a good reputation is another matter. These areas of the online marketplace abound with messages that are never read, or worse, messages that generate hostile responses. Building a positive reputation on a newsgroup or forum takes time, and it requires tact. Here's how guerrillas do it.

Lurk first, post later

Before you post anything to a newsgroup or forum, monitor its activity and read messages on it for at least a week. It takes that long for you to learn the group's etiquette. Some of the points you need to fully understand include:

- what's acceptable and not acceptable in the way of promotional messages
- what's considered an appropriate message length
- which topics are of the most interest to the group's members
- which group members are the most active, and which of them have views similar to yours
- which messages or message titles draw the most replies

Read messages diligently and learn what kinds of information and which methods of expression are regarded the most highly. You'll quickly learn how to become one of the good guys.

Use descriptive topic names

The names you give your postings should arouse curiosity and encourage group members to read your messages. When you reply to a message, your newsreader or forum software automatically suggests *RE: something* as the new message name. It's tempting to let the newsreader suggest a message name for you, but the problem is that lots of people do the same thing. If your message title is *RE: something* and there are six others with the same title, yours won't stand out. Worse yet, it'll be lumped in with all the others. If there are half a dozen messages whose topic names are *RE: Butterflies*, anyone who reads and isn't interested in the first one of them will probably never bother to open the rest of them. Your topic name should explain the main point of your message, and it should stand out from the crowd.

Don't be crass

Whatever you do, don't simply post your marketing message or an ad for your business. This is the surest way to draw lots of flames (poison-pen replies) from all but the ad-related discussion groups and forums, and it may permanently damage your reputation. If you've already made this mistake, an abject apology that includes some useful information or a useful comment about another member's posting may help restore you to the group's good graces.

But this isn't to say that you can't pitch yourself. It's all a matter of doing it properly. Here's a message you might post to a newsgroup about gardening if you wanted to promote your online garden supply business:

```
I've been enjoying the discussion here for awhile,
and would like to ask for some help. I'm in the lawn
and garden supplies business and am looking for useful
information to post on my Web server. I already post
excerpts from articles in Green Thumb News, as well as
a list of seasonal gardening tips for four different
regions of the United States. Does anyone here have
ideas for other selections of information?

Thanks for your help!

George Beasley
------------------------------------------------------
Garden City Online
http://www.gardencity.com, email: info@gardencity.com
The Gardener's Source For Supplies & Info
------------------------------------------------------
```

Rather than a sales pitch, this message acknowledges the group's expertise and then asks for help. This message may provoke further discussion about what constitutes useful gardening information. It may encourage any experts on the group to send articles they've written as potential additions to your Web site. It will definitely put your Web site's name and address before a group likely to be interested in it, and it will almost certainly attract some visitors.

Don't be banal

One mistake newbies make when attempting to join a discussion is to post a message just for the sake of posting one. When America Online first allowed access to newsgroups, a lot of groups had to suffer through messages like *Hi. Is this the Internet?* If you're not sure about how to post a message or whether or not you're in the right newsgroup, check out the news.announce.newusers newsgroup and read its general information messages.

Even if you know you're in the right place and you know how to post a message, don't reply to someone else's comment by simply agreeing with them. Posting a message that repeats someone else's message and says you agree is a waste of time for everybody in a discussion. If you don't have something new to add, keep lurking until you do.

Provide useful information

Each discussion group has its own ideas of what "useful information" is, but you can increase your chances of hitting the mark.

- Don't assume people are interested in your subjective opinions until you've developed a reputation as someone whose opinions matter. Instead, back up your opinions with citations from other sources, or base your comments on actual experience.
- If you come across a short article or a message on another group that you think the current group's members would appreciate seeing, post it (as long as it's not copyrighted), and include some comments of your own about it.
- If you've written an article that you've stored somewhere online and you think the group's members might find it interesting, include some of the article's information in a message and direct members to the article's address.
- Respond to questions posted by other members if you can offer some constructive advice, but don't claim experience or knowledge you don't have. If you can provide a partial answer, do so, and try to direct people to others who know more. This will show group members that you're not just in the game for yourself.

Use a company signature

Create a signature for your messages that identifies your business and its online address. Customers can't find you if you don't tell them how. *(See "Your signature" on p. 76.)*

Choose a handful of targets

You only have so much time in a day, and you can devote only so much of it to forums and newsgroups. Don't overdo it. As you're shopping around, look for two or three groups whose topics most closely relate to your business, and focus on those. Establish your presence in one group at a time. Stay away from groups that are so active that you can't keep up with them or so inactive that nobody ever posts messages in them. You should be able to come up with a short list of forums or newsgroups that

YOUR DISCUSSION GROUP BUDGET

Time is a busy entrepreneur's most precious commodity, and participating in discussion groups may seem a poor investment of your time compared with passive marketing techniques such as Web sites and advertisements. But discussion groups give you a way to develop solid, ongoing relationships with potential customers that you can't easily get by advertising or having a storefront. Rather than dismissing discussion-group marketing out of hand, guerrillas find a way to work some of it into their daily schedule.

To make discussion group marketing work for you, decide how much time per day you're willing to spend, and then spend only that much time. If you have only five or ten minutes a day to spend in discussion groups, then focus your energy on just one group and become a regular contributor to it. Obviously, you'll increase your time budget for this activity if your efforts result in new customers, but if you don't get results in one group, try others.

And don't limit your efforts to the Internet. For a $10 or $20 monthly fee, you have access to lots of active discussions on any of the major online services. This can be a bargain investment if you end up attracting several new customers each month. And it won't cost you anything to investigate: every online service offers a free trial period during which you can browse and check out its forums.

match your market. If you try to keep up with more than three active groups, you probably won't be able to keep up with any of them.

Participate frequently

Check every forum or newsgroup for new messages at least every day or two, and try to respond to questions or add helpful comments to the discussions whenever you can. Frequent postings keep you visible, and if you wait too long to respond to a previous message, people won't remember the prior discussion.

Propose a conference in your forum

If you're in a forum on an online service, send a note to the forum's administrator and propose holding a conference. Your pitch to the administrator should include a description of yourself and your experience as well as some noteworthy accomplishments. The pitch should convince the administrator that you know your stuff and that your area of expertise would make for an interesting and popular conference for the forum's other members. *(See Chapter 9 for details.)*

If your pitch is accepted, the administrator will announce your up-coming conference in the forum's What's New area. If your subject is broad enough and you schedule the conference at least two months in advance, you may also be able to get the administrator to propose an an-nouncement about it on the online service's welcome screen or What's New list. *(See Chapter 6)*.

SIX STRATEGIES FOR DISCUSSION GROUP MARKETING

Here's a list of key points to remember as you go about promoting your business in forums and newsgroups.

1. Do your homework.   Diligently seek out forums and newsgroups that relate to your business as closely as possible. The more closely a discussion group's topic relates to your business, the more likely its members are to become your customers. Lurk on any group for at least a week before you even consider posting a message to it. Make sure you understand the group's culture and etiquette before you join the discussion.

2. Don't waste the group's time.   Post messages that are on the topic, and that add to the discussion. Don't simply agree with others, and don't post blatant ads. Back up your opinions with facts.

3. Be helpful.   If you see a posting or article someplace else that your group might appreciate (and its author allows it to be reproduced), post it with your comments. Whenever someone posts a question and you can provide all or part of the answer, do so. This is the best way to gain other members' respect.

4. Use a company signature.   People can't find you or your online store if they don't know your address. Sign every message with your name, company name, and address.

5. Be attentive.   Check your newsgroups and forums every day or two for new messages, and participate in the discussion whenever you have something to add. Frequent postings equal visibility.

6. Be patient.   Success doesn't happen overnight. Group members must learn to trust you by the quality of your contributions to the discus-sion. Some people may not have an interest in your product or service for months, but if you persistently and patiently stay involved, they'll remember you.

8

Bulletin Boards

Bulletin board systems are miniature versions of commercial online services. Although the rise of the Web has driven most successful BBS operators into becoming ISPs for their local communities, BBSs are still a good place to focus on specific groups of people who might be receptive to your message. Rather than catering to hundreds of thousands of subscribers with information and services designed to suit the largest online audience, each BBS serves a smaller slice of cyberspace. BBSs serve individual cities like Houston, subject areas like real estate or fishing, or other specific communities such as programmers who use Microsoft languages. BBSs tend to have loyal and active groups of subscribers, so your marketing efforts on them have a good chance of falling on receptive ears.

The trick to BBS marketing is finding one or two boards whose subscribers will be keenly interested in what your business offers. There are more than 20,000 BBSs in the United States alone, so you'll have to do some hunting, but you're sure to find a board whose topic fits your marketing purposes like a glove. There are hundreds of different BBS topics, including computer games, Christianity, vacations, politics, home brewing, shortwave radio, reptiles, software development, health, real estate, self-employment, and law enforcement.

When you find one or more boards that match your target market, you can use many of the same guerrilla marketing techniques covered in Chapters 4–7. Most BBSs have e-mail systems, file libraries, and chat systems. Many host one or more forums, and some have conferences and classified ad sections as well.

In this chapter, we'll see which BBS features can support your marketing campaign, how to find a BBS that matches your target audience, how to start your own BBS if you don't find the right one, and how to promote your company's identity and generate sales through the bulletin board of your choice.

MARKETING OPPORTUNITIES ON A BBS

A BBS is like a commercial online service, only smaller. Like an online service, subscribers dial a phone number to reach the BBS and then use the resources available on the BBS to communicate with each other, play games, read news, download information, shop, or access the Internet. Some BBSs are free, but most charge a subscription fee between $25 and $150 a year.

The main differences between a BBS and a commercial online service are size, features, and access.

- A BBS typically has only a few thousand subscribers.
- A BBS often has a text-based interface rather than the graphical ones used by most commercial services.
- A BBS has fewer features than an online service.
- A BBS usually has one local phone number or 800 number you use to access it instead of hundreds of local numbers across the country.

But from a marketing standpoint, you use the same features to pursue your marketing goals on a BBS as you do on an online service. Let's see how these work on a bulletin board.

E-mail. Nearly every BBS has electronic mail that allows members to communicate with one another. Many BBSs these days also have mail *gateways* to the Net, so you can exchange mail with other netizens from your BBS. You normally have to be a registered member or a paid subscriber to a BBS to have a mail account on it.

Forums. Most BBSs have one or more forums. These work like the forums on online services, although the interface probably won't be quite as classy. On the other hand, people who join a forum on a subject-specific BBS will be much more likely to stick to the discussion topic.

Chat rooms and conferences. Chat rooms are online social gatherings that don't stay on a particular topic, so they're not a promising avenue for marketing. However, conferences on topic-specific BBSs are a great place to build an online presence.

File libraries. File libraries are the most popular feature on a BBS. Libraries on topic-specific BBSs are a good place to post useful articles or information that enhance your reputation.

Classified ads. Boards that host classified ads have the advantage of letting you zero in on a particular geographic area or letting you sell highly specific items to a target audience. You can market diving equipment on a divers' BBS. If you live in Los Angeles, you can offer your job skills on a Los Angeles employment board.

HOW TO FIND THE RIGHT BBS

You could spend hundreds of hours and hundreds of dollars dialing all over the country and poking into BBS systems at random before you found even one that met your marketing needs. But time is more valuable than money to a guerrilla, so here are some shortcuts.

Magazine references

First, get a copy of *Boardwatch* magazine. *Boardwatch* is the leading monthly report on the BBS industry. Edited for people in the BBS business, it covers news about BBS technology and general developments in other online communications markets such as the Web and commercial online services. *(See Appendix for contact information.)*

Every month *Boardwatch* lists a couple of hundred BBSs with the name, phone number, and a brief description of each. You can go through the list each month, weed out the BBSs that don't meet your needs, and find others worth checking out. Along with the list, there are individual ads for BBSs throughout each issue, especially in the classified ad section at the back. Each ad offers a more complete description of a BBS, such as the specific features it offers, the number of dial-up connections it has, and what its subscription rate is, if any.

By browsing through just one issue of *Boardwatch*, you should find one or two BBSs that can deliver the subscriber base you're seeking. And if you like what you see in one issue, following the magazine for a few months will produce even more results.

Boardwatch also runs a list of list keepers — BBSs that maintain lists of other BBSs. Each BBS list keeper focuses on a particular selection of BBSs, so you can obtain lists of BBSs that focus on specific topics or geographical areas. For example, several BBS list keepers maintain lists of BBSs that relate to issues regarding the handicapped. Another keeps a list of BBSs related to firearms. Some lists are geographic, such as a list of BBSs in the 713 area code. By dialing up the right BBS list keeper, you just might find a dozen or more BBSs that are right up your marketing alley.

Aside from *Boardwatch*, you'll find ads for and some news about

BBSs in other magazines that cover the online world, such as *Internet World* and *NetGuide*.

Newsgroups about BBSs

There are also a couple of dozen newsgroups devoted to BBS news. You'll find them in the alt.bbs hierarchy in your list of newsgroups. Try alt.bbs.lists for referrals to hundreds of different boards.

If you're using a Web browser like Netscape Navigator to look at the BBS newsgroups, you'll find that many of them can be accessed directly via the Web. Inside a newsgroup message announcing a particular BBS, you'll find a Web link to the BBS, and you can click it to display the BBS in your Web browser.

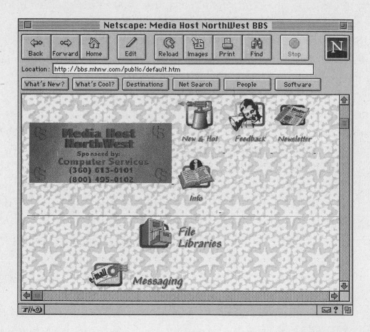

This board is a collection of programs and utilities for PCs. This is the Web version, but you can download graphical access software and dial into it directly as well. Most of the successful BBSs now offer access via the Web.

Online services

All the major online services carry at least some references to BBSs. If you're an America Online subscriber, for example, the BBS Corner offers a list of BBSs. You can view the list by geographic region or by subject, and you can search for BBSs by name. Other services such as CompuServe and Prodigy have similar information.

EVALUATING A BBS

Once you've put together a list of potential BBS targets, it's time to go online and start exploring. You may find more BBSs that match your marketing target than you can keep up with, so you'll want to zero in on the cream of the crop.

Every time you dial up a BBS, you're asked to log on, just as you would on an online service. Every BBS allows you to log on as a visitor or guest, although you probably won't have access to all of its features unless you actually become a member or subscriber.

If the BBS has a subscription fee, you'll usually be allowed to register anonymously as a guest to check out all the features it offers. If the BBS doesn't have a subscription fee, you'll probably be asked to register by entering your name, address, and phone number in order to see and use all of its features. In either case, you should be able to move far enough into any BBS to evaluate it without having to commit any money to a subscription. When evaluating a BBS's marketing potential, there are several aspects to consider.

Access

Some BBSs have more than one hundred dial-in lines to give lots of callers access at the same time; others have two or three lines and end up producing a lot of busy signals. If you have trouble connecting with the BBS, other people will probably have trouble too. Look for another board that is easier to connect with.

Most BBSs have local calling numbers, which probably means subscribers will either be local or they won't spend a lot of time in any one calling session. The largest boards offer 800-number access for a flat hourly fee of about $12, or they offer connections through public data networks like SprintNet, which have local dialing numbers in every major city. If several boards have roughly equivalent features and content, choose the one that's easier and cheaper to dial, because it will attract more subscribers.

Finally, find out if the board places a limit on the amount of time a caller can be connected. Many boards manage call-in traffic by limiting each caller to a certain number of minutes per call or to a certain number of minutes per day. Make sure these restrictions aren't unreasonable: a one-hour limit is reasonable, but a fifteen-minute limit probably isn't.

Features

Check out the BBS's main menu to see what kinds of services it offers. Here's an example.

```
THIS IS THE N.A.C.D. MEMBER'S AREA

Access to this area is limited to Members ONLY.
----------------------------------
<G>oodbye, <T>ime, <-> Top Menu, <B>ack to Previous Menu




<D>ive Site Reports ... Water Conditions, etc.
<F>orum ... Member's Open Message Area
<E>quipment Forum ... Equipment Ideas, Defect reports, etc.
<L>ibrary ... Assorted Text Files, Articles, etc.
<M>ail ... Electronic Mail to Other Users
<W>anted/For Sale ... Items for Sale or Wanted by Members
<C>ombined read ... Read all boards you have access to

Command:
```

This is a free BBS. In order to see this menu, all you have to do is register as a member by typing your name and address. Notice that this board (for the NACD, the National Association of Cave Divers) has a general forum, an equipment forum, a library, a mail function, and a classified ad area. This is a small BBS focused on a very specific subject, yet you can see it has several features we could use for marketing. You could join one or both of the forums, upload an article to the file library, or run a classified ad. On most BBSs, forums are moderated.

A BBS doesn't have to have dozens of features or forums in order to suit your marketing purposes. What it needs is a steady and active subscriber base that is interested in the same topic you are.

You can see the features here, but to really find out how active the board is, you have to explore beyond the main menu.

File libraries

File libraries are a major drawing card for any BBS, so have a look. Do the categories of files look useful? Are there lots of files? Let's look at the file library on the NACD BBS.

```
Listing of Library Files available on the NACD BBS.

When the prompt asks for your choice, please enter the number of the article.
If you choose to download these articles, an error correcting protocol (such as
ZModem) is highly recommended).

 1 - "The Physiologic Basis of Decompression" by Richard Vann, Ph.D.
     This is must reading for those interested in a greater under-
     standing of the physiology of DCS.

 2 - Australian InWater Recompression treatment for DCS.  This is
     a description of the Australian method of inwater recompression
     treatment of DCS, includes treatment tables.  This is included for
     your information only.  Neither the NACD or the SYSOP of this BBS
     recommend or advise the use of this information in the actual
     occurence of a diving accident.
```

This is a small library, with only seventeen files listed. All the files are articles about scuba diving. While the library is small, however, it's potentially very useful to a marketing guerrilla. If you were a travel agent specializing in scuba diving vacations, your article about cave diving in the Aegean Sea might interest subscribers and promote your services. Many boards have file libraries that contain software such as pictures or utility programs, but there's always at least one library category for articles like the ones in the preceding example.

Forums

Look at the board's forum or forums to see if the messages are serious or frivolous. On page 166 is a sample from the NACD BBS.

```
Section has 37 Msgs, #115 to 894
Starting number, <CR>=First:

Msg # From                 To                   Subject                  Board Name
----- ------------------   ------------------   ----------------------   ---------------
 115  ED SUAREZ            TO ALL TEKNA SCOO    SEA HORSE TECH SYSTE     EQUIPMENT FORUM
 237  RONNIE HALL          ALL                  CYKLON 5000 VS ODIN      EQUIPMENT FORUM
 289  R SECONN             ALL                  FARALLON SCOOTER         EQUIPMENT FORUM
 327  ED SUAREZ            TO ALL               PLUS RATINGS FOR STE     EQUIPMENT FORUM
 337  ED SUAREZ            ALL BEUCHAT ALADI    LOW BATTERY WARNING      EQUIPMENT FORUM
 349  ED SUAREZ            TO ALL BEUCHAT AL    MORE ALADIN DIAGNOST     EQUIPMENT FORUM
 397  ANDREW MESHEL        ED SUAREZ            PLUS RATINGS FOR STE     EQUIPMENT FORUM
 402  ED SUAREZ            ANDREW MESHEL        PLUS RATINGS FOR STE     EQUIPMENT FORUM
 418  GLENN KIMBLE         ALL                  DRYSUIT WANTED           EQUIPMENT FORUM
 558  RONNIE BELL          ALL                  WANTED  DRY SUIT IN      EQUIPMENT FORUM
 576  ED SUAREZ            ANDREW MENDELSSOH    USDIVERS M2 WARNING      EQUIPMENT FORUM
 583  ANTHONY MARTINEZ     ALL                  DIVE-RITE MODULAR VA     EQUIPMENT FORUM
 587  ANDREW MENDELSSOH    ED SUAREZ            USDIVERS M2 WARNING      EQUIPMENT FORUM
 588  ANDREW MENDELSSOH    ANTHONY MARTINEZ     DIVE-RITE MODULAR VA     EQUIPMENT FORUM
```

These messages look like elements of a serious discussion, although you can see that some classified ads have crept in, as in message number 558.

This particular BBS shows messages by number, rather than by date. There are thirty-seven messages in all, and half the ones on this first screen are from the same person. This isn't encouraging. It would be better if there were more messages with more authors.

Another way to judge a forum's activity is by the message dates. This forum doesn't list message dates — we have to open a few messages to see the posting dates inside them. Messages here are numbered in ascending order, so the one with the highest number at the bottom of the list will be the most recent. Forums can have dozens or hundreds of messages, but you can choose an option to display only those posted after a certain date or those above a certain number.

On most BBSs, including this example, the classified ad section is just another forum. The NACD's Wanted/For Sale forum looks just like the preceding example.

The Interface

No matter how intriguing a board's subject is, it won't get much action if the BBS software supporting it is difficult to use. The BBS program determines how a board looks and works, and there are more than three dozen commercially available bulletin board programs that BBS operators (or *sysops*) can use when they set up their systems. A few BBS operators write their own software, but as you explore the BBS world, you'll notice that many boards look and work the same because they're run on the same software.

Still, different BBS operators have different ideas about ease of use. The better BBSs have a Help option or a list of commands that's available everywhere, while other BBSs force you to do more guesswork.

If you're used to a nice graphical interface on a commercial online service or a graphical shell account from an ISP, you'll find lots of BBSs to be quite primitive in comparison. In many cases, though, you'll be able to download special software on your computer that gives you a graphical interface to the BBS, just as if you were using Prodigy or AOL.

Once you've explored a handful of boards, you'll have a general sense of how they work. If at this point you still find a board difficult to use, take your marketing attack elsewhere unless the board's topic and subscriber base is so perfect for your purposes that the hassle is worth the trouble.

Activity

Most BBSs have one or two thousand subscribers, but if those subscribers are active on the board and they're receptive to your marketing messages, they can do a lot for your bottom line. However, it's hard to tell just how many subscribers a board has or how active they are. Some ads you'll find in *Boardwatch* may claim a certain subscriber base for a BBS, but most of the time you'll have to do a little detective work to find out just how active a board is.

As you browse a BBS, check the dates of forum messages or the dates when files were uploaded. Look at the variety of names attached to forum messages or uploaded files, and see if there are lots of names that appear over and over. That's the measure of solid activity. A board could have 20,000 subscribers, but it won't do you much good if there are only 10 regulars.

MARKETING ON A BBS

The specific marketing techniques are determined by the BBS feature you're using at the time. The fundamental techniques have been covered elsewhere in this book. *(For advice about marketing with e-mail, see Chapter 4. For classified ad strategies, see Chapter 6. For information about marketing in forums, see Chapter 7.)*

In addition to this basic advice, here are a few BBS-specific pointers that will help your attack succeed.

Know the policies

Every BBS has policies regarding commercial messages and general behavior. In most cases, these policies are posted in an information file that is automatically displayed when you register, or that you can display from the board's main menu. Read these policies and follow them. The BBS may have a library where you can upload a file describing your business, for example, but you'll find that out a lot more quickly if you read it up front rather than having to stumble into the appropriate library to discover it.

The general information file will also tell you how to contact the board's administrator or sysop. Sysops are the kings of BBSs, and what they say goes. Sysops can help you make the most of the BBS, and they can cancel your account if you step out of line. If you're not sure about whether it's okay to do something, clear it with the sysop first.

Know the board

Even if you've reviewed the board's general rules of behavior, watch what others do on it before posting messages yourself. By reading other forum messages, ads, or library files, you'll quickly get a sense of how to go about promoting your business. Some boards prohibit commercial announcements completely, while others have a special forum or library for them. A board that frowns on blatant commercial announcements doesn't prohibit you from marketing, however. It just requires you to be more subtle about it. *(See Chapter 7.)*

Your marketing campaign should also take the board's capabilities into account. It won't do much good to promote your Net storefront in a BBS forum if the BBS doesn't provide access to the Net. Instead, you'll have to offer to provide a catalog or information about your services directly through the BBS mail system or one of its libraries.

Tread lightly

A BBS is like a small town. A bad reputation is much easier to get and much harder to get rid of than it is in the relative anonymity of a major online service's forum or a Net newsgroup. Because they have so much more traffic, an online service or newsgroup may have a fairly short memory: you might step over the line with a blatant ad one month and then have the luxury of dealing with a mostly new audience when you try a different approach the following month. But on a BBS, you're more likely to deal with the same group of people month after month. You should be much more careful not to offend anyone.

In the beginning of your campaign, focus on providing useful information by posting nonpromotional articles in the BBS libraries or answering questions in the forums. For example, you might post a forum message alerting other members that you've just uploaded a new article to one of the BBS libraries. In this case, you're just alerting people to some new information, which is a lot different than posting an ad for your business.

Make a commitment

One of the advantages of the smaller subscriber base on a BBS is that with some persistence and a spirit of helpfulness, you can become one of the board's leading lights. Even on an active board, a handful of subscribers usually stand out as key members, people to whom others on the board turn for answers and advice. By making regular visits to a BBS and always trying to post useful information, you can become a respected leader. And if people also know that you offer products or services that can help solve their problems, you'll probably gain lots of customers in the bargain.

SETTING UP YOUR OWN BBS

Marketing on someone else's BBS carries many of the same restrictions you face on an online service or on the Net because you have to conform to the customs and tastes of a user community that was there before you were. If you set up your own BBS, you're the ruler of your own online world. Naturally, you'll want to create a world that many others find attractive and interesting, but you'll have a lot more leeway in terms of promoting your products and services. You can post your company name right on the board's welcome screen, offer a catalog of your products in a library, and even schedule conferences with yourself as the speaker so that you can share your wisdom and build your reputation with others.

Company-sponsored BBSs are a successful part of many marketing campaigns. Computer hardware and software companies have used them for years as a way to communicate with their customers, offering price lists, product descriptions, and technical support. Now, consumer-oriented companies such as bookstores, office supply stores, newspapers, art galleries, and auto buying services are finding that having their own BBS is a good way to expand their market into cyberspace.

For example, Penny Wise Office Products in Edmonton, Maryland, hosts a BBS that callers reach through an 800 number. Once on the BBS, callers can browse its catalog of merchandise and place orders online. Penny Wise has been operating its BBS for six years now, and has many steady customers on it. Combined with the company's online storefronts on CompuServe, America Online, and GEnie, the BBS accounts for 20 percent of Penny Wise's multimillion-dollar annual sales volume.

Even if you don't market products directly, your company BBS can help enhance your reputation. The Raleigh, North Carolina, *News & Observer* newspaper operates a BBS called NandO.net. The BBS provides Internet access for the Raleigh community and also distributes the *News & Observer* electronically. NandO.net opened in February 1993 with five dial-in lines and now has more than a hundred lines due to its popularity. The board also features a children's educational area called Nando Land and offers online editions of books and articles in such categories as literature, American history, world history, and poetry.

NandO.net supports itself by charging subscribers $20 per month for full Internet access. But by offering lots of free information along with free subscriptions for kids and the handicapped community, the *News & Observer* also enhances its reputation as one of the community's good guys.

What you need to run a BBS

Running a BBS requires investments in hardware, software, and time. On the hardware and software side, you can get started for less than $2,000 with an inexpensive PC clone, a modem, an inexpensive BBS program, and a single phone line. As your BBS grows in popularity, you can add disk storage, more phone lines, faster modems, and a multiplexer that allows several callers to reach the BBS at once. To get an idea of how much it will cost and what it will require, pick up a book about starting and running a BBS. *(See Appendix.)*

On the time side, you have to plan time for designing the board as well as for running it. You'll need several weeks to figure out what you want to put on the board and how the information will be organized. You'll also have to gather the material you'll be offering. When the board is up and running, you'll need a sysop or administrator to take care

A BBS VERSUS A WEB SITE

Most successful BBSs today provide not only specialized content, but Internet access as well. Each month, *Boardwatch* magazine is a good place to start getting information if you're thinking about going into the ISP business.

But even if you don't want to go into the ISP business, your market location may make a BBS attractive for other reasons. If you operate a small business with a local market, setting up a PC with a couple of phone lines is a reasonable alternative to creating a Web storefront because you're only serving a local audience. Why put your storefront up in an international marketplace when you have no intention of serving anyone more than thirty miles away? With a local access phone number, you'll automatically screen out most of the callers outside your market area.

If you have a local-market business and you're not comfortable with the ins and outs of setting up a BBS, you can still set up a Web site. But in that case, try to locate it on a local ISP's server so that the people dialing into the ISP in your area will have greater exposure to your store.

of it. The sysop monitors the board's activity, takes care of any problems, answers subscriber questions, posts new information, and deletes old information when it's no longer useful. You can do all this yourself, or you can find a consultant to do it for you.

If you do it yourself, you'll find that the major BBS software companies usually offer lots of help. Each of them has its own BBS that stores answers to frequent questions, and you can e-mail the company's technical support staff for help in ironing out specific problems as they arise. If you'd rather hire a consultant, the best way to find one is through a referral. Find a BBS that you like and then contact the sysop or owner. Most successful BBS operators are happy to talk about their experience, and eventually you'll get a reference to a consultant who can help you. *Boardwatch* magazine features articles about the ins and outs of BBS management.

Three keys to BBS success

The three most important goals in choosing BBS hardware and software are accessibility, expandability, and ease of use.

Accessibility. Your board is useless if people can't connect with it. Make sure you offer easy telephone access with as many lines as necessary. If you're going for a national audience, get a connection to the

Internet. Going on the Net expands your promotional opportunities a hundredfold, and it increases your potential audience about a thousand-fold. Even if you're not on the Net, offer your paid subscribers an 800-number access option for a flat monthly fee. With a cheaper phone connection, people will feel freer to spend more time on your system.

Expandability. Many a BBS operator has suffered from success by choosing a system that became increasingly difficult to expand as membership grew. Some BBS packages place limits on the number of subscribers or the number of dial-in lines. Moving your BBS off one software package and onto another is a major undertaking that you should avoid if possible.

Usability. There are lots of BBSs to choose from, and no matter how unique the information yours offers, people won't call it regularly if it's disorganized and difficult to use. Give careful thought to the board's layout of features. All major features should be visible on the main menu, and callers should be able to navigate back to the main menu from within any feature with one or two steps at the most.

Some BBS programs give your board a graphical user interface with windows, menus, and icons, while others are text-only. If your BBS has a graphical interface, it will be more attractive to customers who are new in the BBS world, but you'll have to supply your callers with a special access program to run on their computers. A well-designed text BBS isn't as inviting, but it's what veteran BBS prowlers expect, and it's available to any caller. The choice depends on the audience you hope to attract.

What to put on your BBS

Your BBS should be an exciting and attractive place to visit. The specific contents will depend on the product or service you're selling, but the features you offer will affect the amount of effort required to maintain the board. Here are some considerations.

What's your marketing goal? Part of your decision about content will be influenced by the board's purpose. If you want to offer information as a way to enhance your reputation in general (like NandO.net), you'll focus on articles and other information files. On the other hand, if you plan to sell products (like Penny Wise), you'll put up a catalog and descriptions of the merchandise, along with some tips about how to use it.

LEVERAGE YOUR BBS WITH GATEWAYS

As we've implied earlier, setting up a BBS doesn't exclude you from marketing on the Net or even on online services. Commercial bulletin board software makers offer gateways that link your board to the World Wide Web and to other users of the Net via a program called *Telnet*. If you set up a storefront on a BBS, you can also make that storefront available to shoppers on the Net.

You can also leverage your BBS efforts on online services. Rather than physically renting storefront space on an online service, you can work with the service to build a gateway from the service to your BBS. Shoppers in the online service will still see your store listing or icon in the service's shopping area, but when they enter your store, they'll actually be taken through a gateway, over the Net, and into your BBS storefront.

What would your customers like? Rather than simply posting a catalog of your merchandise, try to post as much helpful information as you can. You can offer buying advice, care and maintenance tips, or pearls of wisdom gained through your years of experience in your field. One way to involve your customers from the beginning is to take a survey in your physical store or through your other customer contact channels and ask people what they'd like to see on a BBS. Offer them some choices, such as libraries of how-to articles, an online catalog, a user advice forum, and so on. If you involve customers in the board's creation, they'll want to check it out once it's up and running.

What's your audience? Your board's content will also be governed by the audience you're seeking. If you want to attract local subscribers, focus on localized information. For example, NandO.net carries lots of information about the state of North Carolina. If you're going for a national audience, you'll want to choose information that will be equally useful and interesting to anyone.

How will you keep callers interested? If you have the lowest prices on your merchandise and you offer speedy delivery, callers will keep coming back to your board. But you can boost caller volume by offering special promotions and collateral information. For example, Penny Wise Office Products features seasonal specials for items such as calendars in the fall, and it has offered lines of ergonomic computer products along with advice for strain-free computer use.

Attracting callers to your BBS

Once you set up your BBS, promote it as widely as possible. Unlike with a storefront in an online mall, nobody will stumble across your BBS by accident: they have to know the number or Web address and have a desire to visit. Here are three ways to promote your BBS:

Advertise. Take out advertisements in appropriate print media. If you have a BBS that promotes your local store, run ads in the local newspaper or the regional computer newspaper. Run a classified ad in *Boardwatch*, *Online Access*, or another Net-related magazine. If you have a physical store, put up a sign inviting people to try your BBS. You might even set up a computer in the store that's directly connected to the BBS and invite customers to check it out. If you publish a mail-order catalog, be sure to feature the BBS option prominently, and consider offering a discount for online orders.

Seek print publicity. Send a press announcement about your board to *Boardwatch* and other magazines that cover the online world. You may get a free mention in the magazine. *(See Chapter 16 for more information about publicity.)*

Once your board takes off, send out a press release that stresses your board's uniqueness and success. You might generate a full-blown article about it and gain thousands of dollars' worth of free publicity. *Boardwatch* does articles about individual BBSs. The featured boards are interesting to *Boardwatch* readers because of their contents, rapid growth, or use of BBS technology. Find an angle you can use to turn your BBS into a news story. If yours is the first local BBS or the first one set up by a local business (and it could well be), this will make interesting news for the local newspaper. A press release about your BBS will probably result in an interview and an article.

Seek online publicity. If your board can be reached via the Net or the Web, promote it through mailing lists and newsgroups. A newsgroup called alt.bbs.internet carries messages announcing new bulletin boards, and there are also Web sites devoted to lists of BBSs.

SIX STRATEGIES FOR BBS MARKETING

As you begin exploring marketing opportunities on BBSs, you'll quickly find yourself knee-deep in details like phone numbers and menu choices. To help you focus on the ultimate goal, remember these key guerrilla strategies.

1. Find the right BBS.   If you're marketing on existing BBSs, search diligently for the one whose topic most closely matches your business and expertise, and choose only the best of those you find. Don't participate in more boards than you can handle: it's better to be a key member of one board than to be a marginal player on six of them.

2. Learn the culture.   Monitor all the features of a board for a week or so before you start posting things so that you're sure you understand the best way to get your points across. Read the board's information file or send a message to the sysop if you have questions about appropriate behavior.

3. Proceed with caution.   If you're going to err, err on the conservative side when posting marketing messages. A BBS is like a small town with a long memory, and it's easy to tarnish your reputation. Protect your reputation as a member of the community.

4. Decide what your board should accomplish.   If you're setting up a BBS of your own, decide what goals you want it to achieve and whether you want to attract a local, regional, or national caller base. The board's capacity and content will depend on your marketing strategy.

5. Maximize access to your BBS.   Your audience expands geometrically if you provide an Internet gateway into your BBS, and the cost of doing this is minimal compared with the audience you'll gain. Even if you're not on the Net, offer a flat-rate 800-number connection to put distant callers at ease about the time they spend on your board.

6. Promote your BBS wherever and whenever possible.   If your BBS offers information, then promoting it is no sin. Promote your BBS on relevant newsgroups and mailing lists, through advertising, and through the methods covered in Chapter 16.

Boosting Your
Online Reputation

E-mail, storefronts, online advertising, newsgroups, and forums are the most common ways to promote your business and build an online presence, but they're not the only ones. There are other important strategies for boosting your online reputation by becoming a respected source of information.

For most netizens, cyberspace is like a huge combined encyclopedia and conference center where the collections of articles and topics of discussion change constantly. Anyone on the Net, in an online service, or on a BBS can contribute an article or add to a discussion, but even the cleverest contributors are soon forgotten unless they contribute regularly and in the most visible areas of the online marketplace.

It's a lot like gaining fame on TV. If you appear on a nationally syndicated television show, you're introduced to millions of viewers across the country. The next day somebody else is on the show and your fifteen minutes of fame is up. Fame is being noticed; enduring fame is being noticed over and over again. That's why national media superstars have promoters who work nonstop to make sure their names aren't forgotten. Whether you gain fame on TV or in cyberspace, your moment in the sun is soon forgotten unless you follow it up with a continuous stream of appearances and noteworthy deeds.

To build an online reputation and maintain it, you have to draw people's attention by providing useful information and then continue to hold their attention by spreading news about that information and providing more new information. You can do this in forums and newsgroups by becoming a regular participant in the discussion, but your comments are temporary and you have to keep making new ones to stay in the spotlight. If you publish information, you create visibility that lasts for months or years.

In this chapter, you'll see how to provide information through online conferences and online publications. Becoming a source of online information increases your credibility far more than an advertisement, and publishing new information regularly helps maintain your good reputation indefinitely.

CONFERENCES

An online conference is the electronic equivalent of a public seminar or speech. An audience gathers to learn from a speaker about a particular topic. By becoming the speaker in an online conference, you get a chance both to show people what you know and how it can help them and to promote your business in the bargain.

The conference takes place in the main conference room of an online service or in a smaller conferencing area in a particular forum or BBS. A main conference room has space for an audience of a thousand or more, while a forum conference might host a few dozen members.

The conference format is questions and answers. A moderator introduces the conference speaker and asks a few general questions to get things rolling, and then members of the audience ask questions of their own. On the computer screen the whole thing looks like a film script, with the names of individuals followed by their comments. *(For an example, see p. 51.)*

Conferences are arranged by the administrators of an online service or of a particular forum. A conference typically lasts an hour. Each of the major online services holds several main conferences every week. Forums and BBSs may host conferences once every week or two, or they may have a regular schedule of chat sessions moderated by specific experts. There are lots of conferences going on all the time, which means lots of opportunities to put yourself in the spotlight.

Once you schedule a conference, the online service, forum, or BBS administrator promotes it. A few days before the conference, the administrator puts up a notice announcing it on the area's welcome or sign-off screen or on the forum or BBS menu.

As you might expect, it's much more difficult to line up a spot as a general speaker on an online service than it is to speak in a forum or BBS conference, but both types of conferences are well worth arranging. In either case, an hour's work will get you the kind of visibility and credibility that would take weeks to get through participation in a newsgroup, forum, or mailing list.

To arrange a spot in a conference and successfully conduct one, you need the following:

- the confidence that you will make a compelling online speaker
- a conference topic that appeals to a large portion of the online audience
- a description of you, your business, your accomplishments, and your expertise that will convince the administrator that you can provide lots of information in a useful way
- a pitch that targets the right conference slot at the right time
- a plan for conducting the conference that will give the greatest boost to your business

Gaining self-confidence

You won't go far in promoting yourself as an online speaker unless you believe you have what it takes to do it. Most people break out in a sweat at the idea of speaking in public, either because they don't feel they know enough about a particular topic or because they can't bear the idea of getting up in front of a group. Your campaign to put on a successful online conference must start with the firm belief that you're up to the job. Let's explode a few myths that might be keeping you from believing you'll make a great online speaker.

You're no expert. Sure you are. If you're at all successful in business, you know more about succeeding in business than most people. And the chances are that your specific business has required you to develop expertise that will be interesting and useful to others. Whether you sell flowers or music recordings or you're a highly paid financial consultant, you know more about that subject than almost anyone else. That makes you an expert. If you're planning to break into online conferencing, it's no time for false modesty.

What you know isn't interesting to others. Each of us has special knowledge, but most of us don't think anybody else is interested in it. But it isn't usually the subject that turns people off, it's the packaging. You may think nobody is interested in learning what you know about turquoise jewelry or leatherwork, but it's really a matter of presenting those subjects in the right light. After all, if Stephen Hawking can turn his knowledge of astrophysics into a best-seller called A Brief History of Time, you can find a way to make what you know interesting to lots of people. *(For ideas about turning your experience into a likely conference topic, see "Choosing a conference topic" below.)*

You can't speak in front of a crowd. Fear of speaking in public has a lot to do with physically standing before an audience and wondering if you'll freeze up, if your hair is out of place, or if your fly is open. In the online world, you don't have to worry about things like this because your presence is just a string of letters across a computer screen. This relative anonymity puts everyone at ease; it's the reason online chat sessions are so popular. People don't actually have to look at each other when they bare their souls or make indecent proposals. And if you're worried about your typing speed or accuracy and how that will reflect on your electronic persona, relax: most participants in online conferences and chat sessions make typos as a matter of course.

You're not clever enough. You don't have to bombard the audience with pearls of wisdom every second. A lot of online conferencing is just like having a conversation. The conference format helps you with this. At the beginning of the session, the moderator introduces you and asks you a few general questions to get the discussion moving. Naturally, you will have supplied the list of questions, so you'll already know the answers. Once you're through the opening, you move into a question/answer session with the audience. If you've chosen the right conference topic, this should be no different than answering questions for customers in your store or on the phone.

Choosing a conference topic

Once you're convinced you can do a conference, the key to making it happen is selling a topic. You have to find a topic that the forum, BBS, or online service administrators are convinced will be interesting to their members. To do this, approach the problem from two directions: what you know and what topics are likely to sell.

First, start noticing the topics of conferences that are already set up. Check out some of the conferences themselves to see how closely the actual discussion matches the topic, how the conference leader handles things, and what sorts of questions and answers are offered. In the process, you'll get ideas about what makes a good conference topic along with a general sense of how conferences proceed.

After you've done some basic conference reconnaissance, think about your business, the expertise you offer your customers, and how

you can package that expertise as a conference topic. A good topic
should be:

- broad enough to attract the widest possible audience
- specific enough so that people get some useful insights
- close enough to your business so that conference attendees are motivated to follow up with you later

One good source of topics is major news or achievements. For example, if you're the author of a successful book or the head of a company
that has been prominent in the news, you may be able to do a conference about it. Online services feature authors, entertainers, and business leaders all the time. Even if you're not in the media spotlight, you
may have a new product or service that's interesting to a group. If your
company makes a unique instrument for airplanes, you should be able
to interest the members of an aviation forum.

If your products or achievements aren't newsworthy in themselves,
turn your expertise into a conference topic. Think about what you know
and how you can present it in terms of solving a problem or answering a
widely discussed question. If you're in a consumer services business like
accounting, insurance, or investment counseling, it should be easy to
come up with a conference topic that has broad appeal and yet allows
for specific insights. For example, *Planning for Your Retirement* would
interest lots of people, and you could structure the conference so that
you offer a handful of useful tips before opening up the discussion for
questions.

If your business is consumer merchandise such as toys or hardware,
choose a subject area for its interest level. For example, you probably
could talk about different types of screws and bolts if you're in the
hardware business, but you'll be much more likely to interest people
with a conference on deck building, house painting, or flooring.

The conference audience and location will also help you focus your
topic. If your conference is in a topic-specific forum, you should assume
more knowledge in the audience. For example, if you're an investment
counselor speaking to an investors' forum, you might choose a topic like
Investing in Derivatives. But if you're speaking in a main conference on
an online service, you should choose a broader topic like *Investment
Profits Without Risk*.

When evaluating any prospective topic, put yourself in the audience's shoes. Think about the members of the forum, BBS, or online

service, and consider some topics you might want to learn about if you were they. Ask yourself whether you would attend a conference on the topic you're considering. If the answer is no or even maybe, move on to a topic that's more compelling.

Once you've come up with a topic, give it a catchy title. The title of your conference is like the cover of a book or magazine. Nobody will get past it if it doesn't arouse their interest. Some good conference titles raise questions or answer them. If you know everything about diesel mechanics, your audience in an automotive forum will be more interested in a topic like *Why Diesels Won't Die* than in a topic like *Diesel vs. Gasoline Technology*. Other titles promise to solve a problem, like *Writing Successful Advertisements*.

Finally, your topic should have some connection with your business. You may know a lot about fly-fishing, for example, but doing a conference on the topic probably won't do much for your auto-leasing business.

Describing your qualifications

With a topic in mind, your next challenge is to convince the forum or online service administrators that you are the perfect person to present it. After all, it won't do your cause much good if you propose a great topic like *High-Power Investing* and the powers that be then decide to approach someone else about doing the conference.

When you propose a topic, the information you provide about yourself, your business, and your expertise should convey the sense that you and your subject were made for one another. One or two paragraphs of text ought to do it. Be sure to explain your experience and qualifications, including any key achievements that prove you know the subject.

Let's suppose your conference topic is *Bargain Vacations*. Your qualifications might read:

> *For the past fifteen years, Jane Waggener has designed exciting low-cost vacations for hundreds of customers across the United States, making it possible for her clients to visit exotic locales like Latin America, Micronesia, India, Greece, Egypt, Japan, Scandinavia, and the Balkans for as little as $500 per person per week, including airfare.*
>
> *Jane has spoken about low-cost travel before a variety of community groups, and has contributed to such magazines as* Horizons

and Travel and Leisure. Her insights about saving on food, lodging, and tours can bring the world within reach for anyone.

The first paragraph offers specific details about Jane's years of experience, her client base, and the vacation destinations she knows about. The second paragraph gives more details about Jane's achievements and the specific areas where she can help people save money. The sketch ends with a little flourish that reinforces the conference topic, along with the idea that anyone can benefit from Jane's expertise.

Keep your qualification sketch down to a couple of paragraphs, but provide as much specific evidence as possible of your experience, its usefulness, and proof that you can share it with others. By itself, having worked in a business for a certain number of years doesn't prove anything: the proof is in the specific achievements and details you provide.

Pitching your conference idea

The final step in arranging a conference is the pitch itself. If you've developed a likely topic and a good information blurb on yourself, the only remaining hurdle between you and success is timing the pitch.

Online conferences are scheduled weeks or months in advance, depending on their size and importance. If you want to be the featured speaker one night on America Online or Prodigy, you'll have to arrange the engagement two or three months in advance, but you can probably set up engagements for smaller conferences a month in advance. The forum or conference administrator can give you information about the amount of lead time for proposing a conference and which specific information is required for the pitch.

The people who schedule conferences are always looking for topics that will generate the most interest from their subscribers or members. To have the best chance of success, your topic should be fresh and timely. Study your online target carefully for several weeks and make notes about the conference topics presented. Don't pitch a topic that's close to one that has just been featured. If the investment forum just had its weekly conference about bonds, wait for a couple of months before pitching your conference about tax-free investing.

You can also increase your chances of success by linking your conference topic with a particular time of year when people will be more interested. If you're in the gardening business, you could propose a conference on spring planting for March. If you're an accountant, you could propose a conference on year-end tax planning for November or early December.

Handling the conference

When it comes time to conduct the conference, make a plan about what you hope to accomplish. List three or four key messages you want to get across in the talk, and then prepare questions for the moderator to ask you that will lead to answers containing those messages. The conference moderator probably won't be intimately familiar with your business or the topic and will appreciate having a starting point. And from your point of view, answering the questions will allow you to convey your key messages and to focus the audience on your topic. If you offer enough questions, the moderator may start the conference off with a couple and then save the others to jump-start the discussion if audience questions drop off later on.

The rest of the conference is easy. Just do your best to answer the questions as if you were talking in person to the individuals asking them. When you can't answer a question, don't try to bluff your way through it. Your audience will respect you a lot more if you admit you don't know an answer and offer to find out than if you try to fake it.

At the end of the conference, make sure the audience members know how to reach you for further information. Ask the moderator to wrap things up by announcing your e-mail address, phone or fax number, or postal address.

Post-conference promotion

Guerrillas save time and money by leveraging their work. When you've done the work to devise, pitch, and put on a conference, leverage it as much as possible. After the conference is over, the transcript (the text record of its proceedings) is usually stored somewhere in the forum, BBS, or online service archives. Find out from the conference moderator or forum administrator where the transcript is stored and then have a look at it. You may be able to use it in other ways. For example, if you offered some especially brilliant insights during your talk, you can direct other people to the transcript. This is the online equivalent of offering a tape recording of your last speech to customers interested in your views on a particular topic.

You can also reproduce parts of the conference as a separate docu-

ment. Read the conference transcript, select a few questions and answers, and then publish them as a Q&A document *(see p. 185)*.

PUBLISHING INFORMATION ONLINE

Information is the coin of the realm in cyberspace. A quick trip anywhere online will convince you that a lot of the scenery is information:
files, lists, databases, and news. Information is as varied as life itself and
as plentiful as the grains of sand on a beach, but everyone who goes
online is always looking for more of it.

In a conference you present information at a given time and place,
but by publishing electronic documents, you can provide information
to a much broader audience indefinitely. By becoming an information
publisher, you gain visibility as an author and respect as someone who
makes useful and lasting contributions to the collective knowledge of
the online world.

Through the information you provide, you give people a chance to
know you and to understand how your knowledge can help them. And
since you're the publisher of the information, you can include a promotional message in every document you produce. You can also store your
published information in your online storefront, giving customers another good reason to visit your little corner of the online marketplace.

The main goals in publishing information are to offer something
useful to your target audience and to promote your business identity in
the process. As long as you achieve these goals, the type of information
and the source of the information aren't important. You'll find that you
have a lot of options. You can:

- prepare original reports and articles on your field of expertise
- compile information from other sources into one handy location
- publish your own newsletter or electronic magazine

If you don't feel up to doing any of these, your company can sponsor
a newsletter, magazine, or directory provided by someone else and gain
respect for helping to support it. Here's how to become an information
provider in three simple steps:

1. Decide which information you want to present and how you want to
   present it.

2. Choose a distribution method and distribute it.
3. Let your target audience know it's there.

Sources of information

Most of us don't think of ourselves as publishers because our ideas about publishing are locked into a vision of paper and ink. But publishing is based on distributing information, and we do that every day as we answer customer questions, offer advice, and even when we display brochures or catalogs about the things we sell.

Another problem we run into when thinking about publishing is that it's a specialized skill reserved for media people. The beauty of computers and the online marketplace is that anyone can be a publisher. There are millions and millions of documents available on the Net, and most of them were put there by people who never published anything in a traditional newspaper or magazine.

All you really need to start your publishing empire are a few nuggets of truth and a place to put them. As long as the information is useful, your readers will thank you for it.

Often, thinking about a particular type of document can help you come up with ideas for information you can provide. Here are some types of documents that can get you started.

Q&A and tip sheets. Think about the advice you've given to customers over the years, and imagine how you could distill it into a short question/answer sheet or a list of tips. These documents are from one to

YOU DON'T HAVE TO BE A WRITER

The most common hurdle in publishing is writing ability. Most people don't see themselves as professional writers, and so they never attempt to write anything for others to read beyond a quick thank-you note now and then. However, anyone with average writing skills can get a few useful points across.

If you're concerned about your writing ability, try writing a short list of tips or a brief note of advice, and then ask a more qualified writer to edit it. Otherwise, you might want to dictate your ideas to someone in your company who can write. If all else fails, you can always hire a professional writer to turn your ideas into print. You might have to spend a few hundred dollars for an article, but you'll end up with a promotional tool you can use for months or years.

a few pages long and cover a particular subject related to your business. If your products or services are varied enough, you might build a whole library of Q&As or tips on different subjects.

If you can't come up with ideas on your own, pull some from a brochure or flier you've seen in the course of your business. If you're in the building supplies business and one of your distributors left you a particularly helpful brochure about choosing roofing materials, for example, you might turn it into an article or tip sheet. If you don't want to rewrite such a document substantially to avoid copyright problems, ask the original publisher for permission to reproduce it as is.

Articles. An article is a longer document that explains or discusses an issue in greater detail. You might start off with a Q&A or tip sheet and then expand one or more of the tips or answers into a full-blown article. A list of tips about choosing the right scuba gear might be expanded into short articles about choosing a wetsuit, choosing a regulator, and the outs and ins of choosing fins.

Again, if your own insights don't lend themselves to article-length documents, get permission to reprint or excerpt from articles you've read elsewhere. You may have access to a trade or industry publication whose articles could help your customers, and you'll win a lot of friends if you share those articles with them.

Newsletters and zines. If you're really ambitious, you can publish a regular newsletter or electronic magazine *(zine)*. These documents feature collections of articles, lists, or anything else you want to put in them. Newsletters are text-only documents focused on a particular topic and are often distributed via e-mail. For example, Guerrilla Marketing Online distributes the Weekly Guerrilla Update to some 10,000 subscribers.

Electronic magazines have more elaborate layouts that include graphics. You'll find lots of these on the Web. In fact, many traditional print publishers offer electronic versions of their magazines on the Web. But lots of publishers are doing magazines that appear only on the Web, like this one from Adobe Corporation:

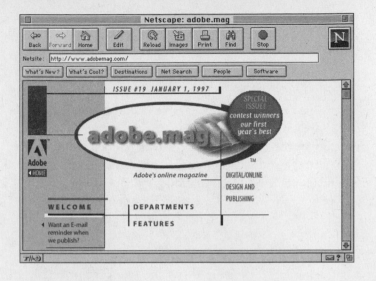

The information in a newsletter or magazine can be your original creation, or you can simply compile and edit information from various sources. For example, the Edupage newsletter is a summary of high-tech news compiled and distributed three times a week by Educom, a consortium of colleges and universities. Edupage's editors read a variety of newspapers and magazines and then write up one-paragraph summaries of technology stories. At the end of each summary, Edupage adds the publication, date, and page number of the original article for those who want to read more.

If you can't come up with information on your own, compile articles you've seen elsewhere (as long as you summarize them or get permission to reproduce them). You can even solicit contributions from other members of a forum or newsgroup that discusses the same topic.

There are hundreds of newsletters and magazines available on the Net, and you'll learn about them and see them in your travels. To see a collection of magazines, check the alt.zines newsgroup, or look in the Magazines category of the Yahoo online directory. Look at other electronic publications to get ideas about what yours might look like.

Lists and directories. Another type of document is a list or directory. Dozens of guerrillas on the Net have already compiled directories of resources available there. People appreciate the service because it can be so difficult to locate resources in the Net's vast reaches. If you're in the travel business, for example, you might prepare and maintain a directory of Internet locations that offer international weather reports. If you're in the auto parts business, you might offer a list of forums, newsgroups, and mailing lists related to automobiles. You could also offer a glossary of terms relating to your business.

The beautiful thing about a list or directory is that you don't have to be a writer to produce one. All you have to do is compile the information and revise it regularly to keep it up-to-date.

Don't forget the promo. Whatever type of document you publish, don't forget to include a short paragraph about your business. The whole point of offering the information is to increase your visibility, and that won't happen if you don't mention your company someplace. Just remember that the information, not your company plug, is what builds your reputation.

The promotional paragraph is like the "brought to you by" message at the beginning of a TV program or on the title page of an advertising supplement in a magazine. The paragraph should be in the document, but it shouldn't be so prominent that it overwhelms the document's information content. Most publishers run a simple notice at the beginning or end of the document, like this:

```
*****************************************************************
****************
Edupage, a summary of news items on information technology, is provided
three times each week as a service by Educom -- a consortium of leading
colleges and universities seeking to transform education through the use of
information technology.

*****************************************************************
****************
```

Distributing information

Once you've prepared information, you'll want to make it as easy as possible for the widest possible audience to get it. There are many ways to display and present information online.

E-mail. You can mention the document in newsgroups, forums, on mailing lists, or on your Web site and then suggest that people request it via e-mail. You then mail the document to them, or set up a mailbot to do it for you. This helps you build a list of interested prospects that you can use for other mailings in the future.

Newsgroups and forums. If you have short lists or articles no longer than a page, you can post them to relevant newsgroups, forums, and mailing lists. If the information piece is longer, upload it to the appropriate forum library.

Web sites and other storefronts. If you have an electronic storefront, the obvious place to store your documents is in your store. Then when you promote the information and tell people where to get it, you bring them into the store as well.

Mailing lists. If you produce a regular electronic newsletter or zine, distribute it to a mailing list of subscribers and place copies of it on your electronic storefront, if you have one. *(For information on finding subscribers, see "Promoting your information" on p. 190.)*

Sponsoring an information provider

There's no substitute for the credibility and visibility you get from producing and distributing your own information online. But if you really can't spare the time to become a publisher yourself, you can gain some visibility by sponsoring someone else. Just find a Web magazine or newsletter that covers a topic related to your business, and then ask the editor if you can sponsor it. Look for a document that's published on a regular schedule and that has a good following.

In the simplest terms, sponsorship amounts to paying for an advertising message, button, or banner at the top of the provider's publication. However, it may also mean giving the publication space on your electronic storefront, trading your products or services to the provider in exchange for the sponsorship space, or offering your products to the publication's subscribers at a discount.

If you don't find a publication related to your business, consider sponsoring the creation of one. Here are some possible scenarios.

- Come up with a great idea for a newsletter, find a writer to put it together, then distribute it through your online storefront or through e-mail.
- If you're an active participant in a newsgroup or forum related to your business, look for other knowledgeable and regular participants of the group and approach one of them about producing the publication with your sponsorship.
- Contact a writer for a magazine related to your business or the author of one or more online articles you read and liked, and approach him or her about doing a newsletter on a related subject area.

Promoting your information

Once you create or sponsor information, you'll want to let others know how and where to get it. You promote your information through the same online methods you use to promote your business. In some cases, you'll want to send a copy of the publication or document or post it on your storefront or on a forum or newsgroup. At other times, it will be better to tell people where to get a copy. Here are some specific strategies.

E-mail. Send a copy of your Q&A, tip sheet, or brief article via e-mail to your previous customers with a note saying you thought they'd be interested. If you have a broader e-mailing list of prospects, send them an announcement saying the publication is now available and what it offers, and then tell them how to get a copy.

Newsgroups and forums. Post the document itself only if it's highly relevant to the discussion. If you've placed a copy of the document in a forum library, it's acceptable to put a notice about your having done that in the forum itself. Otherwise, find a way to mention your document and its location in the course of the discussion. If you've just completed an article about the care and feeding of gecko lizards, for example, watch for questions about this topic on reptile-related newsgroups or forums. Respond to the questions when they appear, and mention your article and how to get it as part of your reply.

Signatures. If you're publishing a newsletter or magazine, add the publication name and its subscription information to your e-mail signature.

Storefronts. If you have an online storefront, set up a library for all the issues of your publication, and promote it as one of your store's departments.

Conferences. Ask the moderator to include information about your online publications and how to get them when he or she introduces you. Also, find a way to work your publication's name into the conference. You might suggest that someone read your publication for more detailed information when you answer a question from the audience.

FIVE STRATEGIES FOR MARKETING WITH INFORMATION

To sum things up for this chapter, here are five key guerrilla strategies for promoting your business with online information:

1. Choose an audience and serve it.   The magazine graveyard is filled with publications that either aimed at an audience that wasn't there, offered perfectly good information to the wrong audience, or offered bad information to the right one. Don't make the same mistakes. Your business has customers and prospects, and they're your target audience. Whenever you propose a conference topic or produce an online publication or document, make sure the information is aimed squarely at the needs of your audience.

2. Tell the truth and don't steal.   People get a good feeling about you when you offer them good information. Satisfied readers frequently spread the word or even forward your publication to others. Unfortunately, netizens will seize on your mistakes like hungry barracuda and tell all their friends about them as well. In fact, they may even parody your publication and post the parody in more places than the original! Make sure any information you publish is accurate and that you have the right to publish it. If you're caught in a lie, an error, or a violation of someone's copyright, your mistake may well shine brighter and live longer than any good you've done.

3. Recycle information.   One of the most wonderful things about computers is the ease with which you can edit and recycle things you've written in the past. Create an article or Q&A document from the transcript of your last conference. Turn your Q&A document or tip sheet into a series of articles. Summarize insights from your favorite newsgroup or forum. Without the right packaging, information is no more than a jumble of words. With the right packaging, you can present the same information in many different ways to serve many different purposes.

4. Keep the presses rolling.   One good document deserves another; one good conference should lead to the next. If you've started to build your reputation as an information source, the only way to maintain it is to keep producing. Citizens of the online marketplace have an insatiable appetite for information, so you can be sure of a ready audience for your next talk or document. The frequency of your publications depends on the type of documents you produce, your distribution method, and your ability to produce them, of course, but you should plan from the beginning to produce a collection of documents. Think in terms of a monthly, bimonthly, or quarterly tip sheet or newsletter, or an ongoing series of articles.

5. Tell the world.   Nobody will know what you've done unless you tell them. Use your forum and newsgroup contacts, e-mail address lists, storefront, conferences, and any other means you can think of to promote and distribute your online documents.

10
One Hundred Online
Guerrilla Marketing Weapons

The online marketplace has vast possibilities for the dedicated guerrilla, but it's a jungle out there. Every week, there are thousands of new people joining the fray, and hundreds of new online marketers will increase the ranks of your competition.

You now know the geography and strategies for your attack. In this chapter, we'll look at 100 specific marketing weapons you can and should use. Your competitors don't even know about most of these, and those that do aren't using very many of them, or aren't using them to their best advantage. Your mission is to understand and use as many of the following 100 weapons as effectively as possible.

1. Name In cyberspace, most customers will first hear about your business by its name. Choose a name that both explains what your business is and sets your business apart from others. You can't rely on your personality or your storefront location to distinguish you from the crowd, so your name should help do it. Vague, generic, or ambiguous names can cost you time and money. One Internet consultant spent a lot of time trying to defend his right to the name *Internet Presence, Inc.* This name didn't suit his business purpose any better than a lot of other names, and it was very much like other names out there. It did nothing to distinguish this business from some others. And while the consultant spent a lot of time arguing over whether he had a trademark on this name, his competitors were busy making money.

2. Product/service niche A unique niche or position for your business is crucial online. You might be able to distinguish your business by its physical appearance or location offline, but these assets disappear in cyberspace. Your unique position in the market is the best way to distinguish yourself from a horde of competitors. This position can be built from the quality of your service, your expertise, your selection, your price, or lots of other possible advantages, but you must have at least one. Find a new niche and fill it, or fill a successful niche better than anyone else. For example, there are lots of online bookstores that offer millions of different titles, but a store called anybook.com now offers to locate old, out-of-print titles as well as current books.

3. Online business plan   Your online efforts should be guided by a business plan that projects your expenses, effort, and earnings at least a year in advance. The business plan also includes your online marketing plan. *(See Chapter 12.)* You can't chart your progress if you don't have a plan. Your projections should be based on diligent research and a realistic understanding of how the online market works for businesses like yours.

4. Mission statement   If you don't know what your mission is, you'll have trouble trying to accomplish it. Come up with one or two sentences that describe your business precisely in terms of your basic business proposition, your customers, and which advantages you'll use to succeed. Make sure all of your employees know your company mission and are striving to execute it. *(See Chapter 12 for more information.)*

5. Identity   Decide exactly what sort of identity you want your business to have, and then make sure everything you do online promotes it. Your identity is reflected in the style of your announcements, the design of your electronic storefront, your participation in discussion groups, your e-mail signature, your attitude about service, and in countless other ways. Your business identity transcends any particular advertisement, storefront, or other online effort you make. It should distinguish you among your competition. Everything you do online contributes to your identity.

6. Theme   A theme is a sentence or phrase that defines your business. Avis Rent A Car uses *We Try Harder.* Kentucky Fried Chicken uses *Finger Lickin' Good.* Pick a theme that crystallizes your main business advantage. Display your theme on your Web site, and if it's short enough, make it part of your e-mail and discussion group signatures.

7. Domain name   If you're operating a storefront on the Web, get your own domain name. Most ISPs will help you register your domain name with the Internet Information Center (InterNIC) for about $100. Having your own domain name shortens your Web address (you can have *www.ourcompany.com* instead of *www.theircompany.com/ourcompany*), and it makes your company appear larger and more substantial in cyberspace.

8. Marching orders list   One of the most difficult problems in daily Internet marketing is staying focused. It's incredibly easy to start out doing one task and then get sidetracked until you forgot why you went online in the first place. But by listing the specific tasks you need to do each day (checking e-mail, checking one or more discussion groups, and so on) and then following the list, you'll be able to get your online marketing job done quickly and completely. *(See Chapter 12.)*

9. Activity log   It's very easy to post things in cyberspace and then forget them. But eventually, some of your postings grow outdated, and when they do, they become negative advertisements for your business. Keep a record that shows the date, purpose, and location of all your online activities, including when you posted messages to discussion groups, when you published electronic publications, when you e-mailed a list of prospects, and when you last changed your online storefront. Check your activity log once a month and remove or update information that's growing inaccurate. *(See Chapter 13.)*

10. Canned messages   Don't wait until the heat of battle is on to compose effective messages about your business. If you anticipate general inquiries about your business via e-mail, spend some time in advance to create a series of generic messages about yourself, your company, and various services or products that you can quickly personalize and send out in response. You may only have one chance to begin a customer relationship, so don't blow it. Take the time to prepare basic replies and marketing messages in advance, and you'll be able to quickly send effective, well-thought-out responses when they're needed.

11. Mail groups or aliases   The more specifically you address your customers' needs, the better. Organize your e-mail contact lists into groups related to different aspects of your business. For example, if you have a group of customers who have asked about your design services rather than your furniture prices, create a special Design group and then create focused e-mail promotions for just that group. By sorting incoming e-mail inquiries into topic-specific groups as you receive them, you'll be much better prepared to create tailored marketing messages for each group.

12. Hot lists   As you surf the Web or an online service and come across useful forums or information resources, add those locations to your Internet browser's hot list or bookmark menu so that you'll be able to return to them easily later. There are far too many locations online to expect yourself to remember where they are, so let your Web browser or online access software help you remember.

13. Writing ability   Graphics are great, but the written word will always be your primary mode of communication online. Effective writing skills are your most important online communication tool. If you can't write well, get a book about business writing and brush up your skills. Poor writing is unprofessional — it erodes your online reputation, muddies your marketing messages, and diminishes your chances of success.

14. Reliability   If you want customers to trust their business to you, be totally reliable in all your dealings with them. Don't promise things you can't deliver, and respect any deadlines you have set.

15. Credibility   When people believe what you say, they trust you and buy from you. You earn credibility through service, honesty, promptness, and sincere efforts to be helpful. You also earn it through consistency, so don't change your marketing plan in midstream.

16. Reputation   Your reputation is the market's awareness of your business identity. Do all you can to promote and protect it in everything you do, from your store's decor to the clarity of your advertisements and discussion group postings. A bad reputation spreads quickly online and is incredibly hard to repair. A good reputation inspires confidence and makes it easier to win business.

17. Signatures   Develop informative signatures and use them to sign all your e-mail messages and discussion group postings. If you're involved in several discussion groups, create a different signature for maximum impact on each group. Create different signatures to promote different aspects of your business or to plug special events or promotions you have under way. Signatures are the business cards you leave wherever you go in cyberspace. Every guerrilla should always use them.

18. Logo   A well-designed, evocative logo can help distinguish your business from others on a Web page. Your logo should convey your business identity through color, design, and its location on the page. A good online logo is small enough that it can be displayed quickly when customers download it.

19. Package   The way you package your online presence says a lot about you. Whether you're posting an article or a forum message or designing a storefront, make sure your packaging is attractive, clear, and well organized. Choose a storefront design that works equally well on any type of computer, and format your articles, newsletters, and e-mail messages so that they look good on any screen. Proofread everything before you put it online.

20. Pricing   Choose prices for your products or services that match your business identity. If part of your identity is your expertise, quality, or superior service, charging a little extra for it shows that you think the advantage is worth it. Tiffany's isn't known for its bargain prices. If your store offers the same products and service as others, then selling at a lower price will give people a reason to buy from you.

21. Decor   In an online storefront, the decor is everything from the name you choose to the presentation and organization of your catalog, price list, order form, and other information. It includes the colors and graphics on your Web site, the number of pages in your store, and the names you give various options. The decor should complement your business identity, but it has to do so within the limitations of cyberspace. Choose a storefront designer who has experience in graphic design and in computer interfaces to create the best decor for your chosen battle-ground.

22. Hours and days of operation   The online market operates twenty-four hours a day, seven days a week, all over the world. So should your business. Cybernauts expect quick responses to their queries and orders, so make sure you oblige them. Check for incoming orders or questions several times a day, and at least once a day on weekends and holidays. (They don't celebrate Presidents' Day in Australia.) Your ability to respond more quickly than your competitors will give people a reason to trust you and will lead to more business in the future.

23. Locations   Every store is equally invisible on the Net. Multiplying your locations increases your visibility. Your online presence should have as many locations as possible. Each Web link you add to your online store is another doorway into it from a different part of the Net. If you link your BBS to the Internet, you add access for millions of new potential customers. If your store on one online service is generating a profit, consider opening up on another online service. And even if you don't have a storefront, you can be in many different places yourself by participating in newsgroups and forums, by publishing information and storing it in many places, by placing classified ads, and by holding conferences.

24. Access   Give people access to your products in as many ways as possible. Use as many storefronts and links as possible to allow customers with different access methods to patronize your company no matter what. It's fine to have a Web storefront, for example, but you should also consider e-mail versions of your company information or catalog for those who prefer to get it that way.

25. Neatness   Neatness conveys a sense of reliability and competence. It helps give customers the confidence to buy from you. Check all your online messages, displays, publications, and discussion group contributions for proper spelling, grammar, and formatting before sending them out into cyberspace. When you compose e-mail brochures, for example, don't use fancy formatting or fonts that won't survive a trip across the Net.

26. Order form   Ordering online can make customers nervous. Your order form should help put them at ease. Make the form clear and compact. If possible, design it to fit on one or two screen pages. Put the Cancel or Clear button in an obvious place so that customers don't feel trapped. Use pop-up menus or checkboxes to make selecting items easier, and use a shopping cart system that automatically totals up the order so that the customer doesn't have to do it. State your guarantee, delivery policy, and return policy right on the form.

27. Guarantee   Help ease natural reluctance to order online by offering an ironclad guarantee on everything you sell. Make sure you explain the guarantee prominently in your promotional literature.

28. Ordering options   Some buyers are skittish about ordering online, so make sure you offer a phone or mail option. Every purchase option you can offer removes a barrier to sales. Penny Wise Office Products has storefronts on CompuServe, GEnie, and America Online, its own BBS, plus 800-number phone and fax order lines. Amazon Books reminds customers that they can give their credit card information over the phone if they'd rather not send it over the Net.

29. Payment options   Give customers as many payment options as possible, including credit cards, CODs, purchase orders, checks, and even an in-house credit plan. If you're expecting overseas buyers, consider accepting EuroCard or JCB cards as well as MasterCard and Visa.

30. Service   Customers are gambling on you until you earn their trust through service. Respond to every customer request as if your business future depends on it; it probably does. If you're too busy to check your online store for incoming orders every couple of hours, get someone to do it for you.

31. Convenience   Online shopping's main advantage is convenience, so make sure you maximize this advantage as you promote and sell your business. Think about what you can offer online to improve the shopping experience for your customers. Maybe you can offer a wealth of information that's difficult to get offline. Maybe you can offer instant pictures of your products. Think about unique online possibilities, and make sure you use them.

32. Speed   Online shoppers expect speedy responses. Strive to make your service and delivery schedules as fast as or faster than those of your competitors. Some companies are slow to answer questions or submit proposals, and a faster response often gets the sale. Ask friends to visit your storefront and report any problems with response time or access. Change ISPs if you have continuing problems.

33. Bandwidth   Bandwidth limits your ability to transmit and receive information online. If you were in an auto race, you'd want to have the fastest car. Buy the most bandwidth that you can afford. Get a fast computer, the fastest Net connection, and the ISP with the fastest and most reliable access. While your competition is waiting for a screen to scroll or getting a busy signal at their ISP, you can be promoting your business.

34. Customer recourse   Develop a consistent policy for handling dissatisfied customers, and explain it clearly in advance. Your policy will put potential customers at ease and will help convert unhappy customers into repeat buyers.

35. Follow-up   Treat customers like people and they'll come back to you again and again. Send e-mail thank-you notes after each purchase, and let your customers know when you have new products or services.

36. Stationery   Display your online address prominently on your business cards, brochures, letterhead, invoices, packing lists, and other documents. Customers will know they have an online option for communicating and doing business with you, and even those who aren't online will respect you for being there.

37. An advertising plan   You'll be presented with hundreds of advertising opportunities as you surf the Net, but to make the best use of your advertising budget, develop a plan in advance. Explore both online and offline advertising options, decide on the ones that best reach your audience for the lowest price, and then follow the plan.

38. Billboards and buttons   Design effective billboard or button advertisements and place them on Web sites or on online services. It's a good way to gain a higher level of visibility for your business, and most small businesses aren't doing it yet.

39. Announcements   Post text notices on What's New areas and on newsgroups that cover new Net features and Web sites. People are always looking for the next new thing on the Net, but they won't find your new storefront if you don't announce it.

40. Classified ads   You can run classified ads for free on dozens of online services, forums, BBSs, and newsgroups. These ads work just as well online as they do in newspapers and magazines. Try different ads and different locations, and use response codes to see which ads work the best.

41. Magazine inserts   It's remarkably inexpensive to have postcard-sized ads blown into magazines or included in a magazine's delivery envelope. Most magazines about the online world offer this service at least once a year. *CompuServe* magazine has inserts like this each month. Inserts are a great way to pull in online business from offline customers by offering a killer price on a particular product or by promoting a contest or service.

42. Direct-mail postcards   Use direct-mail postcards to announce your new online presence or to announce special promotions. You may encourage an infrequent online traveler to log on and take a look at what you're offering.

43. Mailbots   If you have an account with an ISP, set up a mailbot to automatically distribute your information when people ask for it. The mailbot boosts your service reputation by sending out information instantly, and it gets you out of the e-mailroom so that you can focus on more important tasks.

44. Print advertising   Buy print or classified ads in magazines about the online world. Use your online address in regular print ads and billboards, too.

45. Brochures   Prepare electronic brochures describing your products or services and have them ready to send via e-mail when prospects ask for more information. Again, use a mailbot for automatic responses to queries.

46. Free information   Netizens are information hounds. By offering free, helpful information on a subject related to your business, you enhance your reputation and encourage people to visit your online store or to contact you. Your offer of free information can spark the beginning of profitable customer relationships.

47. Catalog   It's easy and very inexpensive to put your catalog online. You can reach far more customers with an online catalog than you could afford to reach if you had to print and mail it. What's more, you can change your catalog as often as you wish for virtually nothing. Web sites like amazon.com or cdnow.com have online catalogs that offer far more merchandise than these companies could in a printed catalog.

48. Newsletters and magazines   Publish an online newsletter or magazine on a topic related to your business. You can write the material yourself or collect it from other sources. Your subscribers will appreciate the information and many will become customers. Mail printed copies of your publication to existing customers as a way to stay in touch.

49. Directories   Compile a list or directory and maintain it. You'll gain respect as a source of useful information, and your business will get extra visibility in the bargain.

50. Surveys   Conduct a survey on a topic related to your business. Post the survey on newsgroups, forums, or mailing lists where you participate regularly, and publish the results when you're done. *(See Chapter 13.)*

51. Books and articles   Publish your own articles or book excerpts to increase your credibility as an expert. Use a ghostwriter if necessary.

52. Reprints   Save your ads, billboard or marquee copy, articles, conference transcripts, newsletters, magazines, and newsgroup postings, and recycle them as informational aids for your customers.

53. News summaries   Publish a daily, weekly, or monthly summary of news specific to your area of business. By publishing on a regular schedule and selecting news related to a certain topic, you'll attract a community of people who value your information.

54. Tips   Come up with a series of short, useful tips about your products or services. These can be one-sentence items or brief paragraphs. If your tips meet with a positive response, you can compile them into collections or expand each of them into longer articles.

55. FAQs   Make notes about questions you're asked, and then write answers to the ten or twenty most common ones. You'll not only be providing valuable information for new customers — you'll save yourself the work of having to answer the same questions repeatedly.

56. Conferences   Hold conferences about your area of business expertise. Conferences give you a chance to establish a bond with dozens of people at once and to show how your experience can help them.

57. Conference transcripts   Research the transcripts of other conferences to find out how others present them, and reuse information from transcripts of your own conferences. It's not hard to turn a conference transcript into a Q&A document.

58. Column in a publication   Contribute a free article or column to a publication in exchange for including your business name and address. Many newsletters, magazines, and newspapers are looking for material, and you can increase your visibility and build your reputation by helping to provide it. If you can't write the article yourself, find a ghostwriter; the fee you pay will be worth it.

59. Samples   Send out free excerpts from an article or newsletter you've published, or post them on relevant newsgroups, forums, and mailing lists. If you're publishing good information, it will lead to subscribers and customers. Most electronic newsletter and magazine publishers offer free samples of previous issues.

60. Demonstrations   If you're in a service business, offer to show prospective customers how you work by performing a partial service. For example, one guerrilla pitches his scholarship consulting services by offering to create a free list of potential scholarships for every interested client.

61. Software   Since most of your customers are using personal computers to visit your online storefront, why not offer a computer-related goodie as a thank-you? Several Web sites offer custom screen-savers that display their company name, and you can do the same. Or maybe you know of a template file or shareware utility program you can offer via downloads from your storefront.

62. Gift certificates   Offer gift certificates for your products or services so that your customers can introduce your business to other people. You can control online gift certificates by issuing them via e-mail and assigning a unique number to each one.

63. Audiovisual aids   Points made to the eye and ear are 68 percent more effective than points to the ear only. Use the power of the Web and of online services to add visual and audible pizzazz to your site with sound files, blinking graphics, and animation.

64. Advertising specialties   Notices in cyberspace are ephemeral, but by printing your name on mouse pads, floppy disk cases, or other computer gear and giving it away, you can keep your online presence in view even when the computer is off.

65. Club/association memberships   Join online and offline business associations and clubs to make friendships through which you can help spread the word about your business. Some of the best business referrals come from owners of other businesses.

66. Community involvement   Become a part of the community represented by your customer base. Participate regularly in forums, newsgroups, and mailing lists, and add your expertise to the pool of knowledge. Your involvement boosts your credibility as a source of information and shows potential customers that you're not just in it for the money.

67. Public service   Show your generosity by devoting a portion of your Web site to a charitable cause. For example, you might publicize the need for contributions to a worthy foundation or post notices asking for information about missing children. Just make sure that the public service projects you undertake are ones that won't offend any potential customers. For example, plugging for the American Red Cross or the American Heart Association is less potentially offensive than asking for contributions to a particular religious organization.

68. Co-marketing and tie-ins   Establish co-marketing agreements with other businesses that complement yours. By joining together, you can share the costs of Web pages, billboards, and other online marketing venues. Arrange to display another company's promotional information on your Web site if they'll do the same with yours. Plug another company in newsgroups, forums, and conferences if they'll plug yours.

69. Directory listings   Seek out online directories of businesses and make sure yours is listed in them. Most directory listings are free.

70. A publicity plan   Most small business owners wait until their business has been operating for awhile (and without much success) before considering the magic of publicity. But publicity can get your business off to a roaring start if you plan for it. Long before you launch your online business, develop a publicity plan that lists the key messages you want to get out about your company, the key online and offline publications where you want those messages to appear, and some specific ideas for articles in each of those publications. *(See Chapter 16 for more information.)*

71. Media targets   Your publicity efforts will be wasted unless you're focusing on the right targets. Spend some time researching the best possible media outlets for your company's story. Investigate online magazines and newsletters, printed magazines, newsletters, newspapers, and radio and TV shows, and find the ones most likely to attract your target audience. Find out exactly which editors or producers at each outlet are responsible for deciding which stories to do, and make sure your publicity releases or pitches go to them.

72. Editorial and media calendars   The best way to generate effective publicity about your company is to pitch article ideas to the publications most likely to print news or articles about your business. But you'll increase your chances of success if you time your article pitches for the specific issues of those publications that will be covering your topic area. For example, if you offer online accounting services and you know a magazine is focusing on accounting in its January issue, you'll want to target that issue about three months in advance with your article idea. By asking your target publications for an editorial calendar, you'll get a sense of what they'll be writing about in upcoming issues, and you'll be able to develop a media calendar that targets specific article ideas at specific issues of specific magazines or newspapers. *(For more ideas about publicity, see "Publicity pitches" below.)*

73. Publicity contacts   The easiest way to generate media stories about your business is to make personal contacts. Research local and regional newspapers, radio and TV stations, and magazines or newsletters related to your business. Find out who the reporters, editors, and producers are who cover your business. Get to know the ones in your area over lunch or coffee. Use these contacts when you put out an announcement about your company.

74. Press releases   Don't wait until the last minute to create press releases announcing your new online business. Plan a series of press releases that will generate interest in your business over the first six months or year of business. Make your company newsworthy and tell the media about it. You'll gain free public exposure and the kind of credibility no advertising can buy. If yours is the first online store of its kind, that's news, and most Internet magazines will print it if you send them an announcement. If your store is the first online business in your city or community, that's news, and your local newspaper will print it if you send them an announcement. You may even make it into the technology pages of *Newsweek* or *Time* if you send an announcement about a unique Web site or service.

75. Publicity pitches   While a press release is an announcement you send to a number of publications, a publicity pitch proposes that a particular publication do a feature article that will focus on your company. It might be about an industry trend (companies in your industry going online, for example, or competition among firms in your business to create the most useful Web sites), or it might be about the type of service you offer and how different companies (including yours) deliver it. To develop an effective publicity pitch, read the publication for which the pitch is targeted to get a sense of the kinds of articles it prints, and then come up with an idea for an article that could include your company. *(See Chapter 16 for more information.)*

76. Press kit   A press kit is a paper or electronic collection of basic information about your company that is the starting point of reference for any reporter or writer doing an article about you. It should include a company background document that explains your business and your company, products, services, and key personnel; one or more press releases about recent company developments; product photos; a list of customer references; a competitive analysis featuring your company and your major competitors; and perhaps one or more article pitches for the specific person receiving the kit. Package a printed press kit inside a portfolio with your business card in it, and create an online press kit that contains the same information. *(See Chapter 16.)*

77. Press follow-up   Once you send out press releases to specific people at your target publications, follow up a few days later with a phone call or e-mail message asking if they saw the release and if you can provide further information. You shouldn't make a pest of yourself, but a well-timed phone call can often make the difference between your story seeing print and it seeing only the bottom of a wastebasket.

78. Testimonials   One satisfied customer is worth three salespeople. Ask your customers for comments on your products or services, and then use these comments in ads, publicity announcements, and other promotional efforts.

79. Sponsorships   Sponsor an online publication, newsgroup, forum, or mailing list. Sponsorships boost your reputation as a member of the online community. You'll also have the chance to display your company name again and again before hundreds or thousands of people.

80. Contests   Holding a contest brings customers into your online storefront and adds visibility to your name. A contest can also become a promotional opportunity when you put a notice about it on a shopping mall's entrance or on the What's New board on an online service. If the contest is clever enough, it may even make news in magazines about the online world. *(See Chapter 13 for more information.)*

81. Special events   Grand opening, pre-opening, and seasonal events all help to create and maintain an atmosphere of excitement and fun around your business. Schedule a pre-opening tour of your electronic storefront, and plan special events every couple of months to rekindle customer interest.

82. Celebrity appearances   If there's a recognized authority on some aspect of your business, ask him or her to make a guest appearance on behalf of your storefront. You could ask customers to submit questions to the celebrity via e-mail, for example, or sponsor an appearance by the celebrity in a chat room on your favorite forum. By connecting your name with that of a celebrity, you bask in the glow of that celebrity's reputation.

83. Human bonds   People buy from people they like and trust. Do everything you can to make each transaction as human as possible. Use personable language in your messages and ads, and address each e-mail response to a specific person. Show genuine interest in people's questions and problems. Follow up to ensure full satisfaction.

84. Word of mouth   Friends telling friends is a tried-and-true method of expanding your customer base. E-mail makes it easy to spread the word. Ask your satisfied customers to pass on their experiences or your promotional message to others who may be interested.

85. Satisfied customers   Satisfied customers will expand your visibility and your credibility. They're proof that you mean what you say and that you'll deliver on your promises. With proper service and follow-up, you'll not only create satisfied customers, you'll know exactly who they are.

86. Market research   Ask questions about a new product or service you're planning. This is a good way to promote your business in discussion groups without blatantly advertising. You'll get valuable advice and curious readers will want to know more about you. Search the Web and Gopher servers for reports and statistics about your industry or potential new markets. You'll find reams of useful information compiled by research analysts and government bureaus.

87. Competitive research   A lot of the people selling in cyberspace these days don't really have a clue about how it works. Formal research into your business, markets, and the demographics of the online battlegrounds will pay off in a better understanding of cyberspace. The better you know your market and your customers, the more likely you'll be to

keep them. And by researching your competition, you'll know exactly
how to stay ahead of them.

88. Discussion group archives   You probably didn't join a discussion
group or forum at its founding. Most discussion group messages are put
in archives when they get old, but these can be a gold mine of information about participants, their interests, and most important, their e-mail
addresses.

89. Server logs   If you have an online storefront, your presence provider should maintain a log that shows how many people access your
store each day and who they are. Study the log regularly. It helps you
gauge the impact of your marketing efforts and find out who is responding to them.

90. Customer mailing list   As you gain customers, store their e-mail
addresses for later use. E-mail is the surest way to inform people about
your company, and your existing customers are your best source of
future sales and referrals. Keep the e-mail addresses of your customers
and stay in touch with them regularly.

91. Marketing savvy   Most of the people doing business online today
know little or nothing about marketing. Your marketing savvy is a powerful competitive weapon, and you should do all you can to increase it.
The Appendix lists dozens of resources you can use to boost your understanding of the online world, consumer attitudes, and proven marketing
techniques. Don't stop learning.

92. Realistic expectations   People who think online marketing is
magic end up sitting around and waiting for the magic to happen. It
usually doesn't. Guerrillas make their own magic through hard work
and savvy. Don't expect your computer to do your marketing for you;
you still have to do it yourself. If you approach the cyberspace market
realistically, you'll do what it takes to succeed there.

93. Ego strength   In the anonymity of the online world, people often
exhibit anger, rudeness, and hostility that they wouldn't dream of showing in person. And no matter how careful you are to avoid offending
someone, you can't avoid getting flamed from time to time. Have the
strength to shrug it off and move on.

94. Curiosity   All guerrillas are willing to go the extra mile, but the
most successful guerrillas never stop looking for new tools, tactics, and
strategies. Become a student of the online world. Make a point of exploring new battlegrounds you haven't seen. Follow up on interesting news

stories in online magazines, and see if you can add new methods to your marketing repertoire.

95. Enthusiasm   Convey enthusiasm about your products or services in every message and advertisement. Excitement is contagious, and it leads to sales.

96. Objectivity   In the absence of evidence to the contrary, most of us think our ideas, our written messages, and our designs are as good as they can be. Guerrillas are always looking for ways to do better. That means constantly searching cyberspace for new or improved ideas, asking for honest critiques and suggestions from customers and coworkers alike, and having the objectivity to realize it when others' ideas are better than ours.

97. Imagination   Most online marketers are so concerned with doing things properly that they stick to proven forms and methods. But cyberspace technology is advancing by leaps and bounds. By breaking out of the mold a little, you can gain a lot of attention. Add some animated graphics to your Web storefront, or try some short video clips to liven up your presentation.

98. Humor   A little comic relief can make your messages or storefront more attractive and exciting. The online world can be intimidating for newbies, and veteran cybernauts often take themselves a little too seriously. Take some of the pressure off your contacts by injecting a little tasteful humor in your discussions, group postings, catalog, ads, or other online messages.

99. Confidence   The online marketplace is still very new, but a lot of businesspeople achieve marginal results there because that's all they strive for. Pursue the online market with the confidence that you will succeed there, and you will. Pursue it as a marginal option that won't mean much to your business, and it won't.

100. Competitiveness   This is simply your drive, your willingness to devote as much time as you can to using these weapons. If you put in twice as much effort as your competitors, you'll be twice as far ahead in the race to profits.

Most of these weapons require only your time and the commitment to use them. Only half a dozen require a significant investment in dollars. Guerrillas know that commitment and imagination can triumph in an attack, so use as much of both as you can.

THE TEN MOST IMPORTANT WEAPONS

You should use as many of the one hundred weapons as well as you can, but there are ten that stand out as fundamentally important to your success.

1. Community involvement
2. Identity
3. Competitiveness
4. Credibility
5. Free information

6. Confidence
7. Signatures
8. Convenience
9. Satisfied customers
10. Service

Why are these so important? Confidence and competitiveness are vital traits you'll need in order to press your attack. Credibility and identity give customers a reason to do business with you. Community involvement, free information, and your signatures are the vital tools for creating visibility. Convenience, service, and satisfied customers will give you a reputation that brings more customers to you and keeps them returning again and again.

But before you tear off onto the infobahn with these weapons in hand, remember this: each of these weapons, and each of the ten most important ones in particular, is a two-edged sword. Use it well and you'll gain customers and profits; use it badly and your online business will fail. Strive for excellence, aggressiveness, and consistency in your use of these weapons and the online marketplace will reward you.

BUILDING YOUR MARKETING ARSENAL

Most of your competitors will use fewer than ten of the weapons we've covered, and few will use more than half of the ten most important ones. Before you begin planning the details of your attack, you should know which of these weapons you plan to use and how you plan to use it. To get started, look back over the list and assign each weapon to one of three categories:

A: You're using this weapon now, or you plan to use it immediately, and you know exactly how you'll use it.

B: You're using this weapon now, or you plan to use it immediately, but you're not using it as well as you could, or you don't know how you'll use it.

C: You have no plans to use this weapon.

Your goal, of course, is to move as many weapons as possible into Category A. Certainly there should be more weapons in Category A than in either of the other two.

Look at each weapon in Category B and plan to implement it in a specific way as quickly as possible. As for Category C, you may think you have no need for these weapons, but in time you'll need them to maintain your advantage over your competition. The online marketplace is still in its infancy, but your competitors will catch on quickly and you'll need all the weapons you can muster to stay a step ahead of them.

Recognize, too, that your list of weapons may change. There are 100 weapons listed here, but improvements in online access and presentation technology, changes in the makeup of the online audience, and good old ingenuity will surely reveal others as time goes by. Stay alert for new ideas and implement them when you can.

With our online battle lines clearly drawn and our weapons at the ready, we're almost ready to begin planning and pressing the attack. Before we do, however, let's look at some key strategies for success as an online guerrilla.

11

Twelve Strategies
for Online Success

Even if you're a diligent student of guerrilla marketing techniques, the
online marketplace has its own rules and limits that change how those
techniques are applied. In your transformation from guerrilla marketer
to online guerrilla marketer, you'll need to adapt your strategies to
online battlegrounds.

If you're not familiar with guerrilla marketing techniques, you can
learn the basic strategies here, but you'll find a more comprehensive discussion in *Guerrilla Marketing*, the basic text for guerrillas everywhere.

THE ONLINE MARKETPLACE IS ANOTHER COUNTRY

Think of the online marketplace as a foreign country. Cybernauts are
people just like you, but the online marketplace isn't just like the familiar, physical world. Computers and online communications enforce
different rules for social interaction and for selling. Guerrillas understand and play by these rules. Just as patting a child on the head conveys
affection in America but is considered an insult in Asia, some of the
techniques you use for face-to-face marketing can do more harm than
good in the online world.

Many a marketer has blundered into the online marketplace with
direct e-mail appeals or newsgroup advertising blitzes, and all of them
have felt the sting of the online community. Canter and Siegel's spam
attack is only the most famous example. These two lawyers posted ads
on thousands of newsgroups and generated so much hate mail that their
ISP closed their account. But dozens of other companies have found
their e-mailboxes stuffed with multimegabyte files of garbage or hundreds of poison-pen letters because they posted an ad on the wrong
newsgroup or sent out direct e-mail appeals without the recipients'
permission.

As a guerrilla, your goal is to market as aggressively and effectively as
possible without ruffling any feathers. The more you understand the
unique characteristics of the online marketplace, the more easily you'll

be able to adapt your strategies for success in it. Before we examine the twelve strategies for success as an electronic guerrilla, it is important to know what makes the electronic marketplace so different from the physical world.

Everybody and everything is invisible

When we go out shopping in the physical world, we see stores, products, and people. Our shopping experience and buying habits are influenced by light, sound, color, or the presence or absence of a crowd. A store can stand out from others by its window display, sign, size, location, or the crowd it draws. When you market in the online world, none of these advantages work for you.

The online marketplace is like a huge, dark exposition hall. The hall contains millions of people and thousands of exhibition booths. There are thousands of signs, banners, and billboards, and billions of pages of information. The trouble is that it's totally dark, and you have to know exactly how and where to reach any person, booth, or document page in order to see what it offers.

Every business is equally visible and invisible in cyberspace. The Web site that costs Digital Equipment Corporation or Silicon Graphics thousands of dollars to maintain is no more visible than the Web site you rent for fifty dollars a month. For large businesses and small, success online comes from making the invisible visible.

If you had a booth in a totally dark exhibition hall and you wanted to draw customers into it, you'd have to reach out to them and tell them where it was and how to get there. You couldn't just put up a big sign, because nobody could see it in the darkness. You'd have to find a way to deliver your message to specific groups of people or individuals. You might hire a team of agents to go out among the people and pass the word. Guerrillas do this all the time at trade shows: rather than waiting and hoping for the crowd to pass by their booths, they hire people to stand at key places around the exhibit hall and pass out handbills. Instead of letting a booth and one sign be their only presence, they expand their presence by distributing their message in many places.

It follows that to gain an effective level of visibility in the online marketplace, you have to distribute your message widely. Rather than buying just one ad or billboard, you post several little signs in various locations where your customers are likely to see them. Rather than simply putting up a more elaborate storefront to improve your credibility, you distribute useful information and build a reputation for expertise and service.

The darkness of cyberspace is the great equalizer; it gives you as much of a chance for success as your largest competitors. In many ways, it's the ultimate guerrilla battleground. Company size and financial resources mean very little; guerrilla savvy and competitiveness will carry the day.

Everything is ephemeral

You can hand out circulars, brochures, samples, business cards, or advertising specialties in the physical world and they'll serve as constant reminders of your identity or message. Leave them on a desk, and they convey your message every time somebody looks that way. But in cyberspace even the cleverest message or the most inviting storefront is no more than an electronic ghost. Every message disappears as soon as the customer moves along or logs off.

Every marketing effort is somewhat temporary because it only remains in the prospect's mind for so long, but messages are even more fleeting in cyberspace. Your marketing efforts must compensate by appearing in more online locations and with greater frequency. You can't rely on a printed brochure to present your message over and over. You'll have to make sure your electronic brochure gets around in the online world.

Things change quickly

In an online world where you can build a new store in a matter of days or change the store's departments with a few keystrokes, the terrain shifts rapidly. Every week dozens of new businesses invade cyberspace, and every month many of those businesses modify their selection of wares or their presentation.

Netizens expect change. Guerrillas satisfy those expectations by regularly offering something new. Your online marketing strategies should incorporate new attractions. Use special promotions, regular publications of new information, publicity announcements, contests, or other means to rekindle interest. The only things you won't want to change are your company name and address.

Shopping is research. In the physical world, we shop and buy things for several reasons. We visit shopping malls with no goals in mind other than to get out of the house, to be among people, and to be entertained.

Sometimes the crowd's enthusiasm for a store or product will transform us from lookers into buyers. We're swept up in the prevailing mood.

When you're shopping online, the only prevailing mood is your own. Shopping in cyberspace is a matter of one person and one computer. There may be hundreds of other people visiting the same online store or shopping mall at the same time you are, but you never see them and you're typically not influenced by them. (Although you may be more tempted to buy an item that's listed as a best-seller.)

You're not even influenced by a store's salespeople when you shop online, because you never interact directly with them. You're far less influenced by the appearance of an online storefront, because it's the information on the screen that affects you, not the atmosphere in which that information is presented. You can't feel, smell, or taste anything online.

You don't go online to experience a crowded mall or some holiday decorations; you go online to explore a world of information. If what shoppers want is to expand their realms of knowledge, then you have to offer compelling information to get their attention. Online shoppers may still be intrigued by a promotion for some product or service they didn't have in mind at all when they logged on that day, but you'd better have a good presentation to make that happen. You have to put the right messages in the right places at exactly the right times.

Online guerrillas recognize that information is the major drawing card for their businesses. You can get by with simply posting a catalog of your products and prices, but unless your selection is vastly better or your prices are clearly lower than in competing stores, catalog information alone isn't enough to draw customers in. Teach people something new, and you'll distinguish your store from your competition. Information is what people seek, and the more of it you provide and the better you are at providing it, the more customers you'll have.

There's only so much bandwidth

No matter what we do online, our experience is limited by bandwidth. Bandwidth dictates the amount of information we can receive through our computer during a given period of time, and there's only so much of it to go around. Bandwidth is affected by all these variables:

- the speed of your online connection
- the speed and display capability of your computer screen

- the speed with which you can read and comprehend information
- the cost of your online connection
- the amount of money you have to spend on your connection

A person with a 56,000 bps modem connection to America Online can take in more information in five minutes than can another person with a 14,400 bps connection. The person with the slower connection will wait longer for graphics to appear, longer for his or her commands to take effect. A limited budget or limited speed means limited access. Bandwidth is time, and time is money. Nobody likes to waste it.

The most effective online messages are those that don't waste the recipient's time or money. Spam artists invite the wrath of the Net community because they waste bandwidth. Marketers who send out mass e-mailings arouse anger and resentment because their recipients have to waste bandwidth reading and deleting the message. Even participants in forums or newsgroups get testy when a message is longer than it should be or when a signature takes up more screen space than normal. Every marketing effort you make online should be designed to make the best use of bandwidth.

Most contacts are made through writing

In your physical store you have a lot of marketing allies that help make the sale. Customers can pick up, feel, smell, and taste the merchandise. They can talk directly to a salesperson. They can even hear testimonials from other satisfied customers.

In cyberspace, your marketing message must be carried through written words. You may be able to help it along with pictures or sounds if you're marketing on the Web, but words do the real selling.

We've known many terrific salespeople who could sell anything face to face, but who couldn't put two sentences together if you asked them to write down a pitch. In the online marketplace, written words are the coin of the realm. Being able to express yourself clearly, effectively, and concisely in writing is essential in cyberspace. If you can't do it, find someone who can.

It's not magic

Despite all the hype surrounding the information highway and the technical allure of cruising through cyberspace, there's nothing magical about the online marketplace. While the Internet does link millions of people, few if any of them are suddenly seized with a desire to buy things simply because they've gone online.

The online marketplace is a different place from the local shopping mall, to be sure. It lets you reach customers you could never reach before, and it lets you do business at times and in places that were off-limits before. But marketing is work, and computers don't do it for you. Guerrillas know that online or off, their success always depends on hard work, dedication, and savvy.

THE TWELVE STRATEGIES FOR ONLINE SUCCESS

Knowing that cyberspace is different from other marketing venues and being able to operate effectively in it are two different things. Knowing how the online world operates will keep you from making serious marketing mistakes. The following twelve strategies will help you adopt the attitudes and skills necessary to succeed and profit in cyberspace.

1. Know how to express yourself

Being able to get your message across in writing is the primary strategy for online success. Effective writing makes or breaks every other strategy you apply. Not knowing how to write online is like trying to sell cars in Japan without being able to speak Japanese. Without the ability to get your message across, you might as well have no message at all.

The most important aspects of writing are clarity, precision, and economy. In promotional writing, it also helps to have a personal voice.

Clarity is important because you're not there to answer questions if your message is muddled. Prospects may be able to send you an e-mail message if they need further information, but your messages should be written so as to minimize general questions. Ideally, the only question your prospect should have is "When can I get it?"

Precision is saying exactly what you want in exactly the right way. Check your messages for spelling, grammar, and punctuation mistakes. If people think you don't care about how your messages look, they'll wonder if you care about the rest of your business.

Economy is important because time costs money in cyberspace. Few people will wade through line after line of gibberish in order to decipher your point. As in print advertising, words are at a premium. The time anyone spends online is precious, and if people are attracted to your message, they'll want to get the facts as quickly as possible.

And ads aren't the only place to be concise. Descriptions of your product or service, order forms, e-mail replies, newsgroup postings, and anything else that you post in cyberspace should be carefully crafted to deliver the most information in the least amount of time. Strive to make learning about your product, ordering, or just contacting your company as easy and efficient as you can.

A personal voice makes it clear that there's a person behind the message. Unless you're giving a conference, you're talking to one person at a time. Your e-mail and newsgroup postings are being read by individuals, not by a crowd, so communicate with that one person. Say "You'll be amazed . . ." instead of "Our customers are amazed." Say "We've come up with a new . . ." instead of "Acme Manufacturing is pleased to announce . . ."

Take the time to hone your writing skills. Test your messages on others before posting them online. If you're no wordsmith yourself, find one to help create and maintain your online presence.

2. Know the terrain

You can't hope to win the battle for online customers if you don't know the battlefields. You wouldn't choose a store location by picking an address off a map. Don't even think about launching an online marketing program without knowing the territory firsthand.

So check out the marketplace yourself. Join several online information services and poke around. Most of the online services have trial offers that give you a few hours of free connect time. It won't cost you much, if anything, to do some basic battlefield reconnaissance. Seek out some BBSs and newsgroups related to your business, and monitor them for a few days or weeks to see what's going on there. Visit some online storefronts, and see how they work.

Learn your way around each battlefield. Find out who is selling on these battlefields now, what they're selling, and how they're selling it. Check out the stores in online shopping malls, and see how merchandise or services are described and sold. Find out whether or not each battlefield has access to the Net and what sort of access it has. Check out the advertising and promotional opportunities on each online service. Look for holes in the marketplace that your product or service can fill. Check out the classified ads.

If you're planning to focus on an online service as your primary battlefield, get some statistics about it. Contact the service's marketing department, and ask for a subscriber profile that includes demographics about the service's user community. Any potential marketer on a service is entitled to such information, and it can help you zero in on a particular audience. For example, GEnie boasts a high percentage of satisfied customers. America Online has the largest subscriber base, with more than 7 million users.

Check out the forums on each online service, as well as the newsgroups and mailing lists on the Internet. Look for ones that relate to your business, and think about how you might participate. If there isn't one, you may want to start one yourself. Forums, newsgroups, and mailing lists are the closest thing to clubs in cyberspace — it's there that you'll build the personal relationships that will establish your online reputation and expand your visibility.

Millions of cybernauts use bulletin boards. There are thousands of bulletin boards covering every subject from job opportunities in Toronto to nutrition in Third World countries. Check magazines like *Boardwatch* for the names of and access information for bulletin boards. The names usually give you a clue about each board's subject. If the name doesn't help, a few minutes on any board will tell you what subject it covers. Many BBSs are now on the Internet, so you may be able to reach them via the Web instead of dialing a direct phone number.

Find out what's permitted on each battlefield. Many online battlefields prohibit commercial announcements, so you'll have to get your message across in other ways. ISPs, online services, and BBSs usually have acceptable use policies that prohibit mass e-mailings or newsgroup postings. Violating those policies can cost you your account and your access.

Even if something is permitted, it may not be effective. Unsolicited e-mail messages in small numbers aren't specifically illegal, but they're frowned upon. Unless your mail recipients already know you, you may alienate them before they even read what you have to say. One California maker of computer accessories sent out 3,000 promotional e-mail messages and got flamed by about 100 recipients. On the other hand, the mailing generated $30,000 worth of orders!

Sometimes just having an Internet address and responding to queries by mail pays off handsomely. The Future Fantasy Bookstore, a small independent shop in Palo Alto, California, has averaged 20 orders per day on the Internet since publicizing its Internet address, and it hasn't ruffled any feathers in the process.

3. Fight on one battlefield at a time

Nobody starts a war by attacking on all fronts at once. Choose the single most promising battlefield and establish your advantage on that one before expanding your attack. If you plan to market mainly through online services, pick the most promising one for your business and then map out a strategy for it. *(See Chapter 12.)* You can always expand your attack after you've solidified your position on the first battlefield.

4. Drill for battle

You wouldn't enter a real battle without knowing how to operate weapons, maintain supply lines, or deploy troops. Don't enter the online marketplace without knowing how to navigate and use its features. Whether you're opening up your own Internet storefront, joining a forum, or publishing information, you'll need to know the mechanics of exchanging information and contacting customers, including:

- how to connect with the Internet or your targeted online service
- how to determine the cost of your online presence and how to connect and put up a storefront in the least expensive ways
- how to get help with any aspect of using a particular network, bulletin board, or commercial service
- how to read, send, file, and forward e-mail
- how to join an Internet mailing list and how to stay abreast of new ones as they appear
- how to participate in a forum or newsgroup
- how to establish and develop an online storefront
- how to post a display ad
- how to post a classified ad
- how to place news and promotional announcements on an online service
- how to contact a commercial service's marketing staff
- how to contact a forum administrator or BBS's sysop
- how to determine the peak usage times on the service or network you've chosen and how to find out if and when it's shut down for maintenance

Think of these mechanics as basics of online business. They're the electronic equivalent of understanding how to turn on the lights or set

THE GUERRILLA ATTITUDE

For typical businesspeople, marketing is an activity that's separate from selling, working with customers, paying bills, and performing other business tasks. They only think about marketing when they have their "marketing hat" on, and that's usually not too often. As a result, they miss most of the daily marketing opportunities presented to them, and what marketing programs they do have under way usually grow stale and ineffective.

For true guerrilla marketers, marketing is everything, and therefore every activity is marketing. Whenever you respond to e-mail, send out information, fill an order, ask for information, participate in a discussion, design a Web page, or do anything else online, look at it as a way to promote your business or your reputation. By thinking about all your online tasks as marketing opportunities, you'll constantly come up with new promotional ideas, and your online reputation will continually improve.

True guerrillas never give up the fight. They look on every business task as a marketing opportunity, and they're always thinking about ways to improve their marketing attack.

the alarm in a physical storefront. You just can't do business without knowing them.

5. Be aggressive

The Internet is no place for wallflowers. At in-person gatherings, shy people can always hope a customer or prospect will waltz up and say hello, but that's not going to happen on the Internet. Your ability to meet people, locate prospects, provide information, and make sales depends entirely on your aggressiveness.

You have to be the one to post messages in discussion groups, send e-mail, and respond to queries. Nobody is going to choose your mailbox out of 30 million and favor you with their attention, and you can't rely on people to simply stumble upon your electronic storefront without having been told where it is and why they should visit it.

Marketing is visibility, and the only way to gain visibility is to earn it. So don't just browse the Internet; get involved. When you're not putting in your two cents' worth, you're invisible.

6. Establish a presence

Nobody will patronize your business if they don't know who you are or where you are. Your online presence may begin with an e-mail address or a storefront, but that's only the beginning. As you pursue your marketing plan, you will develop and expand your presence by getting your name and address, your identity, and your message in front of as many people as often as possible.

Most of your future customers won't be shopping when they hear of you. Instead, they'll be seeking information or trying to solve a problem. Remember, information is the key commodity on the information highway. Although your electronic storefront or e-mailbox may be your key *sales* presence, the *information* presence and reputation you develop is what will bring customers to that storefront or mailbox.

Your product or service is the solution to a problem, so don't be afraid to offer it. The key to sales is finding people with that problem (or making them aware that they have it) and then letting them know that your product is the solution. Be forthright in mentioning your product or service, but be sure to do so in a helpful and informative way.

Choose a good user or screen name. Select one that reinforces your business identity.

Establish your store name. If you have an established business name that's well known, use the same one on the information highway. If not, this is your chance to pick one that promotes what you sell. For example, Penny Wise Office Products is a name that conveys the type of business as well as its competitive advantage.

Participate in forums. Target forums whose members are the most likely prospects for your business, and then become an active source of information on them. Don't use the forum just to post messages about your product or service — many forums specifically prohibit commercial messages. Instead, check the posted messages for information requests or problems, and then respond to those you can be helpful with. If you've chosen the proper screen or user name and you include it in a signature at the end of each message, you'll pitch your business every time you provide a helpful answer. *(See Chapter 7 for more information.)*

MOST CYBERNAUTS ARE OFFLINE

Cyberspace is such a world in itself that we tend to forget that most of our customers spend most of their time offline. Factor this reality into promotions for your online business. Use print advertisements, publicity, direct mail, stationery, signs, and other offline means to promote your online business. *(See Chapter 16 for more information.)*

Start a forum. Commercial online services have dozens of product- or vendor-specific forums set up by companies like Microsoft, Lotus, or Novell to provide information and online support for their customers. But a number of companies are discovering that they can polish their online presence by sponsoring more general discussion groups as well. For example, Performance Systems International, an ISP, sponsors an Internet discussion group relating to the commercialization and privatization of the Internet. Although PSI doesn't directly promote its own products and services through the forum, anyone active in this forum knows that PSI is the sponsor. PSI gains a reputation as a source of information, and when customers shop for Internet services, they remember that PSI is one of the Internet's good guys.

Since there are limitless possibilities in establishing special interest forums, you should be able to find a venue that helps you promote your business. If your company sells motorcycle accessories, for example, you could build credibility by starting a motorcycle special interest forum on a service that doesn't have one or by starting a newsgroup or mailing list on the Net. *(See Chapter 7 for more information.)*

Hold conferences. By sharing your expertise with an audience, you'll build credibility and visibility with a lot of people at the same time. *(See Chapter 9 for more information.)*

Publish online. Your published tip sheets, articles, newsletters, and other documents help increase your credibility over an extended period of time. You can combine information from other sources or create your own material. As long as the publication has your company name on it and it contains useful information, it will add to your visibility.

Get mentioned in print-magazine articles. Your business may be newsworthy enough for you to become the subject of an article in the online service's subscriber magazine or even in a business-related article in a magazine like *Home Office Computing* or *Internet World*. Start checking these magazines every month for stories that use other business sources, and develop a pitch for an article that includes you as a source. *(See Chapter 16 for more information.)*

7. Be attentive

Internet users are accustomed to quick responses. Somebody requesting information via snail mail might wait days or weeks for a catalog, but Internet users expect responses within twenty-four hours. Whatever battlefields you've chosen, make sure you check them regularly for opportunities and queries. Respond to all requests immediately. If you check a target newsgroup only every few days, you may miss the opportunity to respond to a comment. In addition, your customers will wait a long time for answers to their questions if you don't check your e-mail to discover they've asked them.

If you have an electronic storefront, the store is open twenty-four hours a day whether you like it or not. Many netizens make their connections after dark when telephone and online service rates are lower. Customers in many foreign countries will reach your store in the middle of the night even if they're connecting in the middle of their business day.

Naturally, you'll want to sleep sometime, and if you're a small business you may not want to staff your store day and night. But that's the beauty of the Internet: you can receive orders without being connected yourself. Your store should offer enough information to conclude most sales or to allow people to post electronic questions. If you're properly attentive to your store and your e-mailbox, you'll be able to answer any questions within a few hours.

8. Be curious

Although you'll probably focus on one particular battlefield at first, don't ignore the rest of the marketplace. Make a habit of setting aside an hour or so every few days to watch for trends or other areas of activity that might expand your efforts. New discussion groups, mailing lists, new forums, and new BBSs are all places you might strike next.

Check the What's New or welcome screen on your online service every time it's updated. Don't just glance at the headlines on the board; check out the actual events or locations being promoted. Every company that gets a notice on the What's New or welcome screen is your competitor, because you're all competing for visibility. Browse shopping malls regularly to find out what the competition is doing, and think about how you can do better.

9. Make personal contacts

Internet pros can quickly tell the difference between those on the sidelines and those in the thick of the action. Since one key to effective marketing is establishing personal contacts, make sure you're not just on the Internet sidelines. Make every contact count, and keep up relationships through frequent contact.

Use e-mail. As you establish connections with others who are interested in your business or other common subjects, add them to your address list, and make sure they get copies of other mail or forum postings you think would be helpful. There are thousands of phantom forums that don't have an established presence on the Internet, but exist through a selected group of recipients who get copies of one another's messages.

Join forums and newsgroups. When you find forums or newsgroups that present opportunities, become a regular on them. Respond to as many queries as you can, as long as you can be helpful. Even if helping someone directs them to another business or product, your referral will build the kind of trust that will eventually lead to sales.

As you develop online relationships with others, build the human side of the relationship. When you provide information or answer questions, include a few personal details that help people distinguish you from the hundreds or thousands of other people sending mail or posting messages. Most netizens read and respond to many messages every day; make yours stand out.

10. Be patient

As with any marketing effort, patience is essential. Once you put your toe in the water with a forum or online store, stick it out for several months. If you've chosen your battlegrounds wisely and you're sincerely trying to be helpful, your name recognition and reputation as a good source of information will spread throughout the Internet like a ripple in a lake. But it's a big lake, and your reputation will spread slowly. Most businesses that set up online storefronts go through several weeks of browsing before they start making continuous sales.

Just because the world isn't beating a path to your door the way you expect, it doesn't mean that things won't work out in the long run. You may end up with referrals from forum members or e-mail correspondents you originally helped months before. Some referrals will come from across the country, across the world, or from people you've never had personal contact with.

Cyberspace is a changing world, but your marketing plan isn't one of the things that should change. Too many changes there mean wasted time and money. Witness the 1994 debut and retreat of MecklerWeb, a World Wide Web site for business-to-business commerce. After touting the site's construction for months in its *Internet World* magazine, Mecklermedia Corporation changed its mind and turned the site into a technology advertising vehicle after only two weeks of operation. All the promotional work and momentum that had built for the new enterprise were lost, and by the end of 1996, MecklerWeb had ceased to exist entirely.

Once you establish a plan for your attack, stick with it. If your storefront's opening rates a notice on the What's New page on your online service or on the Web, don't just sit back and wait for miracles to happen after the messages have stopped appearing. Think of a new angle or promotion that will put you back on the What's New page soon.

If you're participating in a forum and you don't get any leads from it, stick it out for several months at least. You can't expect people to storm your electronic storefront the first time you mention that you have one, and even if they do, they probably won't buy right away. The biggest cost is in preparing for battle and starting the attack. The incremental cost of maintaining an attack is so low that there's no reason not to do it.

11. Be consistent

Once you've established a certain presence on the Internet, don't change your approach. The information you put out, and the way you put it out, establishes your online identity, so strive for consistency. This not only includes becoming a regular feature on a forum or in someone's e-mailbox — it also means providing the same kind of information in the same tone.

Consistency is important in any marketing effort, but it's more important in cyberspace than it is in face-to-face contact. When someone can see you, part of their comfort comes from your physical presence. In the online world, however, you're an electronic ghost — you could be gone tomorrow unless you continually reassure people that you're still there. Consistency builds trust, and trust is essential to doing business online.

12. Follow up

As leads and sales proceed from your efforts, make sure you follow up with a personal note of thanks via e-mail. Stay in touch with all your customers to make sure their experience with your product or service is a positive one.

Following up not only tells the customer that you care, it provides opportunities for you to mention new products or services and to ask for referrals. A brief mention of a new product in a follow-up note might foster a new sale, or it might be forwarded by your customer to someone else. E-mail is so easy to read and forward that you could end up with half a dozen new customers for each one you thank.

PART III

Managing
Your Attack

12

Planning the Attack

You now know what your options are for your online marketing attack. The next step is to prepare for battle. Your battle plan, or online marketing plan, is a detailed blueprint of your attack. Creating the plan will help focus and refine your thinking about what you hope to accomplish online, how you hope to accomplish it, how much it will cost, and how long it will take. Once you've finished the plan, you'll have a set of step-by-step marching orders to follow that will keep you on track. And as your attack proceeds, you'll be able to compare your results with your initial projections and make adjustments as necessary.

Your online marketing plan will become part of your overall marketing plan. It has six parts:

1. a mission statement that uniquely defines your business
2. a set of goals you hope to achieve with the plan
3. a list of resources you'll need to carry out the plan
4. a list of targets you'll attack
5. a set of weapons and tactics you'll use to attack each target
6. a calendar that guides you through battle

If you already have a basic marketing plan for your business, you have a head start with the mission statement and goals. As you'll see, though, even these areas will need some modification for the online battles ahead.

THE MISSION STATEMENT

Your business mission statement is a sentence (two at most) that describes your reason for being in business and why you'll succeed. The quick answer to this is "To make a profit," but if that's your only goal, you'll probably fail.

Businesses succeed because they provide things people want at prices they're willing to pay — and at prices that are high enough to produce a profit. Profits may well follow from providing useful goods or services to satisfied customers; however, if your focus is only on profits, you'll have a hard time putting enough energy into the products or services to achieve the customer satisfaction that will produce them.

To create a detailed mission statement, start by writing down phrases that describe your business, its reason for success, and its competitive advantages. You should end up with a dozen or two phrases that explain why you'll win in the online market and how you're different from the other guys. When you're finished, look over what you've written and boil it all down to its essence.

Why your business should succeed

Your business should succeed because you fill a unique need or because you fill a common need better than your competition. The mission statement in your online marketing plan must include reasons why people will want to buy from you in cyberspace. You may already have a mission statement that works for you in the offline world, but some competitive advantages like your store's size or your sales staff mean nothing online. The following are some competitive advantages that might apply in cyberspace.

Location. Your online location may bring you customers you couldn't reach before. The online market makes buying convenient by allowing sales from all over the world at any time. The Virginia Diner can sell its peanuts to customers in Japan via the Web. A CompuServe subscriber in Britain can shop in online stores that ship from Canada.

Convenience. You may also have chosen an online location because you can make life easier for your customers via the Net. For example, United Parcel Service and Federal Express let their customers track the progress of shipments via Web sites.

Added value. Your online business may offer faster service, lower prices, or quicker access to information than people could get either offline or from your online competitors. Penny Wise Office Products offers additional discounts to its customers who regularly order online. Amazon Books lets customers search and order from its database of more than a million books.

Uniqueness. Your online business may be the only one of its kind. Of course, the online market is more crowded every day, so uniqueness becomes harder and harder to come by, but you can still carve out a niche for yourself through specialization. As bookstores have popped up on the Net, some have begun to specialize in specific genres. You might, for example, open the only Net bookstore that specializes in cookbooks.

Visibility. All the major hamburger chains sell the same product, but their market share has a lot to do with visibility. McDonald's, Burger King, and Wendy's spend millions on advertising to fight for visibility. There are lots of auto and credit card companies, but Hyundai and American Express have been particularly aggressive in placing banner and button ads on heavily traveled Web sites, and 800-Flowers frequently buys buttons at the entrance to AOL's online shopping mall.

Credibility. People buy securities through Charles Schwab instead of Al's Discount Stocks because Charles Schwab has more credibility. The company has been recognized as a leader in the discount brokerage business for many years. You can gain higher credibility than your online competition by offering reliable service and valuable information for your customers. For example, Amazon Books confirms each order via e-mail within a few hours after receiving it via their Web site.

Service. Your key business advantage may be service. Jiffy Lube and Oil Changers have built large franchises on the simple idea that people don't want to spend an hour or more waiting for an oil change at a gas station or dealership. Since netizens expect speed in all their transactions, your company might use a mailbot for instant responses to information requests or offer a text-only view of your Web site for those who won't wait for graphics.

Pricing. Discounting has been a major competitive force for over a hundred years, and competition for the price-leader mantle is fierce these days. Still, it's a mantle worth having. If you're in a business where shoppers can easily compare your prices with those for identical merchandise, then you'd better be ready to back up your low-price claims with a guarantee. Price guarantees are a hot sales button in many retail businesses. But if you're selling something harder to come by, your prices must only be perceived as low. For example, you might sell art posters or hot sauces on the Net for prices identical to what customers would pay in a store, but they're perceived as low because there are few other companies in the same business.

Quality. If you can't compete on price, justify your higher prices by offering better quality in the products or services you sell. Nobody buys stock through Merrill Lynch because their commissions are the lowest, but because they offer investment expertise. Ace and True Value hardware stores can seldom compete on price with Home Depot or other warehouse chains, so they emphasize their superior expertise and service. Your online business can exude quality through superior presentation, service, and by providing more information than the other guys.

Selection. It's far easier to offer a large selection of merchandise online because cyberspace is much cheaper than physical space. You can store a whole electronic catalog in disk space that can be accessed by thousands yet costs only $20 a month. Online bookstores, music stores, office supply shops, florists, and other businesses compete by offering a broader selection of goods than their competition.

Building your mission statement

Once you've written down all the phrases you can think of that distinguish your business from its competition and provide concrete reasons for your anticipated success, it's time to distill them.

Look over the list and prioritize the phrases in order of importance. At the top of the list, put the phrases that convey clear, unassailable advantages. If yours is the only auto repair BBS in the Cleveland area, that's an advantage that isn't likely to be challenged. But if your Web storefront has the largest selection of floral arrangements or it's the only one selling vacuum cleaners, your advantage could erode any day. When you choose a territory, be prepared to defend it.

By prioritizing the phrases you wrote down, you'll probably find that only the top two or three make it into your mission statement. That's fine, as long as they're phrases you can successfully defend over time. Your final mission statement should be primarily based on one of the competitive traits mentioned in the previous section. It should state what you sell, to whom you sell it, and why you're the best. The following examples emphasize the competitive traits outlined above:

WrenchNet is Cleveland's one-stop online source of foreign and domestic auto parts and auto repair advice. (This BBS stresses location, convenience, and expertise.)

Infotime Research is the only company specializing in fast and reliable patent, trademark, and licensing searches for the aerospace and biotechnology industries. (This company touts its uniqueness, service, and expertise.)

Gaming Technology is the world leader in design, installation, and maintenance of electronic lottery systems for government and chari-

---

DISCOVERING YOUR BUSINESS MISSION

If you don't have a clear idea of how and why your online business will succeed, here are some steps you can take to figure it out.

1. Write down one-sentence answers to questions that will define your business, such as: "What do you sell?" "Who do you sell it to?" and "Why will they buy it from you?"

2. Surf the Web for similar businesses. As you browse each Web site, write down statements about how each business differs from your answers to Step 1 in two columns labeled Better and Worse. Think in terms of the competitive advantages outlined on pp. 230–232.

3. Revise the answers in Step 1 to address your competitors' advantages or take advantage of their disadvantages as listed in Step 2.

4. Organize the new "answer" statements into a coherent mission statement like those shown on pp. 232–233.

---

table institutions. (This statement implies visibility, quality, and credibility.)

Bonus Bookmart offers the largest selection of books on the Internet with the lowest prices in the world. (This company claims the low-price crown and stresses selection.)

InstaPix's online graphics service delivers professional-quality image files to art directors and graphic artists within minutes. (This stresses quality and the added value of the Net's speedy delivery system.)

Each of these statements stakes out a business niche that gives the company a competitive edge in its market. Your mission statement should describe real traits of your business that set it apart from the crowd.

The reality check

When you finalize your mission statement, make sure it's one you can live up to. It may sound great to say your company is the largest supplier of fruit baskets in cyberspace, but you have to be able to support that statement with deeds. If you have competitors who already occupy the niche you'd like to occupy, your mission statement should provide compelling reasons why you think you can capture it. For example, *WinCo will become the leading online vendor of window coverings by offering a superior selection and color graphic samples on its Web server while guaranteeing the lowest prices.*

SETTING GOALS

It's difficult to plan for an outcome if you don't know what outcome you want. Your goals spell out exactly what you hope to achieve with your online marketing plan. The more specific you can be, the more detailed your plan. You may start out with a general goal like "Develop a large, solid base of satisfied customers," but your goal statements should ultimately be much more specific.

Different goals lead to different expectations. To get started, write down every realistic goal that occurs to you. Maybe you want to develop a profitable business from scratch in the online marketplace. Maybe you want to have the first and biggest online yacht brokerage in Canada. Maybe you're going online to increase your mail-order or in-store sales by going after customers with a different medium. Maybe you're trying to improve your credibility with your offline customers by offering an online option. Maybe you just want to gain online experience to prepare for the future.

Each of these goals leads logically to different expectations. If your only goal is to gain experience, you'll probably meet it whether your business succeeds or not. If you want to be the biggest business of your type, you'll have to measure success against your competitors. Set a goal worth reaching for, but not one that creates unrealistic expectations, and leverage your strengths. Compaq didn't set out to sell more personal computers than IBM; it set out to capture the market for portable computers because it had a superior design. It was only after Compaq established its leadership in portable computers that it began to set its sights higher. If you set your sights too high or expect an online presence to deliver value that your products or services don't have, you'll be disappointed.

Focusing your goals

General goals like *bigger, biggest,* or *best* are fine, but it's hard to aim for them because they're difficult to measure. Lots of companies are flopping around in cyberspace because their goals aren't focused enough. One way to make your goals more specific is to relate them to your business as it is today.

Picture your business after a year of online marketing, and come up with a realistic idea of where you think you'll be. Will your online storefront be large enough to support a new employee to take care of it? Will your art gallery in Petaluma develop customers in Europe and Japan who represent 10 percent of your sales? Will your metal-stamping company gain five new accounts among the *Fortune* 1,000 or develop three steady customers in Mexico? These are goals you can shoot for.

If your online marketing plan is only part of your business, think about your goals in terms of their impact on your overall business. How many customers will you gain online? How many new leads per week will your consulting business generate? How will your online sales stack up against sales from your other marketing efforts? How many international customers do you hope to gain online?

If your online marketing attack represents the launch of a whole new business, think about when you'll return your investment. Will your efforts pay for themselves at the end of a year? Six months?

Your income projection

Once you've listed your goals, translate them into dollars and cents. Make a spreadsheet that projects your anticipated monthly income for each month for a year or two following your first attack.

Most online businesses generate little or no income in their first month or two of operation. Don't expect big sales right away. The biggest reason small businesses fail is undercapitalization: they don't have the money to keep running until they start turning a profit. By projecting no sales in the first couple of months, you can plan to have the money on hand to keep going. And if your sales do happen to take off right away, so much the better.

By thinking through your income projections for the first year or two, you'll have a much clearer view of exactly what you hope to achieve. Your experience online will soon tell you whether or not your goals are realistic. If you think carefully when setting goals and do everything you can to achieve them, you may surprise yourself.

ALLOCATING RESOURCES

Your next task is to decide how much money and time you can commit to achieving your goals. If you're already following an offline marketing plan, your online attack is an extension of it. You may be justifiably excited about the possibilities of online marketing, but whatever you do, *don't abandon or compromise your other marketing efforts.* Unless you do all your business or generate all your leads online, think about your online attack as an enhancement of, not a replacement for, what you're doing successfully already.

Think about the different resources you'll need to commit to your online efforts. These resources will be in addition to those you spend offline. You should think about your available resources before you choose the specific battlegrounds, weapons, and tactics you'll use, because you need to be realistic about how much you can commit to your online attack. Time is just as much of a resource as money, and if your online plan is undercapitalized in either area, it will fail. So make some hard-nosed decisions about what you can afford before you commit yourself.

Money

Whether you set up a storefront on the Web or simply get an account on America Online, your efforts will cost some money. Come up with a total figure you can spend to start up your online effort, and then another figure to maintain it each month. Once you have some figures, do your homework and research both startup costs and monthly maintenance costs for various online options. Here are some expenses you may need to consider.

Equipment. If you don't have a computer now, or the one you have can't reasonably be devoted to your online marketing attack, you'll have to buy one. Figure on the cost of the computer, a modem, furniture and space for them, and perhaps a new phone line for dial-up access. (If you're starting a BBS, you'll also need bulletin board software and related equipment.)

Online access. This can include setup charges for an online account and monthly phone and ISP access charges.

An online presence. If you're planning to set up a storefront or purchase advertising space, decide how much you can commit to design, production, placement fees, and maintenance.

Salaries or fees. If you're paying one of your employees to manage your online attack, figure the cost of the time he or she will spend on it. If you'll be using a consultant, include a project fee to get started and then perhaps an hourly or monthly fee for as-needed work later on.

Using the same spreadsheet you created for your income projections, make new categories for each monthly expense, and then divide your total monthly dollar commitment among them as necessary. When you're finished, you'll have a good picture of how you think your business will proceed financially and when you'll begin turning a profit. You'll know in advance just what the online enterprise has cost you every step of the way. You'll also have a yardstick against which to measure your actual results.

Time

Computers are great, but they don't run themselves. It takes time to create an online presence, and time doesn't materialize out of thin air. We wish we had a buck for every software package small-business owners bought and never used because they didn't have the time to learn it. Everyone thinks they'll somehow find the time to do new things, but time is a finite resource, and you can't get more of it without spending less of it on something else.

We'll get into the details of making a calendar later in this chapter, but for now it's important to realize that preparing for and pressing your online attack will require regular attention. Your online store or mailbox will operate twenty-four hours a day, but somebody has to make the online contacts, participate in discussion groups, check for orders in the e-mailbox, or monitor the position of your classified ads in forums. You or one of your employees will have to spend at least some time on these activities every day.

The amount of time you'll need depends on how you attack the online market and how far along you are on the learning curve right now.

- If you're new to computers, plan on spending time every day for a few weeks just getting comfortable with one.
- If you're just learning the ropes of cyberspace, you'll need an hour a day for a month or so to read some of the books recommended in the Appendix.
- If you're exploring your online marketing options, you'll need at least an hour a day to check out the various battlefields, get familiar with the terrain, and decide where and how you'll attack.
- Once you have an idea of how you want to proceed with your plan, you'll have to continue your daily commitment for a few more weeks researching the best options for the attack. You may meet with con-

sultants, review service contracts from ISPs, plan a storefront's design, or prepare your e-mail signature and other marketing materials.

- After you launch your attack, you'll spend from a half an hour to an hour a day maintaining it, and another hour or two per week on top of that keeping up with online developments and exploring further marketing options.

We're not listing all these time expenditures to scare you off, but to make you realize that planning and launching an online marketing attack requires a serious commitment. One of the key strategies for guerrilla marketing online is to build a presence by becoming a regular member of the online communities that represent your target market. The only way to do this is to spend the time it takes to participate in discussion groups, read and send e-mail, and pursue the other strategies in this book. It's not really any different from getting started with an offline business: there's a lot of up-front time and money to be spent before you settle into a profitable and workable schedule.

Look over the time estimates just listed and ask yourself if you or an employee can make this commitment. If the answer is no, change your online marketing plans and reduce your expectations.

BUDGETING YOUR ONLINE TIME

It would be nice if you could simply open a storefront and then watch the business flow in without ever going online again, but your online visibility comes from continuous effort and participation. You should constantly be planning new ways to make your business visible, whether it's scouting out new advertising sites or directories, adding to your Web site, participating in discussions, or planning an online publication or conference.

The best way to remain visible is to go online every day, but that doesn't mean you have to cheat other areas of your business. Set a time commitment you can live with — ten minutes a day, half an hour a day, or whatever — and then tailor your marketing plan to fit within that budget. If you don't have the time to participate in discussion groups right now, maybe you can start with a Web site, an e-mail address, and listings in a few online directories. If you don't have time to design a storefront right away, start with classified ads and an e-mail address.

It's better to start out small and do it well than to make big plans and do them badly. If you have the time and money necessary to pursue your plan to its fullest, you'll find that the results will be worth it.

CHOOSING TARGETS

When you know how much time and money you have to devote to your attack, you can start focusing on the right battlegrounds. Compare your available resources with the resources required to attack on each front, and then make the best match. Each of the battlefields covered in Chapters 4–9 has its own time and cost requirements.

To match your resources with the requirements for battle, list each of the battlefields in one column on a piece of paper, and create two columns to the left for time and money. Then enter your realistic estimates for the resources you'll need for each battlefield. The specific resources you'll need to commit depend on several variables such as your ISP's charges, the number of discussion groups or mailing lists you participate in and how active they are, and the type of Net storefront you have. Here's a quick survey of key battlefields to help get you started, along with some tips for saving money or time with each one.

E-mail

An e-mail address that reaches the entire Net will cost you less than $20 a month. It will require anywhere from a few seconds to an hour or two a day to check your mailbox and read and respond to your mail. If you're doing direct e-mail solicitations, you'll spend time creating the message you send out and compiling the list of addresses to which you send them.

To save time responding to e-mail inquiries, prepare some canned messages in advance so that they can be quickly personalized and sent out when the time comes.

You can save mail-checking time by setting up your mail program to go online and check it automatically several times a day. Then all you have to do is read what comes in: you save the time you'd spend waiting to connect and download mail each time. If you send out a lot of information, a mailbot can handle that chore for you.

Mailing lists

You'll spend from five minutes to half an hour a day reading the traffic from a mailing list and sending appropriate messages of your own when you want to add something to the discussion. If you start your own mailing list and moderate it, you'll spend from an hour to two hours a day evaluating messages for it.

To save time and money with mailing list subscriptions, see if there's a digest option you can use. Some lists let you set a digest option that delivers the list's traffic compiled into one long message, rather than pummeling your mailbox with dozens of separate messages each day.

An online storefront

It will cost anywhere from $100 on up to design and construct an online storefront, depending on whether or not you design and build it yourself, where you locate it, and how elaborate it is. To the basic design and construction costs, add the cost of your time or the salaries or consulting fees of others to prepare the text and graphics you'll want to put in the store, the time you'll spend testing and refining it, and the time you'll spend publicizing and promoting it. Finally, you'll have to spend time checking the store or your e-mail address for orders and processing them.

Classified ads and business directory listings

Classified ads or business directory listings are free in lots of places on the Net. The only other costs are the time you spend locating the ad areas or directories, crafting and posting the ads or directory listings, and spending a few minutes a day checking your e-mail for replies.

Buttons and billboards

These can be free if you agree to host others' Web site buttons on your site in exchange for their hosting your button, but you can also spend up to $100,000 a month for billboards or banners on major online services or high-traffic Web sites. Many Web malls charge by the year and require payment in advance. Add expenses for the design of the button or billboard. Your time investment depends on whether you design the billboard or ad yourself and on what sort of response mechanism the billboard has. If you set it up so people can reply to a mailbot, the only messages you'll have to respond to yourself will be orders.

Forums or newsgroups

You'll spend five to fifteen minutes a day reading and responding to traffic on a typical forum or newsgroup. You may also have to pay long-distance telephone charges to reach some BBSs. If you host your own moderated newsgroup or forum, you'll spend an hour or two a day reading messages and deciding whether or not to post them.

Your own bulletin board

From $5,000 to $20,000 isn't an unreasonable amount to plan for a computer, modems, software, and some design consulting for a two- or four-line BBS. You can do it for less if you figure out everything for yourself, but that will require several extra weeks of your time.

Once the BBS is up and running, you'll spend from an hour a day on up maintaining it, responding to subscriber inquiries, and so on. The most active BBSs need two or more full-time people to maintain them.

Choosing battles you can win

Once you've eliminated battlefield options you can't afford, you'll probably still have several choices. At that point, think about each option and look for the best fit with your product or service. E-mail is an obvious choice, because you'll want an online address where you can be reached. Beyond e-mail, we can divide the battlegrounds into active and passive ones.

Active battlegrounds require your constant attention. These include discussion groups and bulletin boards. Passive battlegrounds hang around in cyberspace delivering your message. These include storefronts, billboards, buttons, sponsorship notices, and classified ads. If you sell a service, the only way to gain customers is to show and tell people about it. You can offer copies of your newsletter or tips on income tax filing on a storefront, but you'll get more visibility and build a reputation more quickly by adding your wisdom to discussion groups. If you sell products, a Web site or online service storefront will give customers a better chance to check them out.

Since you'll have a finite amount of time to devote to online marketing, think hard about where you can spend it most effectively. If you're not good at writing, you may do better by working with a consultant to prepare terrific copy for your classified ad, storefront, or monthly newsletter rather than trying to get your point across in newsgroups or forums.

As you travel through cyberspace, your battlefield reconnaissance will help you decide which battles are the ones you can win. When you've decided, write down the battlefields you plan to attack in the order of their importance.

CHOOSING WEAPONS

With your list of battlefields in hand, it's time to choose the weapons you'll use to attack them. Refer to the list of weapons in Chapter 10 and think ahead to the actual attack and how you'll proceed.

Before you can attack, you'll need some basic tools such as a computer, an online account, and basic training as a cyberspace warrior. Don't forget to plan time to acquire and master these.

Underneath each battlefield, note the guerrilla weapons you'll need for success. If you plan to participate in discussion groups, for example, you'll need a signature ready to go before you do. If you're going to use a storefront, you'll need a design for it, and you'll have to gather the material you want to display. Write down all the weapons you can prepare in advance. You shouldn't have to scramble to create a weapon during the heat of battle. Here are some weapons you should have at the ready:

- your business name
- signatures
- press releases and publicity targets
- information packages you'll mail out on request
- one or more cover letters you'll attach to information you mail out on request
- information you'll publish online
- mailbots
- your company logo
- classified ad copy
- a storefront design
- a catalog
- billboard designs
- a list of target discussion groups
- an order form

As you envision each battle and list the weapons and tactics you'll use, you'll see the battle plan taking shape. Next to each weapon, write down an estimate for the time you'll need to prepare it. Include the basic tools like Internet training and an account. If you find it hard to estimate times, break each weapon down into component tasks like this:

WEAPON	TIME
Internet account	1 week
Internet navigation training	2 weeks
Signatures	3 days
Logo design	2 weeks
Add online info to stationery	3 weeks
Write press release	1 week
Classified ad	3 days
Storefront layout	4 weeks
Storefront contents (text, photos)	3 weeks
Storefront software design	3 weeks
Select target forums/newsgroups	2 weeks
Lurk on forums/newsgroups	2 weeks

When you're finished, you should have a very good idea of how long it will take to prepare each weapon. You'll need this information when you prepare your attack calendar.

MAKING AN ATTACK CALENDAR

Just as a spreadsheet helps you plan your cash flow, a calendar helps you plan your time. Your online marketing attack will have two parts: the preparation phase and the actual attack. The preparation calendar will give you a clear idea of the amount of time per day and the number of weeks it will take you to prepare your attack. It will also help you decide just when to launch your attack. The attack calendar will provide daily marching orders for battle.

Visualizing the attack

By now, your head is spinning with weapons, tactics, strategies, and battlegrounds. Here's how to calm the storm. Think ahead to Day One of your online attack, and visualize what you'd like to have happen on that day. Plan the ultimate launch to your marketing attack, and then prepare accordingly.

Ideally, you'll want every person in your target market to know about

your business and to be curious enough to ask you for more information
or to visit your store. And if your plans succeed, you'll want to be ready
to make sales. How will you make all that happen on Day One? Like the
general of a guerrilla army, you'll have to prepare.

Listing preparation tasks

The preparation phase can be broken down into specific tasks. Make a
list of activities in the following categories.

Basic training. You'll need an online account and an ability to maneuver in cyberspace. Starting today, schedule time to buy a basic
Internet guide and read it, buy a computer and modem and learn how
to use them if necessary, find the right online service or ISP, and get an
account. Train your employees, too.

Reconnaissance. Schedule time to start surfing the Web or an online
service and locating the discussion groups you'll want to join. Find out
how and where to place classified ads, who to contact about pitching a
conference, and how to get listed on the Welcome or What's New
screen. Learn exactly where your battlefields are and how to participate
in them before you launch.

Another part of reconnaissance is locating online business directories
and relevant print magazines. Find out where to send a directory listing
or announcement and how much advance notice they'll need so that
the notice or article appears on your launch date.

Weapons. As you conduct reconnaissance, make some time to prepare the weapons you'll need on the day of the attack. Some of these
can be prepared a day or two before the attack, and others have to be
readied a month or more in advance. For example, to arrange for a
magazine article or directory listings that appear on or near the day of
your attack, you'll have to prepare announcements and listings well in
advance and send them soon enough so that they'll appear when you
want. Magazines like *Internet World* or *Boardwatch* usually need six
weeks' or two months' advance notice if they're to include your announcement in news sections, and they'll need three months or more to
prepare a full-blown article if that's what you're shooting for.

If you're opening a storefront, you'll need to plan its design, layout,
and order form, collect its contents, and get them to your presence
provider or mall operator. You'll need a few days to write classified ads
and prepare e-mail signatures or to set up a mailbot. If you plan to

accept credit cards online and you don't accept them now, you'll need at least two weeks to set up a merchant account.

Drilling for battle. Hone your weapons and sharpen your skills before you launch the attack. Start lurking in newsgroups or forums so you'll know exactly how they operate. Try out your storefront design from different computers, and make sure it works. Test your mailbot or mailing list server. Train your employees to handle online transactions so that they can do it quickly and efficiently.

Making the preparation calendar

Using a weekly or monthly planner (or better yet, a project management program if you have one), start from today and schedule your preparation tasks according to the time you have available. At this point, don't work toward a specific launch date — just schedule out the tasks over a period you think is reasonable, and then see what sort of launch date that leads to.

Rather than choosing general blocks of days or weeks for each part of your preparation, schedule specific tasks for each day. This will help you discipline yourself to get it done. Set up milestones for progress that include deadlines for having certain research completed or weapons finished. If you're working with others on your attack, assign specific responsibilities to each person on the team.

When you're finished, you'll have a detailed calendar of events that spells out what's being prepared when, who's responsible for it, and when each task is due to be completed, as shown on the next page.

June Marketing Tasks

Sunday	Monday	Tuesday	Wednesday	Thursday	Friday	Saturday
				1 Activate Net account (Jeff)	2 Basic Net training (all)	3
4	5 Begin store layout (Jeff & Lisa)	6 Build newsgroup list (Odette)	7 Review store layout (all)	8	9 Store layout due	10
11	12 Assemble Store Contents (Lisa), E-mail Sigs (Jeff)	13	14 Review E-mail Sigs (all)	15	16 Final E-mail Sigs due	17
18	19 Classified Ad #1 (Odette)	20 Prepare news announcement (Lisa)	21	22 Newsgroup list due	23 Begin newsgroup lurking (Jeff)	24
25	26 Classified Ad #1 due	27	28 News announcement due	29	30 Store contents to designer	

When to attack

The beginning of your attack comes at the end of your preparation phase, but setting a specific attack date means striking a delicate balance between readiness and opportunity. If you're like most people who learn about online marketing, you'll probably want to begin your attack as soon as possible. You'll have a target date in mind when you'd like to launch your online presence, and ripeness, as Shakespeare said, is all. If you open your chocolate-oriented Web site just before Valentine's Day, for example, you may cash in on orders for that occasion during your first two weeks in operation. If you're opening a tax information center or promoting your accounting services, January or February would be much better launch times than June or July.

But while a season or event can give you a marketing boost, you can't allow your marketing plan to be driven totally by a deadline. The armies that succeed are the ones that are well prepared, and rushing off into battle for the sake of a deadline will do more harm than good. Many a Web storefront has been mentioned in *Newsweek* or *Internet World* before it was really ready for the attention such announcements brought, and customers ended up frustrated. Don't pull the trigger on your attack before you've seen for yourself that everything you need is up and running.

Your preparation calendar will help you plan a reasonable time frame in which to prepare your attack. If the attack date is crucial, you can juggle the schedule a little or assign more people to the job so that it gets done more quickly, or delay some secondary battle preparations while you concentrate on the main event. Use your calendar as a guide, and it will keep you moving steadily forward.

Scheduling the attack

Starting with Day One of your attack, schedule specific tasks for each day on your calendar. Begin with your attack on the most strategic of the battlefields you've chosen, and plan to spend some time every day maneuvering in that battlefield. Allow a week or two to get used to your attack schedule on the first battlefield before attacking the second most strategic battlefield. If you're using discussion groups, choose the most important one first and establish a presence and a regular schedule of activities there before moving onto the next newsgroup or forum.

The important things about your attack schedule are:

- pressing the attack every day (several times a day if you're checking an e-mailbox or storefront)
- expanding the attack from one battlefield to another in an orderly way

Don't make the mistake of assuming you'll work all these activities into your day or week somehow. If you do, the chances are you won't get them done. Instead, make them a regular part of your day as you would other crucial business activities. Here's a strategy guide to help you schedule activities based on frequency.

Daily: Check your e-mail, storefront, and discussion group activity. Respond the same day to any queries or orders. Mail order confirmations and post discussion-group contributions. Check the positions of classified ads.

Weekly: Check the activity log from your storefront. Review the responses to different classified ads, and modify your ads or choose new targets if necessary. Add news or promotional items to your storefront. Cruise the Net to scout your competition, and look for new battlefields.

Monthly: Read monthly online magazines. Look for publicity angles for your business. Create new information documents (Q&As, arti-

August Attack Schedule

Sunday	Monday	Tuesday	Wednesday	Thursday	Friday	Saturday
		1 **D-Day: AOL ad, mailing list presence**	**2** Check ad position, e-mail, mailing list	**3** Check ad, e-mail, mailing list	**4** Post newsgroup ads, check AOL ad, mailing list	**5** Check ads, e-mail
6 Check ads, e-mail	**7** Check all ads, mailing list	**8** Check all ads, mailing list	**9** AOL forum, check e-mail, new AOL ad	**10** Check all ads, forum, mailing list	**11** Check all ads, forum, mailing list	**12** Check ads, e-mail
13 Check ads, e-mail	**14** Check all ads, forum, mailing list	**15** Post article and announcement, check all	**16** Check all	**17** Check all, prepare forum survey	**18** Review AOL ad results, check all	**19** Check ads, e-mail
20 Check ads, e-mail	**21** Review newsgroup ad results, check all	**22** Post new newsgroup ad, check all	**23** Check all	**24** Post survey on forum	**25** Check all	**26** Check ads, e-mail
27 Check ads, e-mail	**28** Check all	**29** Check all	**30** Check all	**31** Check all		

cles, and so on), publish them, and let others know about them. Locate new media outlets for publicity. Seek out new Web links or directory listings. Search for fusion marketing arrangements. Research newsgroup archives for past comments related to your business.

Quarterly: Run a new promotion for your store. Add a new department to your store. Prepare an informational article or brochure, and e-mail it to your existing customers. Plan a direct-mail campaign.

Your monthly attack schedule should look something like the calendar above.

The first battlegrounds for this attack are a classified ad on America Online and participation in a mailing list. August 1 is D-Day here.

As the month progresses, our attacker maintains the initial attack and expands on new fronts. He checks the position of the AOL classified ad, posts ads in newsgroups that carry them, checks his e-mailbox for responses, begins participating in a forum, uploads an article to the forum library and posts an announcement about it, plans a survey for the forum and then posts the results, and evaluates his ad responses.

The events are spread out so that the attacker becomes comfortable with the first ones before adding others. Eventually, routine matters like checking e-mail or noting the position of a classified ad won't have to appear on the calendar anymore. Notice that the calendar lists active tactics as well as passive ones, such as reviewing the results from the ads on AOL and the newsgroups. And when specific postings are planned (such as the survey on the twenty-fourth), the calendar includes the task of preparing such postings in plenty of time to get them ready (in this case, on the seventeenth).

Prepare a calendar like this for at least the first two months of your online attack, longer if you plan to roll onto major battlefields more gradually. Eventually, you'll use the calendar only for planning new marketing pushes, and all the checking and evaluating will become part of your daily routine.

13

Secrets of a Successful Attack

Guerrillas know that being the best doesn't mean you have to be the biggest. Your online competitors may have more money or more time to buy more weapons or operate on more battlefields than you. But you can still outmaneuver them with superior market savvy, strategy, and tactics.

WHAT CUSTOMERS WANT

Your first mission is to gain the best possible understanding of your online customers. People shop and buy online for different reasons than they buy offline, but most of your competitors don't know that. Many companies take their existing products and marketing strategies and transfer them untouched into cyberspace.

But there are specific reasons shoppers go online. Your attack should leverage these reasons to their fullest potential. Here are some reasons for online shopping that you can turn into competitive advantages for your business.

Safety   Crime is Topic A among many Americans, and the situation isn't likely to change soon. Many people don't feel safe shopping in a crowded mall or department store, especially at night. They'll feel much safer shopping from their PC at home, provided your shopping and buying processes reassure them.

We explained some ways to increase buyer comfort in your online storefront in "Design for buying comfort" on p. 109, but here are some more ways to make cyberspace feel safer for your customers.

- Include your telephone number in your e-mail signature, ad, or storefront information. Most customers feel better talking to someone about their order.
- Say how long you've been doing business. Businesses often use terms like "since 1970" or "established in 1947" to reassure customers about their permanence, and you can do the same online. If you've

been marketing or selling online for more than a year or two, that makes you a cyberspace old-timer as well.

- Offer to provide references from satisfied customers, or include a few testimonial phrases in your marketing information. Mail-order catalogs use testimonials to reassure their customers, and you can, too.

Convenience   It's a lot easier to pull a chair up to the old PC and shop from the den than it is to get in the car, fight traffic, burn up some gas, find a parking space, and plunge into a crowd. Your attack should emphasize this convenience. Remind your customers about the difference. You might even offer a "Winter Driving Safety Special" or a "Fuel Efficiency Special" to emphasize the convenience and economy of shopping at home.

Service   Many people leave stores in shopping malls without buying because they can't find sales help. Holiday times are particularly tough for finding service. Your customers can avoid long checkout lines, crowds, and shopworn merchandise by buying from you. In your storefront, have a department or option labeled *Sales Help* or *May I Help You?* to answer frequent questions. Remind customers that they can order twenty-four hours a day, seven days a week without waiting in line.

Information   Even if they can find sales help, most consumers don't find the salespeople in stores to be knowledgeable enough. Today's superstores that sell so many different types of products make it even tougher to find someone who really knows their stuff. Information can be your key advantage in the online marketplace, so make sure you use it. A store salesperson would have to hunt for the product's brochure, and catalog salespeople don't always have a lot of information about their products. You can satisfy even the most research-minded consumer by providing all the information anyone could want about your products. AutoVantage Online, the online car-buying service, offers used-car pricing information as well as detailed new-car prices. AutoVantage customers can get pricing information in seconds without having to endure a sales pitch.

In a storefront or online catalog, post the prices, model numbers, size, weight, color, and other specifications of everything you sell. Organize information into logical departments like *Color Choices, Specifications,* and *Purchase Options* so that customers don't have to hunt for the information they need. Include collateral information like product reviews, user tips, and Q&A sheets. If you're marketing from an e-mail address, offer to send free information about your products, or reports or guides about your service. This kind of information is difficult or impossible to get quickly outside of cyberspace.

Price   Your online presence has the lowest overhead in the business world. Pass some of the savings on to your customers, and make sure they know you're doing it. Offer discounts for online orders, or set up a sales club for regular customers that gives them an extra 5 or 10 percent off all online orders. The Shoppers' Advantage service on CompuServe and America Online promotes savings of 10 to 50 percent for shopping online. AutoVantage Online offers big discounts on car sales and leases. Offering a lower price is a powerful incentive that helps overcome any discomfort customers have when buying online.

ORGANIZE FOR BATTLE

Every trip through the online marketplace brings an assault of information. Names, addresses, and ideas fly at you wherever you go. E-mail messages and addresses, newsgroup postings, server and document addresses, appear on the screen one minute and are gone the next. Unless you make an effort to capture and organize this information, you'll spend a lot of time backtracking to recall it later. That reference to a directory of consultants that you suddenly want to locate will be buried among hundreds of newsgroup postings, and you'll have to dig through them to find it. The article you posted to several forums now needs to be updated, but you can't remember all the places where you posted it. You'll save yourself a lot of time and frustration if you know exactly how to lay your hands on anything you've read or published in the past. Here are some things to organize.

Discussion group messages   People have a way of mentioning other Web sites, articles, directories, or consultants that you may need in the future, but you'll never remember how to find them if you don't save the information when you first see it. Copy and save any interesting messages. Either copy the whole message into a word processing document or copy the important information out of the message and into a file on your disk. Set up a series of word processing documents that categorize information with names like Web sites, Directories, Consultants, and Reports, and then copy whole messages into them. Or use a database program to clip and save important references in different categories.

E-mail messages   Create a series of directories or separate mailboxes in which to store incoming mail. Like a stack of organizer trays on your physical desk, these will help you retain and organize messages according to content. Use one mailbox to store messages that need an immediate response (and then respond to them as soon as you're done collecting your mail). Use another mailbox to store messages you'll follow up on later. Create individual mailboxes or directories for replies to different newsgroup postings you made. If you conduct a survey, for example, store the replies in a mailbox called Survey Replies.

An electronic Rolodex   Starting from Day One, build a database file of online contacts. These are the people you contact or who contact you each day. In each database record, list the person's name, company name, e-mail or URL address, and a note about who they are and why they're important. Every contact is a potential customer or source of valuable information, and it's easy to forget these contacts as they float by in the cyberstream. If you don't want to set up a special database file by yourself, there are several different "contact manager" programs such as Sidekick, ACT, and Now Contact that are already set up specifically for information like this.

Activity logs   Whenever you put up information online, whether it's a newsgroup posting, a classified ad, an uploaded file in a forum library, or a catalog on your storefront, keep a record of what it is, where you posted it, and when you posted it. It's easy to publish a document in several different places on the Net and then forget where you put it. Then when the document needs to be revised or replaced, you can't remember exactly where all the copies are.

Bookmarks, group lists, and hot lists   When you find a particularly useful newsgroup, forum, Web site, or other online location, use your search utility or browsing software to add it to a list of favorite places. Every online service lets you create a list of favorite places. Every Web browser has a hot-list or bookmark function where you can store URLs for Web sites you visit frequently. Newsreader software lets you create a custom list of groups you like reading. Search utilities like Veronica, Archie, and Anarchie let you store addresses of favorite resources. When you visit a site that looks interesting, add it to your list so that you can return to it easily later.

When you're in doubt about whether a reference is worth saving, save it anyway. It's better to save too much and end up with a lot of stuff you don't need than it is to consign one important piece of information to the vast darkness of cyberspace. You can always do a semiannual

housecleaning on your hard disk to get rid of information you really
don't need.

FOLLOW UP RIGHT AWAY

It's easy to get caught up in the hustle and bustle of online activity,
flitting from one discussion group to another and prowling the Web.
References to new sites, ideas for new marketing arenas, and thoughts
about an ongoing discussion and other visions dance through our heads
in an unceasing chorus line. But if you let such visions dance out of
view, they may be gone forever. Act on your impulses as quickly as
you can.

Check out new resources. When someone mentions a new Net
resource or Web site and it sounds interesting, check it out right away,
before you log off for the day.

Respond to discussion group postings. Hardly a day will go by when
you don't have an idea or comment about something you read in one of
the newsgroups you're following. But unless you respond immediately,
the moment is lost and the opportunity is missed. If you don't respond to
a message within a day or two, the discussion has moved on to another
topic and your point falls on deaf ears. If you have something useful to
say, say it that day.

Follow up with prospects. It's incredible that people with e-mail
addresses take days or weeks to respond to queries, but they do. Service separates the pros from the amateurs, so make sure you're iden-
tified with the pros. A prospect looking for information may ask several
sources. If you get that information out the fastest or if you're the only
one who sends it, you're the one who will get the business. Use mailbots
whenever possible, and follow up within an hour of any specific request
for information that you receive via e-mail or your storefront.

Follow up after the sale. Make a sale and you make a sale. Establish
a relationship and you're well on your way to repeat business and a lot
of referrals. Your follow-up should include a thank you, and you can
sweeten it by offering some helpful information about the product or
service. If you sell a bracelet through your jewelry store, follow up via
e-mail with a thank-you note and some advice about cleaning it.

Thank people for references. If you get a referral from anyone else,
be sure to send a thank-you note via e-mail. An honest appreciation for
favors past may lead to more favors in the future.

STAY CONNECTED ON THE ROAD

Everyone travels or goes on vacation now and then, but you won't want to make potential customers wait for replies until you return. If you're going on vacation, arrange for someone else to monitor your online business. At the very least, you can have someone send out a message that says you're away and will return on a specific day. This way, prospects won't think their e-mail wasn't delivered or is being ignored.

If you travel on business, invest in a laptop computer that will allow you to check your e-mail on the road. You can buy a used laptop that will do the job for well under $1,000, and if you travel a lot, the investment will be worth it. If you travel only occasionally, have an employee or friend check your e-mail and relay messages to you via fax or phone.

INVOLVE THE CUSTOMER

It's so easy to flit through cyberspace that it takes an extra effort to build customer relationships. Yet relationships are what lead to sales, repeat sales, and profits. You build relationships by:

- giving customers an emotional stake in your business (arousing curiosity, empathy, or excitement)
- multiplying the number of times they contact you
- increasing the quality of each contact

The following are some proven ways to build customer involvement.

Contests

If you run a contest with a good prize, people will want to find out if they've won. When you launch a new product or service, run a contest to choose a name for it. Give one of the newly named products away to the winner. You can even combine a contest with a survey, soliciting names for the product first and then posting a survey to choose the best one. Give each voter an incentive to participate by offering a small discount or a giveaway item such as a tip sheet or a buyer's guide.

Contests get people involved with your business, and they also increase your visibility. If you run the contest on an online service or BBS, you'll be able to announce it on the What's New list. If the contest is wild enough, it might even make the Welcome screen or a magazine column devoted to online happenings.

Limited offers

Offer something extra to the first ten, twenty, or fifty people who respond to your e-mail message or visit your storefront. It's easy enough to count responses by monitoring the server log or by just counting the replies in your mailbox. Holding a race to see who can respond first will make visiting your business a higher priority for online browsers.

Teasers

Instead of spilling all the beans about your product or service in a newsgroup posting, billboard, or classified ad, tell just enough of the story to get prospects interested in knowing more. PR companies and marketing departments frequently do this sort of thing before trade shows. They know their exhibition booth will be competing for attention with hundreds of other booths, so they get people involved by whetting their curiosity, curiosity that can be satisfied only by a visit to the booth.

Members of discussion groups love getting the inside story. In the weeks before a MacWorld computer show a few years ago, one computer company teased readers on a CompuServe forum by telling them about some of its new Macintosh PowerBook products. The company hinted that it had one revolutionary product that would be unveiled only at the show. The booth was jammed.

The trick to doing this online is to offer just enough information. Give too little information and readers won't be curious; give too much and you won't get a chance to explain further. The makeup of your teaser depends a lot on the product or service you're offering.

If you're offering a service, get people involved with teaser notices like this:

> You're paying too much income tax, and we can prove it. Send for our free tax guide.

People love to get something for nothing, and your brochure or demo lets you show exactly what you can do.

If you're selling a product, the teaser might explain what problem the product solves, or what benefits it provides, without saying what the product is. Apple Computer's first ads for the Macintosh were about breaking the bonds of conformity, not about computers. People flocked to Apple dealers to see what the machine actually looked like. Television ads featuring rocks and trees drove auto buyers into Infiniti show-rooms to see the actual car when the line was introduced.

Discussions

Each person visiting your storefront is alone, unless you can show them that other people visit the site as well. Many sites feature hit counters that show the number of accesses made to the site during the current week or month, but numbers are just numbers. However, if you provide a space on your storefront for one or more discussions about your products or services, you'll have proof that others visit your site.

Discussion areas give customers a place to ask questions, to interact with other customers, and to learn. Some of your visitors will develop relationships with others that bring them back to the site regularly, and even casual visitors will see that others find your site interesting enough to congregate there.

Change histories

Set up a department in your storefront that details the history of the site and lists the changes you've made. This immediately shows customers that you're working hard to keep the site fresh, but it also gives you a chance to acknowledge the contributions of others. If you solicit suggestions about your site in a survey (see "Surveys" on p. 258) and then make changes based on them, list each change with the name of the person who suggested it. This gives your visitors an ownership stake in your site that they just can't get in other ways.

Mailing list subscriptions

E-mail is the best way to maintain an ongoing relationship with your customers, but sending unsolicited e-mail is a good way to generate flames and lose your online account. If just one person complains to your ISP about an unsolicited e-mailing, you'll be warned that further complaints will cost you your access. Do it again and you'll be hunting for a new ISP.

But that doesn't mean you can't build a mailing list. You just have to convince people that you'll be sending out information worth having, and then get their permission to send it. When you mention your newsletter, article series, directory, or other publication in a discussion group posting, tell people how they can subscribe and how often they'll receive mailings. Most people don't want their mailbox stuffed with product announcement messages every day, but they don't mind receiving a mailing once a month or so. Your listing of new yachts for sale, reviews of hot new books, or a list of quarterly investment tips may find a welcome audience, and it gives you a way to establish ongoing contact with your market. (But don't forget: offer to remove people from your mailing list if they don't find the information useful.)

If you have a storefront, include an option to subscribe to your mailing list on your home page, and then explain the frequency and content of the mailings at the top of the subscription form.

Surveys

Newspapers survey their readers periodically about which features they like or don't like. Manufacturers ask all sorts of questions on their mail-in warranty cards. People love to give their opinions, so ask them about your business. Lots of successful Web sites include customer surveys.

Introduce the survey by explaining that you're going to make some changes or additions to your product line or services. This way, people know something new is in the works. Explain what you're doing now, and invite people to check out your storefront. Ask people for advice about your approach, or for suggestions about new products or services they'd like to see, or for changes to the design of your store. If you have some changes in mind, mention them and ask people what they think.

At the end of the survey, announce when the results will appear. Offer to send them via e-mail to anyone who requests them, and post them on your storefront. And when you send the results, mention how you used them to change your business. People will want to see the changes for themselves.

If you're posting your survey to a discussion group, follow these guidelines.

- Announce who you are, why you're taking the survey, where else you're doing the survey (if you're posting it to several groups), how you'll use the results, and when you'll post the results. Running a blind survey makes people suspicious and cuts down your response rate, so reassure them that you're not simply trolling for e-mail addresses to be used in a spam attack.
- Post the survey results promptly. Comment on the results and invite others to comment. This holds up your end of the survey bargain and also keeps the group involved in your business.

- Explain which of the changes you've made to your business.
- Thank everyone for participating.

EXPAND YOUR STRENGTHS AND CUT YOUR LOSSES

Time, money, and bandwidth are finite. Make the most of yours. Come up with a reasonable testing period for each battlefield you attack, and then evaluate it regularly. If you've given a particular battlefield a shot and it's not producing results, then devote that part of your resource budget to another one. Here are some guidelines for what's reasonable for each of the main battlefields.

Classified ads   Try a classified ad for a week or two and see what happens. If it doesn't ring any bells, try a different ad or a different location. If you spend fifteen minutes a day checking classified ads that aren't bringing in queries or customers, that's fifteen minutes you might be better off spending in a discussion group.

Discussion groups   Spend at least a month actively participating in a discussion group. We'll be surprised if you don't generate at least a few leads this way. In evaluating a discussion group, factor in the information it provides as well as customer leads. For example, joining a marketing-related mailing list may not bring you any customers for your online shoe store, but it's a treasure trove of marketing war stories and news about online marketing technology.

Storefronts   When you commit to setting up a storefront, commit for a year. The work you'll put in to establish the server deserves a chance to be rewarded. Many storefronts report initial spurts of interest followed by a drop-off. Use promotions, new information, and other weapons to revive interest.

Publications   If you decide to publish a newsletter, give it time to build readers. Figure at least a year to develop a loyal subscriber base. Even if you never develop a base, distributing the newsletter and announcing it give your business good exposure. You may end up keeping the publication just as a reason to keep putting your name out there.

DON'T OVERLOOK THE BASICS

It's easy to get carried away by the potential of online computing. Computers are pretty reliable, so we assume that once we set things up on a computer, they'll continue to work flawlessly forever after. The online world can also be so absorbing that we can start overlooking other basic aspects of our business. We end up chasing the techno-butterfly that might bring us profits instead of focusing on tried-and-true ways to success. Don't let this happen to you.

Check your weapons. There's a big difference between using weapons and using them well. Is your mailbot working? Could you be using it to distribute three different information kits instead of one? Remember, mailbots can respond to different e-mail messages by sending out different files, so you can use one mailbot to respond to different groups of prospects.

Are your e-mail messages and signature formatted so that they look good on any screen? The most carefully designed signature may turn into garbage on certain screens, and most people find it annoying to have to reformat messages to read them easily.

Are your discussion group postings generating positive responses from others? If you're not adding useful, provocative posts to a discussion group, your reputation is headed in the wrong direction. It's okay to be controversial, but if everyone else on the group vehemently disagrees with your message, you can quickly get a reputation as an unproductive member of the discussion.

Is access to your storefront fast and reliable? Is your order form clear enough so that orders can be processed without delay? You can set up a great storefront, but if people can't reach it or one of its features isn't working, it can be doing you more harm than good.

Maintain your other marketing efforts. Don't let your online marketing attack interfere with your other marketing efforts. If you're using your fax machine's telephone line to access the Internet, you may be reducing access for customers who want to fax orders to you. If your best receptionist or telephone operator is busy answering e-mail, you're no longer putting your best foot forward on the phone. Think carefully about which of your resources can best be deployed in each portion of your overall marketing plan.

Back up your data. This is a chore most computer users hate, but it's vital. The addresses, messages, hot lists, and other data you gather during your online attack are as valuable to you as the customer list in your filing cabinet. And don't think that having printouts of your records gives you an adequate margin of safety — imagine what it would be like to have to type all that data back into your PC. Back up your computer's disk to save not only your data, but the software you use to go online. If you don't, a disk failure will force you to install and set up your software all over again and rebuild your contact database. All disks fail eventually, and such a failure can derail your attack for weeks or months if you're not prepared.

Your marketing attack will take guts, grit, savvy, and determination, but if you're willing to use these traits you will succeed. You'll be helped in your initial attack by the excitement of striking out onto new battlefields. But as the attack wears on, you'll need to maintain the momentum. In the next chapter, we'll see how to keep the ball rolling.

14

Sustaining the Attack

You'll spend a lot of time and energy preparing your initial salvos into the online marketplace. The first days of your attack will be charged with excitement and anticipation. You'll probably be rewarded for these efforts with a lot of attention at first as your fellow cybernauts get to know you and your business. But as the weeks go on, the surge of attention may subside.

At this point, you'll realize that online marketing requires the same patient and persistent effort to bring sales that offline marketing requires. Cyberspace isn't a magical cure for all your sales ills, and it can be discouraging when that reality strikes. You may become a less frequent visitor to the newsgroup that you once prowled daily. You may spend less time surfing the Net for new opportunities and ideas or thinking of ways to spruce up your storefront.

Apathy is a dangerous thing in any marketing effort, but it's especially dangerous in cyberspace. When you have a physical store, a print advertising campaign, or a mail-order catalog, you can get away with a little apathy now and then. On those days when you're feeling lazy, your storefront, ad, or catalog are still out there carrying some of the marketing load. But apathy online means that your classified ads lose their positions on forums, you drop from sight in your target discussion groups, and your storefront loses its appeal. In short, the presence you worked so hard to create begins to crumble like a sand castle at high tide.

In the online marketplace, you have to keep up your marketing attack, day in and day out. Your attack must continually build your online presence and draw customers to your business. Maintaining your online presence requires two things: keeping your key messages in front of your online market and maintaining your enthusiasm.

You won't be able to accomplish the first objective if you lose your zeal for cyberspace, so let's attack the apathy front first.

MAINTAINING YOUR ENTHUSIASM

Probably the hardest part about maintaining your attack is retaining that initial excitement and enthusiasm for your online efforts. As you settle into a routine of posting messages, checking mail, and monitoring your storefront, the new and exciting quickly becomes ordinary. But success over the long haul means keeping your key messages in the marketplace, continually searching for new markets, and finding new approaches to existing markets. And doing these things requires you to remain enthusiastic and committed to your marketing attack. Here's how to keep up your excitement level.

Tune in to online news

Apathy comes from hopelessness. Hope comes from new ideas. Every day in cyberspace brings exposure to new businesses, new discussion groups and conferences, and new ideas for marketing online. But you won't know about any of these unless you tune in to a source of news for your online market.

- If you're marketing primarily on an online service, check the What's New area every day, and follow up on new stores, promotions, services, and conferences.
- Subscribe to at least one marketing-oriented mailing list so that you'll see new ideas every day or two. Even if you're marketing primarily via one of the online services or a BBS, you'll get new ideas about improving your presence from knowing what people are doing throughout cyberspace.
- Check out the Guerrilla Marketing Online Web site for the latest marketing news, secrets, and war stories.

To stay focused on marketing, stay in touch with a source of marketing ideas. You can subscribe to a daily marketing tip via the Guerrilla Marketing Online Web site, and there are dozens of other marketing-related discussions happening online. These discussions are often where the online marketing pros hang out. You'll always find a lively discussion going on about the best ways to get your messages across and attract customers.

Attend online conferences

On online services, you'll find regular conferences about online marketing-related topics. Make a habit of attending these conferences, if only to lurk and see what kinds of questions and answers are being offered. Attending conferences will make you comfortable with the online chat procedure and will lower one of the barriers to proposing conferences of your own. It will also give you ideas about how to improve your marketing efforts.

Read all about it

Subscribe to one major online magazine or newspaper and read it. Publications like *Internet World, Boardwatch,* and *NetGuide* aren't the most up-to-date sources of news, but they do offer in-depth coverage of online services, new sales tools or information resources, and general trends in the evolution of cyberspace. You'll learn about new Web browsers, new ways to protect credit card information online, and what's going on with America Online, CompuServe, and other services. By the time you read this, there may be a monthly or even weekly print publication devoted specifically to online marketing and sales. Every issue will give you new techniques to try and resources to check out.

Business or marketing publications give you a broader view of how online activities fit into the overall picture for other businesses. Magazines like *Adweek* or *Sales & Marketing Management* cover online advertising and marketing trends. *Adweek* occasionally does special reports about online advertising and how some of the country's largest ad agencies are planning campaigns for today's Net and tomorrow's interactive television. Reports like this show you how the pros are attacking the online market.

Publications like the *Wall Street Journal, Business Week, Fortune, Barron's, Forbes, Inc,* and *ASAP* regularly tell you how America's most successful companies are jockeying for position in the online market. They report on mergers and strategic alliances between telephone companies, cable TV companies, and other firms that are shaping the future of cyberspace. The *Wall Street Journal* has been staying on top of the strategic plans of online movers and shakers like Netscape, Microsoft, and America Online. *Business Week* also does regular reports on online commerce, and *Newsweek*'s Cyberscope column covers online events.

Computer magazines are another information frontier to explore.

Cruise your local newsstand every month, and browse major magazines like *PC Computing, MacWorld,* and *Computer Shopper.* You can skim through these and zero in on articles about modems, communications software, and the Internet.

Whether or not you find something you can use in every issue of every magazine you read, you'll be staying on top of a changing landscape. Guerrillas know that understanding changing weapons and battlefields and taking advantage of them is the path to continuing victory.

KEEPING YOUR MESSAGES IN THE MARKETPLACE

The pace of change in the online market makes it a challenge to continue your attack. You must promote your identity with a consistent set of key messages you developed when you made your online marketing plan. But you also have to find new ways to package those messages so that they don't grow stale. It's like consumer products marketing. Soap and cereal haven't changed all that much over the past few years, but marketers are constantly changing their packaging. Storekeepers shift the same products into new displays to maintain buyer interest. Those boxes of Cheerios that sat on a low shelf for weeks suddenly begin flying out the door when piled in a pyramid at the end of an aisle. Sales of Tide jump a little every time Procter & Gamble changes the box.

In cyberspace, your soap and cereal is the information you post about your business. Whether it's a discussion group message, a classified ad, a storefront, or a billboard, every bit of information you put out is an ad for your business. But information grows stale much more quickly in cyberspace than it does in print, so you have to keep changing the package. When you run the same ad once a week in your local newspaper and keep it up for three or six months, your consistency promotes an image of stability. Try the same thing in cyberspace and netizens will wonder if you're still in business.

The key to maintaining your identity is to find new packages and locations for your messages and products without changing your basic pitch. Here are three strategies.

- Repackage your messages to maintain your visibility with the same audience without boring them.
- Repackage your products to penetrate new markets.
- Find new locations for your messages to expand your market.

REPETITION, REPETITION

Anybody can get a little visibility by posting one message on a screen where others see it, but real visibility is share of mind, not just a share of a particular screen.

The only way to get share of mind is to repeat your message in as many places and as many ways as possible. Most people have to see a message nearly two dozen times before they act on it, so build repetition into your plans for online visibility.

Repackaging your message

When you're putting your messages before the same audience again and again, you need to find creative ways to keep the readers' attention. Like a diamond whose facets reflect light in hundreds of ways, your basic message can be refocused to renew interest. All you have to do is turn the jewel a little. The trick is to think about your product's various features and benefits and turn each one into a message that enhances your basic theme.

Tide has had the same basic package design for decades. That familiar orange box is such a fixture in the detergent section at the market that Procter & Gamble would be nuts to abandon it. But while people want the familiarity of Tide, they don't want to feel they're being left in the dark ages of detergent technology. So Procter & Gamble continually freshens the box's appearance by changing its size or shape, putting new banners on the front, or promoting new benefits. Tide's fundamental message is that it cleans clothes better than other brands, but the brand's managers have found hundreds of ways to say that over the years so that the product remains a best-seller. A hundred years ago, dirt was dirt and soap was soap. Thanks to Tide and other detergents, we now have ground-in dirt, greasy dirt, dozens of different stains, and an army of enzymes and other cleaning agents with which to fight them.

You can do the same thing with your online product or service. Suppose your product is a book about vacationing in New Zealand. Your basic message is that your book is the ultimate guide to travel in New Zealand. You participate in the rec.travel newsgroup as a means of promoting the book. In that one newsgroup, you could post separate messages oriented around travel costs, the South Pacific, long air flights, aboriginal cultures, forgotten outposts of the British Empire, vacations in the Southern Hemisphere, and exotic destinations where people speak English. You're still selling the same book, but you're pitching its many benefits in different ways.

One sure way to repackage your message is to align it with a current event. Every day, the newspapers carry at least one story related to your business, and your opinions about the subject make a suitable topic for discussion. If you're an investment counselor, rising interest rates give you an ongoing topic against which to frame your message about maintaining investment value over time. If you're selling during a Presidential election or the summer Olympics, find a way to tap into the high visibility of these events by linking your company with them in some way. By following the news regularly, you'll have an unending source of discussion topics that can give you fresh entrees into your discussion group.

Freshly packaged messages work in an online storefront, too. Your tip of the day or week can change. You can offer a specific feature like news updates or the latest tips on using your product that keeps people coming back. You can even run topic-related specials. A report on rising auto thefts leads naturally to a Crime Buster Special on auto alarm systems. A news item about proposed cuts in Social Security leads naturally to a pitch for investment services.

Don't forget your existing customers, either. Even though customers know your business and what it can do for them, they need to be reminded that you're still around. Stay in touch with a quarterly e-mailing. Send out tip sheets or news updates related to a topic in the media. Send out e-mail greetings for holidays. Every message helps to maintain your visibility.

The lesson for online guerrillas is clear. Once you've worked hard to establish your online presence with a key message, build on it through repackaging.

Tailoring your product for new markets

While you're refocusing your message to maintain visibility and excitement within one market, think about repackaging your product for new markets. Dave Asprey of the West American T-Shirt Company had been wholesaling custom T-shirts to local stores and street vendors in San Diego for four months when he decided to go online. He came up with a great T-shirt for coffee drinkers and posted a notice about it on the alt.drugs.caffeine newsgroup.

Dave got more orders for that shirt in two months than he'd had for all his other shirts in six months of offline marketing efforts, so he expanded from there. His T-shirt line now includes creating custom shirts for other newsgroups.

Dave is lucky to be selling a product that can quickly be changed to suit different markets, but no matter what your business, you can find ways to expand your market by creatively tailoring your product to suit it. Again, think of the different benefits your product or service offers, and you'll see how it can serve different markets. With thousands of discussion groups and forums in cyberspace, you can target many different market segments.

Suppose you have a book about exercise. You might start out by joining a forum on health and fitness, but you could expand into specific forums on various forms of exercise or various sports. Last time we looked, there were dozens of Usenet newsgroups on different sports, including scuba, skiing, skydiving, skating, golf, and triathlon. Athletes of all kinds need to maintain their strength through exercise, so your book can help all of them.

To help jog your thinking about new markets, save a copy of the Usenet newsgroup list from your newsreader, or consult a directory like Harley Hahn and Rick Stout's *The Internet Yellow Pages*. Browse the selection of forums on your online service. Check out lists of BBSs in *Boardwatch*. You'll see dozens of new markets you can attack.

Seeking new locations

Even if you have just one product, one key message, and one key market, you can still increase your visibility by finding new places to post your message.

- If you have an online storefront, look for new directories and Web sites where you can list your business. And don't just think about national Web directories like Yahoo; consider local or regional directories maintained by smaller ISPs. If you don't have a link on as many of those directory pages as possible, you're missing lots of customers.
- Whatever your business, develop a publicity angle for it and seek media targets where you can pitch it. *CompuServe* magazine does articles about its online merchants, services, and subscribers in every issue. *Internet World* and other online magazines have news sections

and columns that announce new businesses. *(See Chapter 16 for more on publicity campaigns.)*

- If you're planning a conference, leverage your effort by changing the title and focusing on two or three markets instead of one. Your conference on low-cost remodeling will probably be welcome on several home improvement forums on different BBSs and online services. All you have to do is find them and target them with your pitch. You can also speak at industry conferences and trade shows to build your reputation.

WHY YOU SHOULD MAINTAIN THE ATTACK

We've said that it takes visibility to market your products online, and it takes constant effort to maintain constant visibility. Here are some more reasons why it's important to maintain your attack.

The market is growing.   One estimate is that one way or another, everyone in the country will be online by the year 2003. Even if you don't believe that, you can't deny that the market is growing. And now that there are set-top boxes like Philips' WebTV that offer Net access to non-PC owners, growth should accelerate. Don't give up just as the market is maturing.

The market is changing.   Within the next five years, new technologies like interactive television will expand your opportunities for online marketing. You won't be able to exploit these new weapons and battlegrounds unless you stay in the fight.

Your competition is growing.   Although serious online marketing has been going on for at least ten years now, we're only at the beginning of the curve. Web-based advertising is expected to increase an order of magnitude, from about $200 million in 1996 to more than $2 billion by the year 2000. Most of your competitors are still holding off on their serious online marketing efforts, but things are going to become much more competitive than they are now. Your continuing efforts will help keep you ahead of the pack.

People forget.   Information seen online one day is forgotten the next, so it's important to keep putting your messages out there to remind everyone. In just one online journey, a typical netizen comes across hundreds of pieces of information. The only way that netizen will remember yours is by seeing it every day or two.

It's a good way to keep your existing customers. Even if all your customers are satisfied, they'll forget about you if you don't stay in touch. Make sure they know you're alive and well by maintaining your presence.

You've made an investment. Any effort and money you put into launching your attack is an investment. Continue your marketing effort and it will pay off; stop your efforts and you've lost it. Most online businesses report that it takes at least three months to start making consistent sales. Don't quit before your efforts have a chance to work.

With the right attitude, the right weapons, the right battlefields, and a little guerrilla creativity, you can sustain your attack indefinitely. In the next chapter, we'll see how you can use online resources to improve your other marketing efforts.

15

Using Online Information

Cyberspace is a great place to spread the word about your business, but it's also the world's largest library. With a little time, you can get the same competitive information that major corporations pay big bucks for without spending a dime. In some cases you'll spend a few dollars to access commercial databases, but in every case the information you'll gain can mean a lot to your bottom line. You'll discover new international markets or suppliers, spot the latest business or economic trends, and find out what customers are saying about you or your competition. And because you're a guerrilla, you'll be able to act on that information much more quickly than your larger competitors.

In this chapter, you'll learn how to tap the power of online information. We'll classify some different types of information and show you how to zero in on them. We'll see how to use Internet navigation and search tools to find information. And we'll get a sampling of just what's out there in cyberspace. The amount of information is so vast that we can only scratch the surface here, but you'll learn enough to discover more for yourself.

CLASSIFYING ONLINE INFORMATION

Unless you're playing a game online, everything you see on your screen is information. That's part of the problem when it comes to finding what you want. There's so much information that it takes some digging to locate any of it. Here are four broad classes of information that will help your business:

- reports and statistics that help you understand markets or trends
- customer and supplier contacts that expand your market or lower your costs
- inside intelligence and market insights about your competitors, your associates, and your own company

- professional advice about marketing, finance, taxes, law, management, and other areas of business

First, we'll look at each category in general. Then we'll see exactly how and where to locate the information you need.

Reports and statistics

Reports and statistics help you spot likely markets and learn more about your competitors. There are thousands of reports from government agencies, statistics compiled by government and private bureaus, and articles that help you understand everything from export laws to crop conditions.

Looking for the best place to test-market your new fruit drink? Check out the Department of Agriculture's database of economic and consumer statistics, and see which state consumes the most fruit juice. Thinking about exporting personal computers to Albania? Find out about regulations and tax laws from the Department of Commerce's report on international business practices.

You'll find information like this in each of the major galaxies of cyberspace: the Internet, online services, and BBSs. Here's a rundown.

The Internet. Of the three information galaxies, the Net offers the most data, and all of it is available for free. It's also the only place where you'll find research studies and reports from many educational and scientific institutions. Here's a sample of what you'll find:

- directories of consultants
- trademarks and patents
- SEC filings
- census figures
- international status reports
- Internet names and addresses
- crime statistics
- federal and international laws
- government reports and publications
- zip codes
- economic and agricultural statistics
- results of public opinion polls
- export guidelines

VALIDATING ONLINE INFORMATION

Anyone can publish anything on the Web or in a library on an online service or BBS. So along with research statistics and government reports, you'll find lots of personal opinions or statistics gathered from very small samples. The fact that something has been published, on the Web or on paper, tends to give it credibility that it doesn't necessarily deserve. Anyone can set up a site and call it the Web's Primary Source of Demographic Information, for example, but their saying so doesn't make it true. Nor does it make the demographic information contained in such a site any more accurate or useful than demographic information you may get from other sources.

The best way to determine the validity of information you receive from any source is to cross-check it with other sources. If one source says Web advertisers are paying $50 per thousand impressions for a typical banner ad, that's interesting; but if three sources say the same thing, it's probably true. Always try to get information on a subject from as many different online sources as you can.

- Small Business Administration industry profiles
- demographics

The list goes on and on.

Online services. America Online, CompuServe, Prodigy, and other commercial services all have selections of information databases. Here are some examples:

- abstracts from more than 50,000 publications
- company and industry reports from major brokerage houses and research firms
- archives from major international newspapers
- a directory of 80 million telephone numbers in the United States
- a listing of all books currently in print
- financial information on European and international companies
- current and historic stock and mutual fund prices
- legal articles

Along with the online services just listed, there are online services geared for specific businesses and professions. Lexis is a database of law citations and legal articles. Specialized services like this offer more detailed selections of data for higher subscription fees.

To access a research database on a major online service like Com-

CHECK BEFORE YOU BUY

Before you spend good money to obtain information online, make sure the same information isn't available for free somewhere else. The popularity of the Net and the growth of the Web in particular have made available information for free to today's cybernauts that very recently cost money to obtain. For example, data services still offer accounts for $35 per month or 50 cents per minute that deliver stock quotations, but you can get stock quotations with a 15-minute delay for free from several sites on the Web (www.nasdaq.com, for one).

So before you sign up for a fee-based information service, search the Web for the same information and see what you come up with. You may not get exactly the same information, or it may not be updated as frequently, but it may serve your purposes just as well.

puServe, you'll usually pay an extra $20 an hour or so. For a service like Lexis or Mead Data Central you can spend up to $200 an hour. The extra money buys you extra information. Commercial services have proprietary databases you won't find on the Net, like 10K filings and corporate credit reports. They're also easier to search through.

BBSs. Government agencies like the Food and Drug Administration sponsor their own BBS systems and distribute reports and statistics through them, although most agencies have now converted these to Web sites.

Customer and supplier contacts

The online marketplace is an international one, and you can find low-cost suppliers or new markets in foreign countries if you know where to look. Business-to-business contacts are fewer and farther between than individual customer sales, but even one contact can mean more to your bottom line than dozens of single customers.

A furniture designer in Houston, Texas, uses CompuServe's International Trade Forum to find overseas manufacturers for her products. Her lower production costs mean higher profits. An electronics distributor found new customers in Europe, Asia, and Mexico by downloading inquiries from the same CompuServe forum. He wins only one bid in fifty, but each contract is large enough to make the effort worthwhile. His international contacts revived his sales during the last recession, and now they represent most of his business.

Among the major online services, CompuServe and America Online have the best selection of business-to-business forums. On the Net, business- or industry-focused discussion groups are the best places to find suppliers and customers. Sales and marketing discussion groups on the Net frequently carry messages from overseas buyers or sellers looking for North American contacts. There are several government Gopher servers that contain the text of new laws, FCC regulations, and other information.

Competitive intelligence

Every guerrilla knows that it's easier to beat your competition if you know what they're up to. Scouting the competition through anonymous store visits and customer interviews is a time-tested method of gaining valuable business intelligence. In the online world, you can get lots of competitive intelligence by shopping your competitors' storefronts and by listening to what their customers say. Discussion groups related to your business often feature comments about your competition.

When computer companies want to learn what people are saying about their latest products, they join up with a computer-related forum online. Dell, Compaq, and many other companies pay one or more employees to do nothing but prowl cyberspace for scuttlebutt about their products or their competition. Members of discussion groups are very candid in their impressions about different products and services.

Professional advice

Online services have forums devoted to professional topics like marketing, accounting, taxes, and public relations. There are also some newsgroups on the Net that cover the same fields. By joining these discussions, you can learn the latest about what's happening in these fields and get lots of free advice about running your business.

FINDING INFORMATION RESOURCES

Your ability to locate the information you want depends on whether you're using the Net, an online service, or a BBS. If you're seeking information on a BBS or online service, you use the service's menus or searching software to locate it. It's fairly easy to navigate to the database or forum you want. America Online makes it easy for small businesses with its Business Strategies area, a central repository for information and forums for small business owners. On CompuServe, the business and professional forums are all located in one area. There are also printed guidebooks for America Online and CompuServe that tell you what's available on them and where to locate it. CompuServe's monthly subscriber magazine also features articles about the service's information resources.

Compared with online services, the Internet is pretty chaotic. There's a lot of information available for free, as long as you can find it. There's no centralized index of files or databases that spans the whole Net, so you have to do some digging to find what you want. You use the Web to access files and databases, but there are so many files and databases that it can be tough to find what you want. It's much easier to locate something if you already know all or part of the file or menu option name or if you know the server's address.

Even if you have the address you need, the Internet presents other problems. The server that hosts a particular database may be too busy doing other things when you need it, or it may be shut down for maintenance. The gateway between that server and the Net may be on the blink. And even if the equipment is working perfectly, some information resources are moved from place to place as system administrators rearrange their files. An address that's correct today may be wrong tomorrow. Online services seldom change the locations of information they offer.

Your key to finding information on the Net will be the search tools designed for that purpose. There are four ways to gather information from the Net: Web directories, Gopher servers, FTP servers, and WAIS servers. Indexes to many WAIS databases are no longer being maintained due to the rise of the Web, and even Gopher and FTP servers are becoming less popular thanks to the Web. So the first place to start your search for information is the Web.

Finding information on the Web

The most popular Web directory is Yahoo (www.yahoo.com), but there are several other general directories, and you'll also find lots of topic-specific directories. Any of these directories can be searched. If you want to see a selection of general directory sites and search utilities and you're using Netscape Navigator, just click the Search button at the top of the screen and you'll see a page containing links to several different search engines. If you use Yahoo or InfoSeek, there's a search blank on every page. Here's the home page from Yahoo:

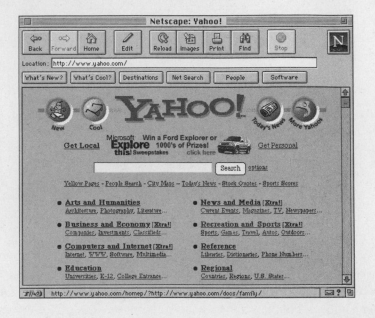

To find information about a subject, type the subject's name into the search blank, and then click the Search button. For tips about how to refine your searches, click the Options link next to the search blank.

After you click the search button, Yahoo will search for sites containing the words you typed and then will list them. For example, suppose you had an idea for a product and wanted to find references to firms that assisted in developing inventions. If you searched for *Invention Development*, the page would look like the one on p. 278.

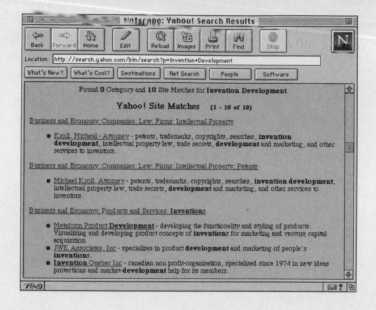

At the top of the page, we see the number of Web pages Yahoo found containing the phrase we searched for. Pages are divided into categories and sites. In this case, there was no directory category that matched our search criteria, but there were ten individual sites.

The pages are listed in order by the number of words in your search phrase matched (complete matches are listed first), by the number of times the phrase appears on the page, and by the position of the phrase on the page (the higher up on the page the phrase appears, the higher that page is on the results list). In each description of a page, the words we searched for are shown in boldface. Notice that Yahoo (and other directories as well) locates single words from our search phrase as well as the entire phrase.

Because Yahoo and other directories simply match the words you type with words found on Web pages, you often get hundreds, if not thousands of matches for your search phrase. But there are ways to refine a search to more precisely find what you're looking for. *(See "How to find things more quickly" on p. 284.)*

Using Gopher servers

Gopher servers display text information in documents and directories, and they provide access to search and retrieval tools such as WAIS,

Veronica, Archie, and FTP. Gopher servers these days store primarily scientific, educational, and government data. Your access to Gopher depends on the type of online connection you have.

- If you have a subscription to an online service, Gopher is an option in the Internet services area.
- If you have a dial-in account with an ISP, you run Gopher software on your own PC.

When you start Gopher, you're automatically taken to a home server. You'll see a menu of choices like this:

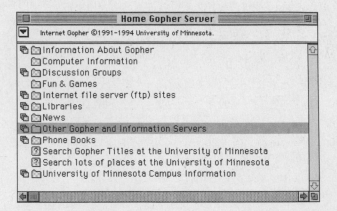

This Gopher server happens to be a computer at the University of Minnesota, where Gopher was invented. You can double-click on any of the folders to see a list of files or other folders inside them. From this

---

GOPHER AND FTP SITES ON THE WEB

Many Gopher and FTP servers are now accessible via the Web. To get an idea of what's out there, use Yahoo or another Web directory to search for Gopher Servers or FTP Servers. You'll see a list of specific Web-accessible servers you can browse.

However, the best way to search for specific documents on Gopher and FTP servers is still to use a search utility such as Gopher, Turbo-Gopher, Archie, or Anarchie. If you don't have a Gopher or Archie utility for your PC, ask your ISP to get you a copy or to tell you where to go on the Web to download a copy.

one window, you can get information about using Gopher, a list of discussion groups on the Net, a list of FTP sites, a list of other Gopher servers, a list of directories, and other information.

Using Veronica

Most of the information databases on the Net are accessible with Gopher, but with more than 5,000 Gopher servers online, there's a lot of data in Gopherspace. In many cases you won't know which Gopher server contains the file you're looking for. That's where Veronica comes in. You use Veronica to search the menus on all Gopher servers. You type a word or phrase for the folder and tell Veronica to find all the menu items with that word or phrase in their names. To use Veronica from our Home Gopher Server, you open the *Other Gopher and Information Servers* folder to see a window like this:

```
┌─────────────────────────────────────────────────────────┐
│ ▣ ═══════ Other Gopher and Information Servers ═══════ ▣ │
│ ▼   Internet Gopher ©1991-1994 University of Minnesota.   │
├─────────────────────────────────────────────────────────┤
│ 🗀 🗀 All the Gopher Servers in the World             ⬆ │
│    ？ Search All the Gopher Servers in the World        │
│ 🗀 🗀 Search titles in Gopherspace using veronica        │
│ 🗀 🗀 Africa                                             │
│ 🗀 🗀 Asia                                               │
│ 🗀 🗀 Europe                                             │
│ 🗀 🗀 International Organizations                         │
│ 🗀 🗀 Middle East                                        │
│ 🗀 🗀 North America                                      │
│ 🗀 🗀 Pacific                                            │
│ 🗀 🗀 Russia                                             │
│ 🗀 🗀 South America                                      │
│ 🗀 🗀 Terminal Based Information                      ⬇ │
│ ⬅ ▯▯▯                                              ➡ ▣ │
└─────────────────────────────────────────────────────────┘
```

You could open the folder called *All the Gopher Servers in the World*, but that option just displays a huge list of server names. You would then have to manually open each server and scan its menu to find what you were looking for. If you know the name of the Gopher server you're looking for, you can click *Search all the Gopher Servers in the World* and find the server by searching for it by name. If you know the Gopher server has Agriculture in its name, you would type *Agriculture* in the search window and the program would find it.

But in most cases, you won't know the server name, and you'll be looking for a menu item on a Gopher server by its title, and that means using Veronica. Suppose you're looking for the Federal Register, a weekly listing of government business contracts put out for bid. You would open *Search titles in Gopherspace using veronica.*

The window opens like this:

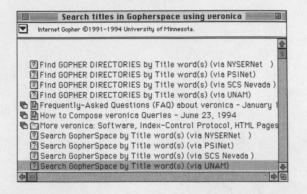

The options here let you search directories — *Find GOPHER ONLY DIRECTORIES* — or all menu items — *Search GopherSpace by Title word(s).* Since you're looking for a specific document (the Federal Register), use the Search GopherSpace by Title Word(s) option and search for that document by name. (If you know the documents were stored in a particular directory, you can use the Find GOPHER DIRECTORIES option to search only the directory names, which is faster.)

This window appears to list the same directory-search option several times, but each option lets you conduct your search on a different server. That's because Gopher servers are often busy. If you try your search on one server and it's too busy, you can try another.

After choosing the Search GopherSpace by Title Word(s) option, you see a box where you can enter the phrase or title you're searching for. When you enter Federal Register and click the OK button, Veronica searches and opens a window showing documents or directories with Federal Register in their names, as shown at the top of page 282.

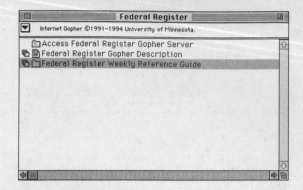

The second item listed is a document that describes the Federal Register. The other items are directories. You can open the Weekly Reference Guide folder to see a list of weekly Federal Register guides. Each guide lists the latest government agency requests for proposals sent out that week, like this:

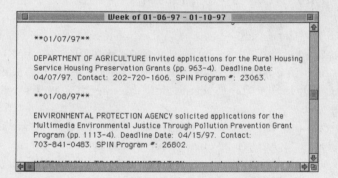

If you're interested in providing services to government agencies, this is a good place to find out what services are being sought.

Using Archie

The home Gopher server also gives us access to the Archie search utility. If you know all or part of the name of a file at an FTP site but you don't know the site's location, you use Archie to find it. To use Archie, we'll open the *Internet file server (ftp) sites* item on the Home Gopher Server. A new window opens, like this:

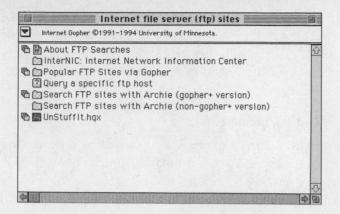

Suppose we want to find a file about the government of Zimbabwe. To search for all files relating to Zimbabwe, we would open one of the *Search FTP sites with Archie* folders and then type *Zimbabwe* in the search window that appears. Archie would search the Net and return with a list of files with Zimbabwe in their titles. We could then click on any of the titles to go to that site and retrieve the file. We would probably get quite a list of files to look at if we searched only for one country name, but by going to each FTP site and looking at the full file name, we'll know if it's the one we want or not. And we could narrow the search by including more words in the search string. Searching for *Zimbabwe government* would yield fewer matches.

The trouble with searches

Search programs like Veronica and Archie should theoretically find exactly what you want, but it's never that easy. Here are some of the problems you'll run into.

You get a bad connection. Sometimes the program can't make a connection to the server you want to search, or the server is too busy to handle your request. If so, you'll see a message saying that Veronica or Archie could not connect.

Your search is too specific. Search programs take you quite literally: if you type *Tennis Shoes* in a search window, neither program will find a file or directory named *Tennis Shoe, Tennisshoe,* or *Tennis.shoes.* Fortunately, you can use wildcards in your search strings to broaden your options. For example, you could tell Archie to search for *Ten** to find any file that begins with *Ten.*

Your search is too broad. You might want to find data about the 1990 census, but if you search Gopherspace for census you'll end up with hundreds of matches and you'll probably get a message that says there are too many matches to list. Instead, it would be better to search for *1990 U.S. Census.*

How to find things more quickly

If you're serious about exploring the information resources available online, here are some tips to help make your searches faster and more efficient.

Read the instructions. Before using a search directory, a utility like Archie or Veronica, or even the search commands on an online service, read the manual or FAQ file. There's usually a directory on the Gopher server that contains information on how to do Veronica, Archie, and other Gopher searches. On an online service, there's a Help file you can use, and individual databases may have dictionaries of keywords you're supposed to use in searches. On the Web, there is usually a link right near the search text entry box that takes you to a page of searching tips. You'll get advice about how to phrase search criteria, how to use wildcards, and how to use searching options to broaden or narrow your search.

Get a directory. Get a good book that describes the resources available on the Net or on an online service. One good general book is *How to Look It Up Online* by Alfred Glossbrenner. There are also books about CompuServe and America Online, and there are many books about Internet resources. Spend some time with these offline, and your searches will go faster once you're connected.

Search within directories. If you're searching on the Web, use the option to search only within a directory, rather than searching all Web pages. The Yahoo home page, for example, lists dozens of different directories that categorize information. For example, if you're looking for a patent attorney, it's faster and more accurate to open the Attorneys directory and search within it rather than searching the entire Web.

Save addresses. Whenever you come across the address of a useful information resource on the Net, bookmark it or write it down for future reference. It can take hours to locate a specific file on the Net, and it only takes seconds to bookmark an address and use it once you have it.

Check spelling. Before starting a search, check the spelling of your search keywords to make sure they're correct. Remember, it's garbage in, garbage out: type the wrong thing and you'll get the wrong result.

Try different combinations. If your first search is unsuccessful, try the same words in other combinations or try adding new words to your query.

Browse. If you use Gopher a lot, browse Gopher servers during your travels to get a feel for how menu item names are specified. You'll get a better idea of the words Gopher and other server administrators use to define menu choices, and your searches will be more successful.

Download. Rather than reading documents online, save them to your own disk and read them later. It's much faster and cheaper to save a group of documents to your disk and sort through them later than to read them online to find the one you really need.

WHY YOU SHOULD DO RESEARCH

Of all the weapons at our disposal, research is probably the one we overlook the most. We're usually so busy using more direct marketing weapons that research gets shoved to the bottom of the list. When we do have some extra time, research stays at the bottom of the list because it seems so academic. It reminds us too much of school or homework. We want to be out there selling, not poking through cyberspace for facts and figures.

That's a shame. The largest and most successful companies use research constantly. It helps them evaluate their market position, plan future products or services, and take advantage of new trends before anyone else. McDonald's wouldn't even think of locating a new franchise without studying the traffic near a proposed location. Home Depot doesn't open a new store until it studies the Effective Buying Income of the area's residents. Yet every day small businesses make tragic mistakes because they don't do enough research. Guerrillas know better.

Make research a regular part of your marketing arsenal. It helps you understand local market conditions, tax laws, and import customs. It helps you make better decisions and fewer mistakes. It can tell you what your customers want and what your competition isn't giving them. It can find you new business partners or suppliers and expand your market across the world.

The next time you have a question about your business, poke around online and look for an answer. The chances are you'll find one.

16

Leveraging Your Online Advantage

Your online attack requires its own focus, but don't forget that it's part of your overall marketing plan. Like every other part of your marketing plan, your online presence should support all your marketing efforts. Sometimes your online presence can help offline sales, and sometimes it works the other way. The synergy is always there if you know how to take advantage of it.

- The Rolling Stones broadcast video clips of their concerts over the Internet, so fans who can't attend the concerts can tune in. The band wasn't selling anything online, but the event helped polish the cutting-edge image of a group whose lead singer is past fifty.
- Well-established phone- and mail-order firms like Lands' End, Spiegel, 800-Flowers, and other vendors offer their wares on the Web. While their printed catalogs already reach millions, going online helps them capture instant sales from those who don't get the catalogs.
- Federal Express and United Parcel Service let you track the progress of shipments online. You can't deliver a package in cyberspace, but an online presence gives these firms a new competitive edge in the service race.
- Ford, GM, and Chrysler can't let you drive a car online, but they offer interactive brochures and product information to whet your appetite for a dealer visit.

In this chapter, we'll see how you can increase the leverage between your offline and online efforts. You'll learn how to use your online presence to build your offline business and how to promote your online presence through traditional marketing channels.

PROMOTING YOUR OFFLINE PRESENCE ONLINE

Every good customer relationship is a human relationship. Nothing you will ever do online will achieve human contact with someone else as well as a face-to-face meeting. In a perfect world where your physical storefront could offer the same safety, convenience, price, selection, information, and twenty-four-hour access as your online presence, customers would prefer to buy from you in person. And under equal circumstances, you'd probably be just as happy to sell to them face-to-face as you would online.

Your main reason for going online is to gain customers and visibility you can't otherwise achieve, but it's much harder to form the human bonds you need for lasting relationships. Fortunately, your online presence can put you in touch with people who can visit you in person or call you on the phone. Here are some specific ways to encourage offline contacts when you're in cyberspace.

Use your full e-mail signature. Include your phone number and your store address in your e-mail signature. Anyone who sees it online and happens to be nearby can stop in or phone. If you're offering value in your product or service, your online contact will turn into a lasting direct relationship.

Invite calls. When someone asks for help in a discussion group, respond with a private message and invite him or her to phone you.

Mention your location in messages. Find ways to give clues about your physical location in discussion group messages. When you start a message or paragraph with *As I was driving through the Lincoln Tunnel the other day*, people know you're in the New York area.

Mention offline shows or conferences you're attending. Business trips, conferences, and trade shows can take you all over the country. When you're planning to attend an event in a different area, post a message about the event in a relevant newsgroup, or respond to another message that mentions it. Ask if anyone else in the group will be attending, and invite them to meet with you at the conference. If you've been participating in the discussion for a while and have made some useful contributions, other members will welcome the chance to meet you face-to-face.

Include printed information with orders. When you ship an order from an online customer, include a brochure, catalog, postcard, or printed information sheet about your offline store. The printed matter becomes a mini-billboard on their desk. Invite people to stop by or phone when they're in the area.

Refer people to offline articles, ads, and promotional events. When you're planning a promotional event at your store or a public

---

PREPARE AN ONLINE PRESS KIT

If you have a press kit for your company (see p. 293), prepare an online version of it. This will give you the option to send your material much more quickly to an editor or writer via e-mail, and it will also prepare you to respond to publicity contacts at online magazines.

To prepare an online press kit, save each of your press documents (backgrounder, press releases, product information, photos, and so on) as separate files with names that indicate what each document contains. Then, store all of the files in a compressed archive so that you can send just one press kit file to your contact. If you're using a PC, you can compress documents with the WinZip utility. For Mac users, the StuffIt program is the standard compression tool.

---

demonstration of your products and services, mention it online so that people in your area can come. Work it into your discussion group messages. Post a notice in your online store. Run a classified ad in a geographically focused newsgroup or BBS.

Participate in a local BBS or Web discussion. Find a BBS or Web site in your local area that hosts a discussion group related to your business, and become active on it. Most of the BBS subscribers will be locals as well, and your online activities will alert them to your offline presence in their community. Even if you don't find a forum related to your business, participating in a general discussion will enhance your local visibility.

All of these activities will alert your online contacts to your location and give them a chance to meet you in person. In-person meetings are the best way to forge lasting human bonds. Use your online presence to facilitate them.

PROMOTING YOUR ONLINE PRESENCE OFFLINE

Visibility is so crucial in cyberspace that you should use every means at your disposal to increase it. Since most of your customers spend most of their time offline, your promotions should include using your physical store, mail-order catalog, print ads, brochures, stationery, invoices, TV and radio ads, and other offline marketing weapons. Alerting your offline customers to your online presence enhances your marketing attack in four key ways:

1. It gives your local customers another option for doing business with you.
2. It allows your local customers to refer your business to others across the state or across the world.
3. It reaches audiences you can't reach online.
4. It enhances your reputation as a modern, growing, and well-managed business.

Planning your offline promotions

Your customers' online experiences with you should be as convenient and professional as they are offline. Before you start inviting people to contact you online, make sure you're ready for any response your effort will generate. Make sure your mailbot, storefront, or e-mailbox is up, working, and being regularly monitored before you begin announcing it offline.

We frequently come across e-mail addresses that aren't checked regularly, and even Web addresses that are no longer valid. It's easy to switch ISPs or online services and forget to change the address on your business card or stationery. If you do this, though, you'll waste your offline promotional efforts and disappoint a lot of online customers.

Through careful planning and research, you should have established permanent e-mail or URL addresses when you prepared your online attack. But if you end up having to relocate in cyberspace, make sure you don't cut off contact with your online customers.

- If you change e-mail addresses, maintain the old address and monitor it regularly for three months after you've stopped publicizing it.
- If you change the address of your storefront, post a link at the old address that directs people to the new one. These days, you can also add a script to your old page that automatically takes visitors to your new site.

Offline marketing messages

It's fine to include your online address on signs and stationery and print ads, but if that's all you do you probably won't attract many new online customers. Most regular cybernauts will see your online promotions, so your printed messages should be targeted at people who aren't regular visitors in cyberspace. They need a reason to log on and visit your online store instead of phoning or shopping in person.

When planning how to promote your online presence in the offline world, think about why your customers would want to shop online. Assume the people reading your messages are reluctant cybernauts, and give them good reasons to take the plunge. Here are some.

Convenience   Your online store is open day and night. Use print ads or signs to emphasize the convenience of ordering at any time from a PC at home or at work. U.S. West ran a television ad for its yellow pages that shows a man searching for an accordion teacher at three in the morning. Tell your customers how online shopping can simplify their lives. Your in-store sign might say, *If you shopped us online, you'd be home now.* If your store has long checkout lines during peak shopping seasons, put up a sign at the register that says, *When you shop online, there's never a line.*

Information   Your online presence probably offers faster access to information, or more complete information, than your customers can get over the phone or in person. An ad touting your online consumer tips or comparative product information gives people a reason to check it out. Or how about this: *3,000 items here, 30,000 more online. Check out our online catalog and order form.*

Lower prices   If you offer discounts for online shoppers, mention that in your store. You could even print price signs that say *$3.49 here, $3.09 online. Let us show you how.*

Offline support weapons

Once you've got some compelling reasons to shop online, you need to combine them with effective weapons. Let's look at some specific ways to promote your online presence with offline marketing weapons.

A demo system   If you have a storefront or online catalog, set up a computer in your store and display the storefront or catalog on it. Invite customers to try it out. Most of your in-person shoppers have never been in cyberspace, so educating them about your online presence is a real public service. If you set up a demo system, make sure you have an employee on hand to help customers use it and answer questions.

Your store   In your physical store you have almost complete control over the size, appearance, and placement of your marketing messages. Use in-store signs, placards, window signs, banners, and even cash register tape to display your online address and invite customers to visit. The information highway is still news to many people; you'll draw new customers who are curious about a window sign that says, *See us on the information highway!*

Stationery   Put your online address on your letterhead, business card, invoice, and packing list. If you have an online storefront, make sure your stationery tells people they can reach you twenty-four hours a day online. Invite customers to send in billing questions via e-mail.

Print ads   Include your e-mail or storefront address in all your display ads in newspapers, magazines, and on buses, taxis, benches, and billboards. When you first begin using the online address, call attention to it by playing up the themes of convenience, information access, or lower prices. If you're on an online service like America Online or CompuServe, put *See us on AOL* in a highlighted box in your ads. The major online services are spending millions to promote themselves, and mentioning your online presence leverages all that promotion.

Radio and TV ads   Include your e-mail or URL address in all your radio and TV ads. Here, too, you can start with special ads promoting your online launch and the benefits of shopping online. Your radio ad might depict someone buying your product from the PC at home instead of going out in the rain. Your TV ad might show a session at your storefront, highlighting the wealth of information available there.

Postcards and direct-mail letters   Send out direct-mail postcards. Announce your online presence, and offer a special discount or gift for those who visit you there. If you send a direct-mail letter, include a color screen photo of your electronic storefront to entice customers into it. If

---

MAKE YOUR URL LEGIBLE

When you add your storefront's URL or e-mail address to a radio or TV ad, make sure it's understandable.

Radio. Lots of radio ads in particular rush through a URL so quickly that visitors would have to be poised with pen and paper in advance to have any hope of writing it down. Don't assume the audience is so well prepared. Instead, include at least one sentence before the URL that mentions your online store so that people can prepare to listen for the address. When it's time to speak the address, make sure it's spoken slowly and clearly so that there's no possibility of ambiguity. If necessary, spell out the URL.

TV. We see lots of URLs on TV ads that are added almost as an afterthought, in tiny print for a second or two at the end of the spot. If you want people to see and remember your URL, make it large enough to be seen on an average TV from across the room, and give it enough time on screen so people can remember it.

you're marketing mostly to computer users, try mailing a postcard teaser with just your online address on it; people will visit your store out of curiosity.

Free software   If you have a BBS, make up floppy disks containing a freeware communications program or your custom BBS interface program. Mail the disks out with an invitation to shop online. This strategy worked fabulously for America Online, which used free disks to build its subscriber base from zero to more than seven million within five years, passing all of its competitors in the process.

Advertising specialties   Print your company name and online address on pens, pencils, coasters, floppy disk holders, mouse pads, screen dustcloths, or other computer-related giveaway items. People will put them by their computers, and your ad message will remind them about your online presence at the right time and in the right place.

CAPTURING OFFLINE PUBLICITY

There may be 30 million or more people in the online marketplace, but most of them won't hear about your business there. Of the millions of people who explore the online world, most barely have their toes in the water. Publicity brings news about your company or activities in front of the reading public, whether or not they're online, whether or not they even have computers.

If news about your company appears in a magazine devoted to online trends, it gives readers an incentive to seek you out. Most of them need one. CompuServe and Prodigy have recognized the need to promote themselves offline since they were founded. CompuServe publishes *CompuServe* magazine, a monthly publication that covers news about CompuServe and features articles about different services or businesses you can explore when you connect. Prodigy mails out a newsletter emphasizing new services or online events. Prodigy also uses telemarketers to phone new subscribers to see if they need help using the service.

When news about your company appears in a general-interest publication, it alerts people to your online presence and may win you some online converts who had remained on the sidelines until then. Every time a story about the online world appears in *Time, Newsweek,* or the *New York Times,* online activity jumps.

Magazines and other print media also offer two benefits you can't get online: portability and distribution. In a magazine or newspaper, people can read news about your online company on a subway train, at a lunch counter, or on an airplane. Print articles in major publications have millions of readers. Print articles can be photocopied or faxed to others who can read them immediately without having to fire up a computer and connect. Finally, articles in targeted media let you tell your customers about your online activities with the credibility of a publication rather than the self-promotion of an ad.

If you're a true guerrilla, you're already pursuing publicity outlets for your business. Your new online presence can give you new exposure or new reasons for repeated exposure in media that have covered your company in the past. The keys to success are coming up with the right weapons and then aiming them at the right media targets.

Publicity weapons

The basic weapons you'll use in media campaigns are:

- a press kit
- a company backgrounder
- press releases
- story ideas or pitches
- contributed articles and columns
- press demonstrations

Let's take a closer look at these.

Press kit   A press kit is a collection of information about your company packaged into a folder or pocket portfolio. It includes a backgrounder about your company, press releases, photos of company executives or of the products you're publicizing, one or more story ideas of pitches, reprints of previous articles about your business, a list of customer references, and perhaps a comparison of your products versus those of your main competition.

Company backgrounder   This document explains in a few pages what your company is, how large it is, when it was founded, who runs it, what it does, why it's successful, and who its customers are. The backgrounder has several standard sections:

- An executive summary that's a one-page collection of key facts about your company such as the name, address, phone and other contact information, date founded, names of main products or services, and names of key executives.

- An overview that describes the market opportunity your company exploits and how your company came to be founded. This puts your company's business in perspective so that readers can see why you are or will be successful.
- A section on products and markets explains in detail the products your company makes, why they're better or different from competitive products, and who buys those products. In the Products section (or separately in a section that follows) you explain your company's strategy for success.
- Brief biographical sketches of your company's key executives.

The backgrounder should provide all the basic information about your company and its products and personnel in one document.

Press releases A press release is a brief document announcing news about your company. This is the first salvo in your campaign for publicity. Properly written, the release reads like a news story to help the reporter or editor who gets it visualize your news as an article or story. The news in this case is that you've gone online, but there are many different spins you can put on this news, depending on your media target. Here are four natural angles you can apply to your news release:

- Your new online presence offers new convenience or lower prices for your customers.
- Your business delivers special information that can't be gotten off-line.
- Yours is the first online business to offer a particular product or service.
- Yours is the first business in your geographic area to expand into cyberspace.

Begin the news release with one of the major news hooks just mentioned, and then expand with a few paragraphs of details. Include specifics of what you're offering online, why it's important for online customers, and how it expands your offline business. Quote yourself or another key employee about the importance of going online. Include your online address. At the end of the release, include a paragraph that describes your business mission, your market, and how long you've been in business. Here's a brief example:

FOR IMMEDIATE RELEASE

Contact:

Jackie Raley, Marketing Director
Wayland Fruit Company
502-555-5521
jackier@pomegranates.com

EXOTIC FRUIT GOES ONLINE
SEEKS INTERNATIONAL MARKETS

Wayland, Florida—July 17, 1997—In a bid to gain an international market for its pomegranates, kumquats, and other exotic fruits, Wayland Fruit today announced the opening of Pomegranates Online, the information highway's first exotic fruit stand. Located on the World Wide Web at http://www.pomegranates.com, the Pomegranates Online storefront displays color graphics of exotic fruit baskets and assortments and allows customers across the world to order at discount prices via the Internet. In addition, the storefront offers a database of exotic fruit recipes, daily bulk pricing updates, a holiday and birthday gift register, and an international fruit newswire.

"Our institutional marketing efforts have brought pomegranates and other exotic fruits to the tables of restaurants across America," said Laurie Mendoza, president of Wayland Fruit. "By moving onto the Internet, we can bring these exotic fruits within reach for millions of international customers who have never seen them before."

Wayland Fruit is Florida's leading purveyor of exotic fruit for restaurants, institutions, and individual customers around the world. Founded in 1981, the company specializes in premium-quality pomegranates and kumquats for discerning palates.

# # #

This is the standard format for a press release, with a title, a contact name and phone number, and FOR IMMEDIATE RELEASE at the top. Notice the first paragraph. It contains two news hooks: Pomegranates Online is the first exotic fruit stand in cyberspace, and the online move is a bid by Wayland Fruit to go international. The next paragraph is a quote about why the move is important, and the last paragraph is a boilerplate that describes the company, its markets, and its market position.

Your press release can be two or three pages long, but don't make it any longer than necessary. The point is to tempt the press with some interesting news and get them to follow up with a phone call and interview. If you have a Web storefront with an appealing graphical look, include a color photo or slide of it.

Story ideas and pitches   A press release may result in a full-blown feature story or article about your business, but often it's just published as a news item. If you're after a longer, more detailed article about your online business, come up with an idea for such a story, and pitch it in a letter or phone call to the appropriate editor at your media target.

The key to a pitch is broadening the focus of your message so that it encompasses a trend rather than just your own news. Wayland Fruit's marketing or PR manager might target a magazine that goes out to restaurant or hotel managers, like this:

James Banuelos
Features Editor
Restaurant Manager Magazine
111 Front Street
Boston, MA 02190

July 24, 1997

Dear Mr. Banuelos:

A year of frosty weather in the southern United States has pushed up prices of exotic fruit, yet restaurant owners are reluctant to raise prices during today's climate of low inflation. What's a buyer to do?

Wayland Fruit is one of a handful of fruit purveyors who are helping restaurants stabilize costs. Wayland recently launched Pomegranates Online, a new interactive buying service on the Internet that allows institutions to use personal computers to place orders, track shipments, and get the latest international grower news twenty-four hours a day.

Other purveyors are offering fruit shipment futures contracts for regular customers as a way to hold down costs.

Please phone me at the number below for more information about this trend, references to some of our electronic customers, and contacts at other firms who are helping cut exotic fruit costs.

Sincerely Yours,

Jackie Raley
Marketing Director
Wayland Fruit Company
502-555-5521
jackier@pomegranates.com

This pitch focuses on an industry trend toward higher exotic fruit costs and explains how Wayland Fruit is helping restaurants hold them down. Notice that it's addressed to a specific editor at a specific magazine. Each pitch must be tailored for a particular magazine and even for a section in that magazine. If the media target was a mass-market consumer magazine like *Good Housekeeping* or *Gourmet*, the focus might be on how consumers are going online to obtain exotic fruits and recipes.

If you're pitching a story by mail, find out which specific editor is in charge of the magazine section or TV or radio show segment you want to reach, and write it up in a letter. Along with the basic story idea, offer to provide references to customers of yours who might be interviewed for the story, and enclose the press release announcing your online business. If you're pitching the story by phone, have the pitch organized and ready to deliver, and have your customer references ready.

Contributed articles and columns   If you're going after an industry-specific magazine or a local newspaper, you can usually write a column or article sharing your expertise. Publications like this are usually hungry for material. They often print reader contributions. As with a pitch, write an article or column that highlights a trend rather than one that blatantly praises or focuses on your own business.

When you're targeting a local newspaper, write an article sharing your experience as the first online business in your area. If the article is well received, pitch the paper about doing a regular column about cyberspace. Your credibility as an expert and the weekly appearance of your online address will draw customers.

When your target is a special-interest magazine, write about online information sources for people with those interests, and include your company as one of them. Your exercise equipment business would benefit if you wrote an article about online fitness forums and sources of equipment. Think about the benefits of your product or service, and turn each benefit into an article for a specific audience.

Press demonstrations   If you're an online pioneer in your business or geographical area and you have an interesting online storefront, set up a demonstration for the press. You may get some air time on the local TV station as you demonstrate online shopping.

Follow-up calls   Unless you're lucky enough to hit a slow news period or find just the right angle, you'll need to follow up your mailed release or pitch with a phone call. Most of the stories that get done are prodded to life with a follow-up call. Call the editors to whom you sent your release or pitch and find out if they got it. If so, ask if they read it, and offer to help supply more information. Editors at busy newspapers see dozens of press releases every day; the ones that are boosted by a follow-up call are more likely to get published.

Choosing media targets

To find the right targets for your publicity campaign, study the media outlets you use now and think about the kinds of stories they run. Every outlet has different types of stories, or different departments. Your city paper has national news, local news, lifestyle coverage, sports, business, society, religion, and other departments. Think about how and where your story will fit into the paper. Do the same thing for TV and radio stations. Every TV news or magazine show is broken into segments that are like sections in a printed newspaper or magazine. Each segment has its own focus.

While noting the different types of stories in each media outlet, look at the stories themselves, and think about how they're written. What angles do they cover? How many different companies or information sources are mentioned or quoted? How might an article about your business be packaged to fit the format of the media outlet you're trying to reach?

To get an idea of how this works, let's look at some target categories, and see how you could attack each one with the weapons covered earlier.

Local newspapers, radio, or TV stations   Set up demonstrations, pitch stories, and offer interviews for radio and TV stations. Send press releases to all your local media. Come up with article pitches for your local paper, or write your own company profile and submit it. Many local papers make local business profiles a regular feature, and some of them are written by the business owners themselves. Pitch yourself as a guest on local radio or TV interview shows.

Online magazines   Send out a press release announcing your business, with a special focus on why it's unique in cyberspace. Online magazines cover the whole online market, but they only have a limited amount of space. If you want to see your news in print, find an angle to use in your press release or story pitch that will make it especially newsworthy.

Special-interest publications   Magazines that focus on your customer base will be interested in stories about your online presence. If you're one of the first to do computer training on the Net, your training industry magazine will be interested in that. Send a press release announcing the opening of your business. Focus your pitches on the benefits of going online for this industry segment's particular group of consumers.

Your online marketing attack will bring a powerful new dimension to your business. You now know all you need to make it work. But guerrillas understand that knowledge is nothing without the willingness to use it. So choose your weapons, target your battlegrounds, and write your own success story in the online marketplace.

GLOSSARY

APPENDIX

- - - - - - - - - - - - -

Glossary

When a definition contains a word in italics, that word is also defined.

acceptable use policy — A code of rules for using an *ISP* account or a portion of the *Internet*.

address book — A personal directory of *e-mail* addresses stored and maintained with one's e-mail program.

agent — a software program or feature that automatically performs a complex function (such as searching Web sites for specific types of products and then ranking the products in order by price) without your intervention.

alias — A collection of *e-mail* addresses stored under one name to facilitate addressing mail to a particular group of users.

Archie — A search utility that surveys all *FTP* sites once a month and builds an index of all software at those sites. The index is stored on an Archie *server* on the *Net*. Short for "archiver," it was written by Peter Deutsch and Alan Emtage at McGill University in Montreal in 1990. There are hundreds of Archie servers worldwide.

backbone — A communications pathway that carries *Internet* traffic between individual networks.

BBS (bulletin board service or bulletin board system) — Any computer system and software with one or more telephone lines that will accept a phone call from another computer at any time with little or no prior arrangement for access.

browser — A program used to access and view information on the *World Wide Web*. Via the Web, browsers also provide access to *FTP* and *Gopher* sites.

channel — A specific discussion carried via *IRC*.

chat session — An area in an *online service* or *BBS* where several users can meet simultaneously and exchange typed messages in real time.

client — a computer or program that accesses information stored on a *server*.

conference — A large *chat* session that features a main speaker and an audience that asks questions.

continuous connection — A high-speed connection to the *Internet* that doesn't require dialing a phone number and which is never broken. It may be a connection via a leased telephone line, a cable TV system, or a satellite system.

cross-post — To send the same message to several different *discussion groups*.

dial-up connection — A connection to the *Internet* that requires dialing a telephone number.

direct connection — A *continuous connection*.

discussion group — An electronic message board on an *online service*, *BBS*, or the *Net* that contains messages focusing on a specific topic.

domain — A category of network on the *Internet*, or a specific network name; also called a domain name.

domain name service — A service offered by an *ISP* that registers customers' *servers* as distinct *Internet domains*.

download — To retrieve a file from an *online service*, *BBS*, or *Internet server*, transferring it to a disk on your own computer for local use.

e-mail (electronic mail) — A means of exchanging typed messages between computer users in which messages are sent to specific addresses and stored in mailboxes.

emoticon — A combination of keyboard symbols that, when looked at sideways, resembles a facial expression, such as ;=).

FAQ (frequently asked questions) — A collection of frequent questions about a particular discussion group, bulletin board, *SIG*, *Internet* service, or other subject, posted for newcomers to read.

firewall — An *Internet* server that is isolated from the rest of an organization's network and so prohibits outside callers from accessing information the organization wants to keep private.

flame — (*v.*) To send a poison-pen *e-mail* letter to another *Internet* user, usually someone who has violated netiquette; (*n.*) A poison-pen e-mail letter.

forum — A name used for a *discussion group* on an *online service* or *BBS*.

FTP (File Transfer Protocol) — A service that allows you to transfer files to and from other computers on the *Internet*.

gateway — A communications link between a network and the *Internet*.

geographic domains — Suffixes at the end of an *Internet* address that denote the country in which a *server* is located. For example, *.us* (United States), *.uk* (United Kingdom), and *.ca* (Canada).

Gopher — A method of locating information on the *Internet*. Also, a type of server that uses that location method, and a software program used to locate such servers. Created in 1991 at the University of Minnesota, Gopher was the first easy-to-use Internet searching and browsing system.

handle — A pseudonym used by an individual participant in a *chat session* or *conference*.

header — The portion of an *e-mail* document that contains the mailing address and subject information.

hierarchy — A category of *Usenet* newsgroups. Usenet is divided into dozens of hierarchies, including *alt* (alternative topics), *biz* (business topics), and *rec* (recreational topics).

hit — A specific occurrence of a user accessing a *server*. Server traffic is sometimes measured in hits per hour or hits per day. An active server has thousands of hits per day (that is, it is accessed thousands of times per day by various users).

home page — The introductory or menu page of a Web site. A home page usually contains the site's name and a directory of its contents.

host computer — See *server*.

HTML (Hypertext Markup Language) — The programming language used to store and present information on *World Wide Web* servers.

HTTP (Hypertext Transfer Protocol) — The communications protocol, or set of technical rules, through which *World Wide Web* information is linked on the *Internet*.

hypertext — A method of cross-referencing computer data through automatic links between words, pictures, or phrases. For example, a paragraph about the history of opera might mention Verdi as one of the great opera composers. Hypertext could be used to link Verdi's name with a page that lists his major compositions, so that someone reading the general paragraph could select Verdi's name to activate the link and get more details about him rather than having to look them up elsewhere.

hypertext link — An automatic link on the *World Wide Web* that connects a word, phrase, or picture with other information elsewhere. When a user selects a linked phrase or picture, that user is automatically connected to the other data to which it is linked.

image map — a graphic on the *World Wide Web* that contains more than one *hypertext link*, so that clicking different parts of the graphic links you to different Web pages.

Internet — An international data communications pathway that links thousands of computer networks together. Also called the *Net*.

Internet mail gateway — A communications path that connects a network to the *Internet* and allows *e-mail* to pass between the network and other networks via the *Net*.

IP account (Internet Protocol account) — A dial-up Internet account that requires you to run Internet Protocol software directly from your computer (see *SLIP* or *PPP*).

IRC (Internet Relay Chat) — A *chat session* function on the *Internet* that has many different *channels*, each of which is topic-specific.

ISP (Internet service provider) — A company or organization that offers *Internet* access to customers for a fee.

LAN (Local Area Network) — A network that connects computers within a single office or building.

Listserv — One of the best-known *mailing list manager* programs; sometimes used as a generic name for a mailing list manager.

lurker — Someone who reads messages on a *mailing list, forum*, or *newsgroup* without *posting* to it.

mailbot — A program that responds automatically to incoming *e-mail*. A mailbot receives e-mail messages and then replies to them automatically by sending messages or files to their authors.

mailer — A program that sends and receives *e-mail*.

mailing list — An electronic discussion carried out with *e-mail* messages rather than with an electronic message board. Rather than *posting* a message to a discussion board, you send it to a mailing list's e-mail address. All subscribers to a mailing list receive copies of all messages sent to that list's address.

mailing list manager — A program that collects and distributes *e-mail* messages to a mailing list.

mail reflector — see *mailbot.*

modem — A device that allows a computer to connect with other computers over standard telephone lines by dialing phone numbers.

Net — Nickname for *Internet.*

netizen — Someone who uses the *Internet.*

newbie — A newcomer to the *Internet* or to an *online service.*

newsgroup — A message board on the Internet that focuses on a particular subject. Also known as a *Usenet* newsgroup.

newsreader — A program that allows you to read *newsgroups* on the *Internet.*

online service — A large commercial *BBS* that accommodates thousands of users at once, offers a wide variety of services and information, and charges a monthly subscription fee.

page — The basic organizational unit in a Web site. Most Web sites consist of several pages, each of which presents a different category of information for the site, such as the company background, product list, price list, and company contact information.

post — (*v.*) To send a message to a *discussion group* or *mailing list*; (*n.*) a message posted to a *discussion group* or sent to a *mailing list.*

PPP (Point-to-Point Protocol) — A communications protocol that allows a computer to become an *Internet* site via a *dial-up connection.* Also a type of Internet connection. When using a PPP connection, you run software on your own computer to navigate the Internet.

Roundtable — The name used for *forums* on the GEnie *online service.*

RTFM — An acronym standing for "Read the f——ing manual," a suggestion to a new user to read the online manual about a program or *Internet* service before asking questions about a particular command or procedure.

script — A program associated with a Web site that performs a house-keeping chore such as counting the number of visitors to a site or adding all the charges on a Web order form.

server — A computer that stores files and makes them available to other users on a network or on the *Internet*.

server log — A record of users accessing a particular *server*.

shell account — A type of *Internet* connection through which your computer establishes a *dial-up connection* with an *ISP's* computer, and you then use software on the ISP's computer to navigate the Internet.

SIG (special interest group) — Another name for a *forum* or *discussion group;* often used on CompuServe.

signal-to-noise ratio — Technically speaking, the relative strength of an electronic signal to the amount of electronic static or interference on a circuit. On the *Internet*, this is the ratio of useful information to meaningless blather.

signature (.sig) — A block of information used to sign the end of an *e-mail* or *discussion group* message. It usually includes an author name, company name, e-mail address, and other information.

site — A distinct location that stores information on the *Internet*, such as a Web site or an *FTP* site.

SLIP (Serial Line Internet Protocol) — A communications protocol or method that allows a computer to connect directly to the *Internet* via a *dial-up connection*. Once you get on the *Net* with a SLIP connection, you run programs on your own computer to navigate the Internet.

smiley — An *emoticon*.

spam — (*v.*) To *cross-post* or mass-mail unsolicited electronic messages to a large number of *discussion groups* or individuals on the *Net*.

sysop — The person responsible for maintaining the hardware, software, or content of a *forum* or *BBS*.

T1, T2, T3, and **T4 lines** — High-speed telephone lines leased from a telephone company that provide an ongoing connection for data transfers.

Telnet — A program that allows you to log onto other computers on the *Internet* and run programs on them remotely.

thread — A group of *discussion group* messages on the same topic, often a sequence of replies and comments about an initial message.

top menu — The menu on a *server* that functions as its table of contents, more commonly known as a *home page*.

Unix — A powerful computer operating system that is used on many *Internet servers*.

upload — To transfer a file from your PC to a *BBS*, *online service*, or a *server* on the *Net*.

URL (Universal Resource Locator) — A standardized address format used for *Internet* addresses.

Usenet — The largest collection of *newsgroups* on the *Internet*.

Veronica — A program that locates information stored on *Gopher* servers. The name is an acronym for Very Easy Rodent-Oriented Net-wide Index to Computerized Archives.

WAIS (Wide Area Information Servers) — A system for searching for files or programs via groups of keywords. Also, *servers* that are set up to be accessed by that system.

Webmaster — The person responsible for maintaining a Web site.

workstation — A powerful desktop computer, usually one designed for engineering or scientific uses that runs the *Unix* operating system.

World Wide Web (also WWW, or the Web) — A collection of information located on many *Internet* servers that can be accessed with a *browser* or by navigating via *hypertext links*.

zine — An electronic publication on one very specific topic, published by one person or a handful of people, and distributed at intervals for free over the *Internet*.

Appendix:
The Information Arsenal

Books

Bryant, Alan D. *Creating Successful Bulletin Board Systems*. Reading, MA: Addison-Wesley, 1994.

Coombs, Jason, and Coombs, Ted. *Setting Up an Internet Site for Dummies*. Foster City, CA: IDG Books, 1996.

Engst, Adam. *Internet Starter Kit for Macintosh*, 4th ed. Indianapolis, IN: Hayden Books, 1996.

Engst, Adam; Low, Corwin S.; and Orchard, Stanley K. *Internet Starter Kit for Windows 95*. Indianapolis, IN: Hayden Books, 1995.

Gilder, George. *Life after Television*. New York: W. W. Norton, 1992.

Glossbrenner, Alfred, and Glossbrenner, Emily. *The Little Web Book*. Berkeley, CA: Peachpit Press, 1996.

Hahn, Harley. *The Internet Complete Reference*, 2nd ed. Berkeley, CA: Osborne/McGraw-Hill, 1996.

LeMay, Laura. *Teach Yourself Web Publishing With HTML 3.2 In A Week*. Indianapolis, IN: Sams.net Publishing, 1996.

Levine, John R., Baroudi, Carol, and Young, Margaret Levine. *Internet for Dummies*. Foster City, CA: IDG Books, 1995.

Levinson, Jay Conrad. *Guerrilla Marketing*. Boston: Houghton Mifflin, 1993.

———. *Guerrilla Marketing Attack*. Boston: Houghton Mifflin, 1989.

———. *Guerrilla Marketing Excellence*. Boston: Houghton Mifflin, 1993.

———. *Guerrilla Marketing Weapons*. New York: Plume, 1990.

Levinson, Jay Conrad, and Godin, Seth. *Guerrilla Marketing for the Home-Based Business* Boston: Houghton Mifflin, 1996.

———. *Guerrilla Marketing Handbook*. Boston: Houghton Mifflin, 1995.

Levinson, Jay Conrad, and Rubin, Charles. *Guerrilla Marketing On-line Weapons*. Boston: Houghton Mifflin, 1996.

Naisbitt, John, and Aburdene, Patricia. *Megatrends 2000*. New York: Avon Books, 1990.

Newby, Gregory B., ed. *Mecklermedia's Official Internet Yellow Pages.* Foster City, CA: IDG Books, 1996.

Popcorn, Faith. *The Popcorn Report.* New York: Harper and Row, 1992.

Randall, Neil. *Teach Yourself the Internet in a Week*, 2nd ed. Indianapolis, IN: Sams.net Publishing, 1995.

Ries, Al, and Trout, Jack. *The 22 Immutable Laws of Marketing.* New York: Harper Business, 1993.

Smith, Bob, and Bebak, Arthur. *Creating Web Pages for Dummies.* Foster City, CA: IDG Books, 1996.

Tittel, Ed, and James, Steve. *HTML for Dummies*, 2nd ed. Foster City, CA: IDG Books, 1996.

Magazines and newsletters

Weekly and monthly magazines and newsletters offer more up-to-date news and help you focus on particular aspects of online marketing or the online world. Most of the publications listed here can be previewed on Web sites. For other magazines not listed here, check out Yahoo's index at: http://www.yahoo.com/Business_and_Economy/Products_and_Services/Magazines/Computers/Internet/.

Boardwatch, 8500 W. Bowles Ave., Suite 210, Littleton, CO 80123 (800-933-6038), on the Web at http://www.boardwatch.com, or via e-mail at: subscriptions@boardwatch.com.

Guerrilla Marketing Newsletter, Guerrilla Marketing International, 260 Cascade Dr., P.O. Box 1336, Mill Valley, CA 94942 (800-748-6444) or (415-381-8361), or via e-mail at gmintl@aol.com.

Home Office Computing, a monthly magazine about home-based businesses with regular coverage of business on the Net. 411 Lafayette St., New York, NY 10003 (800-288-7812), or on the Web at http://www.smalloffice.com.

Inter@ctive Week, a weekly tabloid about the business of the Internet. Check it out at http://web1.zdnet.com/intweek/.

Internet World, the oldest and still one of the best general Internet magazines. Mecklermedia Corp., 11 Ferry Lane West, Westport, CT 06880 (203-226-6967), or on the Web at http://www.internet-world.com.

NetGuide, another good general Internet magazine. 600 Community Drive, Manhassett, NY 11030. (516-562-5000), or on the Web at http://techweb.cmp.com/ng/home.

Online Access, a general Internet magazine with good coverage of on-line services. Chicago Fine Print, Inc., 900 N. Franklin, Suite 310, Chicago, IL 60610 (312-573-1700).

The Web, 501 Second St., San Francisco, CA 94107. (415-267-4586), or on the Web at http://www.webmagazine.com.

Wired, Wired Magazine, 520 Third St., Fourth Floor, San Francisco, CA 94107 (415-222-6200).

Yahoo Internet Life, Ziff-Davis Publishing, One Park Ave., New York, NY 10016. (212-503-4790), or on the Web at http://www.yil.com.

Newsgroup, mailing list, and FAQ information

FAQ locations. The following newsgroups are storage locations for FAQs:

alt.answers

comp.answers

misc.answers

news.answers

rec.answers

sci. answers

soc.answers

talk.answers

For more beginner information about the Net, see

news.announce.newusers.

Directories of Internet mailing lists

These directories list mailing lists on dozens and dozens of topics.

http://www.internetdatabase.com/maillist.htm

http://ds2.internic.net/cgi-bin/tochtml/maillist/0intro.maillist

Online services

America Online, 8619 Westwood Center Dr., Vienna, VA 22182 (800-827-6364)

CompuServe, 5000 Arlington Centre Blvd., Columbus, OH 43220 (800-848-8990)

Delphi Information Service (800-695-4005), or e-mail: info@del-
  phi.com
GEnie, P.O. Box 6403, Rockville, MD 20849-6403 (800-638-9636)
Prodigy Services Co., 445 Hamilton Ave., White Plains, NY 10601
  (800-PRODIGY)

Web directories, shopping malls, and search engines

The best places to start your search for information on the Net are
directories. Here are some of the most popular ones.

AltaVista, a fast Internet search engine maintained by Digital Equip-
  ment Corporation at http://altavista.digital.com/
Apollo, an Internet shopping mall. http://apollo.co.uk
BizWeb, a Web directory at http://www.bizweb.com/
CommerceNet, an organization of large companies doing business
  on the Net, and also a business directory at http://www.commerce.
  net
EINet Galaxy, a directory of shopping and information at http:
  //galaxy.einet.net/galaxy.html
IndustryNet, a directory of business-to-business services. Automated
  News Network, Pittsburgh, PA (412-967-3500), or on the Web at
  http://www.industry.net
InfoSeek, one of the largest Web directories and one of the most popu-
  lar search engines at http://guide.infoseek.com/
The Internet Mall, a directory of retail stores on the Net at
  http://www.imall.com.
Internet Shopping Network, an Internet shopping mall for computer
  products at http://www.internet.net/
Lycos, a search engine and directory at http://www.lycos.com
NetMarket, an Internet shopping mall at http://www.netmarket.com
WebCrawler, a Net search engine and directory service at
  http://www.wcbcrawler.com
Yahoo, the most popular Net directory, at http://www.yahoo.com

Note: The names and addresses of the databases listed here are accurate at this writing, but things change on the Net. If you don't find the
resource at the location we've listed, use a search engine to locate the
directory by name, or use one of the larger directory systems such as
InfoSeek or Yahoo to browse in the appropriate category for the directory you want.

Other information sources

Gopher directories: Galaxy maintains Gopher Jewels, a collection of links to the best Gopher servers, organized by information category, at http://galaxy.einet.net/GJ/.

Yahoo also lists Gopher resources at http://www.yahoo.com/Computers/Internet/Gopher/.

FTP directories: Tile Net lets you search all Anonymous FTP sites by keywords in file names. You can also search by country, Internet domain name, or FTP site name. Tile Net is at http://tile.net/ftp-list/.

There's also a list of FTP resources on Yahoo at http://www.yahoo.com/Computers/Internet/FTP_Sites/.

Government information directories: http://www.yahoo.com/Government/.

National Trade Data Bank: This contains over 300,000 documents from the Commerce, State, Treasury, Defense, Agriculture, Labor, and Energy Departments, as well as the CIA, Federal Reserve Board, and International Trade Commission. On the Web at http://www.statusa.gov.

SBA Home Page: This Small Business Administration's server offers information about the agency's programs and services. Reach it on the Web at http://www.sba.gov.

Professional advice

To find out what the pros have to say, participate in a professionally oriented discussion group or mailing list. Here are three options.

Law: The misc.legal newsgroup is a good place to learn what lawyers are saying about the law.

Marketing: Visit the Guerrilla Marketing Online site at http://www.gmarketing.com for the latest Guerrilla Marketing information. The HTMARCOM mailing list is also a good source of information for marketing, with a special emphasis on Internet marketing. To subscribe to HTMARCOM, send the message SUBSCRIBE HTMARCOM <your name> to the address listserv@cscns.com.

Taxes: The misc.taxes newsgroup offers some advice and professional contacts from accounting professionals, although there's also a good bit of whining about the IRS.

Jay Conrad Levinson's
Guerrilla Marketing International

From the success of the Guerrilla Marketing books sprang Jay Conrad Levinson's Guerrilla Marketing International (1986), a company founded on the understanding that most businesses are not IBM or AT&T and don't have huge marketing budgets to work with, a company organized with the purpose of helping businesses learn to use the power of guerrilla marketing instead of the brute force of enormous budgets.

To learn more about Guerrilla Marketing services and products, write, call, or e-mail Guerrilla Marketing International, P.O. Box 1336, Mill Valley, CA 94942. 415-381-8361.

Now You Can Continue to Be a Guerrilla Marketer with
The Guerrilla Marketing Newsletter!

Now you can continue being an informed Guerrilla Marketer with *The Guerrilla Marketing Newsletter*. It provides you with state-of-the-moment marketing tips and insights to maximize your business profits.

To subscribe to *The Guerrilla Marketing Newsletter*, call 800-748-6444. The subscription rate is $59 a year for 6 issues.

Get the Complete Guerrilla Arsenal!

Guerrilla Marketing: Secrets for Making Big Profits from Your Small Business   ISBN 0-395-64496-8 $11.95

The book that started the Guerrilla Marketing revolution, now completely revised and updated for the nineties. Full of the latest strategies, information on the latest technologies, new programs for targeted prospects, and management lessons for the twenty-first century.

Guerrilla Financing: Alternative Techniques to Finance Any Small Business   ISBN 0-395-52264-1 $10.95

The ultimate sourcebook for finance in the 1990s, and the first book to describe in detail all the traditional and alternative sources of funding for small and medium-size businesses.

Guerrilla Marketing Attack: New Strategies, Tactics, and Weapons for Winning Big Profits   ISBN 0-395-50220-9 $9.95

A companion to *Guerrilla Marketing*, this book arms small and medium-size businesses with vital information about direct marketing, customer relations, cable TV, desktop publishing, ZIP code inserts, TV shopping networks, and much more.

Guerrilla Marketing Excellence: The Fifty Golden Rules for Small-Business Success   ISBN 0-395-60844-9 $9.95

Jay Levinson delivers the 50 basic truths of guerrilla marketing which can make or break your company, including the crucial difference between profits and sales, marketing in a recession, and the latest uses of video and television to assure distribution.

Guerrilla Selling: Unconventional Weapons and Tactics for Increasing Your Sales   ISBN 0-395-57820-5 $9.95

Today's increasingly competitive business environment requires new skills and commitment from salespeople. *Guerrilla Selling* presents unconventional selling tactics that are essential for success.

The Guerrilla Marketing Handbook   ISBN 0-395-70013-2 $14.95

The Guerrilla Marketing Handbook presents Jay Levinson's entire arsenal of marketing weaponry, including a step-by-step guide to developing a marketing campaign and detailed descriptions of more than 100 marketing tools.

Guerrilla Advertising: Cost-Effective Tactics for Small-Business Success   ISBN 0-395-68718-9 $11.95

Jay Levinson applies his proven guerrilla philosophy to advertising. Teeming with anecdotes about past and current advertising successes and failures, the book entertains as it teaches the nuts and bolts of advertising for small businesses.

Guerrilla Marketing for the Home-Based Business
ISBN 0-395-74283-8 $11.95

Usually undercapitalized and short on relevant marketing know-how, home-based businesses have specific marketing needs. Using case studies, anecdotes, illustrations, and examples, guerrilla marketing gurus Jay Levinson and Seth Godin present practical, accessible, and inspirational marketing advice and the most effective arsenal of marketing tools for America's fastest-growing business segment.

Guerrilla Marketing Online Weapons
ISBN 0-395-77019-X $12.95

Here are 100 online marketing strategies to help businesses take advantage of the Internet's great marketing potential. From e-mail addresses and signatures to storefronts, feedback mechanisms, electronic catalogs, and press kits, *Guerrilla Marketing Online Weapons* will help any business, small or large, define, refine, and put its message on the Net with ease.

The Way of the Guerrilla   ISBN 0-395-77018-1 $19.95

An invaluable blueprint for future business success, including advice for both new and seasoned entrepreneurs on everything from preparing a focused mission statement and hiring responsible employees to delegating, finding more time for family and the community, and sustaining one's passion for work. By following *The Way of the Guerrilla*, enlightened and successful entrepreneurs will discover that a balanced life is the means to achieving emotional and financial success, now and in the century to come.

These titles are available through bookstores, or you can order directly from Houghton Mifflin at 1-800-225-3362.